R. W. PETHYBRIDGE was born in Skipton, Yorkshire, in 1934. He is a graduate of Oxford University and the Institute of International Studies at Geneva, and was a member of the first Oxford-Moscow University Exchange in 1958. He has taught at the Institute of International Studies at Geneva and is the author of *A Key to Soviet Politics—The Crisis of the Anti-Party Group* and *Witnesses to the Russian Revolution*. He is currently teaching Soviet government at the Centre of Russian and East European Studies in the University of Wales.

A History of Postwar Russia

BY

R. W. PETHYBRIDGE

A PLUME BOOK from
NEW AMERICAN LIBRARY
TIMES MIRROR
New York, Toronto and London

© George Allen & Unwin Ltd., 1966
All rights reserved. No part of this book may be reproduced
without written permission from the publishers.
Library of Congress Catalog Card Number: 65-25147
This is an authorized reprint of a hardcover edition
published by The New American Library.

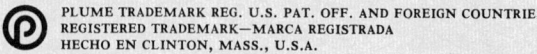

PLUME TRADEMARK REG. U.S. PAT. OFF. AND FOREIGN COUNTRIES
REGISTERED TRADEMARK—MARCA REGISTRADA
HECHO EN CLINTON, MASS., U.S.A.

SIGNET, SIGNET CLASSICS, MENTOR AND PLUME BOOKS
are published in the United States by
The New American Library, Inc.,
1301 Avenue of the Americas, New York, New York 10019,
in Canada by The New American Library of Canada Limited,
295 King Street East, Toronto 2, Ontario,
in the United Kingdom by The New English Library Limited,
Barnard's Inn, Holborn, London, E.C. 1, England

First Printing, March, 1970

PRINTED IN THE UNITED STATES OF AMERICA

TO MY PARENTS

PREFACE

The aim of this book is to introduce both undergraduates and the general public to the study of postwar developments in the Soviet Union. Many detailed accounts of isolated topics already exist, and are listed in the bibliography. There are also more general works that treat either foreign or domestic policy, but as far as I am aware there is no book that attempts to correlate the two. I have drawn on the large body of information now available in English and Russian and have tried to present an intelligible narrative account of events affecting Russia between 1945 and 1961.

The task has proved to be fiendishly difficult. Apart from the usual problems connected with the compression and omission of material in a book of this kind, the controversial nature of the subject and its raw modernity have confronted me with other troubles. In this country a growing number of university undergraduates are now studying different aspects of the Communist world, and outside the universities the general public is taking a livelier interest in this same area. It is for them that I continued with my book, though I am keenly aware of its shortcomings.

The narrative ends with an account of the Twenty-second Party Congress, held in October 1961. Beyond that point the outline of Soviet affairs is altogether too misty to allow of any clear interpretation at the present time. It may become evident in the future that Khrushchev's recent fall heralded changes as great as those that occurred after Stalin's death. We cannot tell yet. But it *does* appear that by the end of 1961 Khrushchev had already put through the great majority of the most significant post-Stalin reforms that are bound to leave a permanent mark on the future development of the Soviet Union and the Communist world.

I would like to express appreciation for the help of Mrs Elaine Davies, who typed large portions of successive drafts, and to Mrs Jean Ulyatt who gave assistance in the closing stages. Mr Brian Murphy kindly read the proofs.

ROGER PETHYBRIDGE

CONTENTS

PREFACE	page 9
INTRODUCTION	13
I. THE IMPACT OF THE SECOND WORLD WAR	17
Soviet Losses—The Psychological Impact of the War—Soviet Gains	
II. STALINISM AT HOME, 1945–1953	49
Stalin and His Aides—The Party—The Drive for Ideological Purity—The Nineteenth Party Congress—The 'Doctors' Plot' and Stalin's Death	
III. STALINISM ABROAD	83
Eastern Europe—Soviet Influence in Central and Western Europe 1945-8—The Development of the Cold War—Eastern Europe 1947-53—Asia—The Middle East—The United Nations	
IV. THE INTERREGNUM: MARCH 1953–FEBRUARY 1956	120
The Significance of Stalin's Death—Domestic Policy —Foreign Policy	
V. THE KHRUSHCHEV ERA: DOMESTIC POLICY	157
The Final Struggle for Power—Politics at the Lower Levels—The Twenty-first Party Congress—The Economic Thaw—Agriculture	
VI. THE KHRUSHCHEV ERA: FOREIGN POLICY	188
The Twentieth Party Congress—Eastern Europe—The German Problem—The Middle and Far East—China—Africa and Latin America—Politics at the Summit	
VII. SOCIAL CONTROLS	219
Instruments of Coercion—Instruments of Persuasion	
VIII. THE TWENTY-SECOND PARTY CONGRESS AND CONCLUSION	242
Domestic Policy—Foreign Policy	
BIBLIOGRAPHY	253
INDEX	257

A History of Postwar Russia

INTRODUCTION

The period covered by this book extends from the closing stages of the Second World War until the Twenty-second Soviet Party Congress in the autumn of 1961. It includes sixteen years of Soviet history—over one-third of the total life span of the Communist regime—with Stalin's death at the mid-point in 1953. The story begins on a note of combined disaster and opportunity for the Soviet Union brought about by the war against Germany, and ends with the Soviet Union's bright vision of its Communist future as recorded at the Twenty-second Congress.

In the course of the present study the author has attempted to illuminate several facets of Soviet affairs that merit particular attention. The relationship between Soviet domestic and foreign policy is the foremost of these. Students of a country other than their own are apt to view it almost exclusively in terms of foreign policy; little importance is attached to its internal affairs and even less to the influence of home on foreign policy and vice versa. In this way the whole image of a country is distorted. The degree of distortion increases as the effects of the country's foreign policy become more problematic for the rest of the world, since national leaders are always inclined to see things in relation to their own problems and to ignore the rest. The reactions of West European and United States leaders to aspects of Soviet foreign policy not specifically aimed at them have for the most part been omitted, though they are described at crucial periods of contact such as the renewal of the Cold War from 1945 to 1948, and in connection with the extended crisis over the future of Germany.

The close ties between Soviet policies at home and abroad cannot be ignored. At the beginning of our period, Stalin's behaviour at Teheran and Yalta in dealing with Roosevelt and Churchill is hardly comprehensible unless one takes into account the contrast between the difficult situation inside Russia and the brilliant opportunities that lay abroad for a power that has always taken advantage of economic and social disaster to implement its foreign policy. Again, the purely internal struggle for Stalin's succession in the Soviet Union had significant repercussions on the conduct of foreign policy between 1953 and 1957. We do not know the exact extent of its influence, but at least it is clear that Molotov's intervention had a disruptive effect. So did Malenkov's 'soft' economic policy as applied in Hungary; immediately followed by Khrushchev's stricter line, it set up violent fluctuations that led directly to the Hungarian uprising of 1956.

The most conspicuous example of the interaction of domestic and foreign policy is to be found in the proceedings of the Twentieth Congress. For once the Soviet Union itself under-estimated the strength of the ties binding the People's Democracies of East Europe to the USSR. Khrushchev's secret speech on Stalin's crimes was intended above all for domestic consumption, but it also led to a series of upheavals in the Soviet bloc that only subsided at the end of 1957 and which left the bloc radically different in character from what it had been before 1956. These upheavals reacted in turn on the Soviet internal struggle for power in the winter of 1956–57. Similarly, it is impossible to fathom the motives behind the introduction of the theory of 'peaceful coexistence' at the Twentieth Congress without some understanding of factors in the domestic scene that favoured the adoption of the new line in foreign policy.

It may be thought that too much space in this book is devoted to foreign policy. Nevertheless, the author contends that such treatment is essential in considering this period of Soviet history. Russian expansion since the Second World War demands close observation, just as does similar British expansion in the eighteenth and nineteenth centuries. Even after 1948, when this expansion virtually came to a halt as far as direct Soviet control was concerned, other aspects of Russian influence played a scarcely less significant role in many parts of the world beyond Eastern Europe.

The border line between domestic and foreign policy with respect to the Soviet bloc is blurred, since within the period from 1947 to 1956 the Soviet internal system served in almost every way as a prototype for the People's Democracies. It was not Molotov, the spokesman on foreign affairs, who set up the Cominform, but Zhdanov, who was originally concerned with domestic matters. Whether we consider Eastern Europe as part of the Russian empire or as the first projection of that Communist supranational society that Marx dreamed of, it is worthy of detailed study as a sounding board of Soviet policy—call it foreign or domestic as you will.

Another aspect of Soviet life that fascinates the author is the subtle interaction between ideology and power politics. The two forces are as closely intertwined as were the religious and secular interests of the mediaeval papacy. These forces are backed by a political machine that follows the Jesuits in professing that the end justifies the means, and which has more power for good or evil than all the religious sects put together. In the years since the Second World War, the influence of ideology on practice and of practice on ideology is perhaps seen at its clearest in Stalin's theoretical musings before his death, in the circumstances of the Soviet-Yugoslav quarrel of 1948, and as the background to the formation of the revised theory of Soviet foreign policy at the Twentieth Party Congress of 1956.

The contrast between the last years of Stalin's rule and the era that began in 1953 also deserves special attention in any study of postwar Russia.

The first eight years differed greatly from the following eight. The last stage of Stalin's rule is as difficult to interpret as any period in the Middle Ages. The poverty of Soviet sources on this period contrasts with their unusual abundance, by Soviet standards, for the years after 1953. On another level, the grand monolithic design of Stalin's postwar policy, with its well-defined turning points imposed by an all-powerful leader, compares strangely with the sudden, unpredictable ebbs and flows reflecting the struggle for Stalin's succession from 1953 to 1957.

In politics the balance tipped from the use of brute force to that of persuasion in managing domestic and external affairs, although both elements were present in varying degrees throughout the postwar period. In economics a more rational approach slowly began to replace dogmatism. Ideology bowed increasingly to the pressure of reality. Changes were not made in a day, and the weight of nearly twenty years of Stalinist rule still hung heavy on all aspects of Soviet life; but if Stalin could have been stirred from his slumbers when his body was removed from the Lenin mausoleum in 1961, he would surely have been astonished at more than one aspect of the Soviet Union. One feature remained that would have seemed familiar to him—a single ruler still commanded the scene; but a glance beneath the outward veneer would have convinced him that appearances somewhat belied the true situation. Even after Khrushchev's triumph in 1957, there was no return to the Stalinist pattern. Khrushchev's power was not as secure as his master's had been, nor was his reputation yet confirmed by history. In 1961 Khrushchev was an ageing statesman still in a hurry to make a lasting name for himself. By 1945, as the hero of the mightiest war ever fought, Stalin could afford to be set in his ways.

This was not an easy book to write. Contemporary history presents many pitfalls to anyone rash enough to record it; Soviet history incurs extra hazards. In the first place fewer sources are obtainable than in the case of other countries; secondly, valuable Soviet sources appear months or years after the event (Khrushchev's secret speech on Stalin at the Twentieth Party Congress in 1956 is the most famous example); thirdly, the present state of international politics induces both Communist and capitalist governments to distort the true face of Soviet Russia, especially with regard to its foreign policy. The author has striven to base this work not on political propaganda from either side of the Iron Curtain, but on known facts and their interpretation by the least-prejudiced scholars, without whom he could never have plucked up the courage to assail such a redoubtable theme. He is greatly in their debt. An additional difficulty arises from the unusually fluid political, economic, and social condition of the Soviet Union since Stalin's death, which set deep currents running that still have not found their bed. It is always harder to depict an object in motion, and the faster the movement the more delicate the task.

Many studies have been written on various aspects of postwar Russia, but to the author's knowledge no short general history has yet appeared covering the period from 1945 to 1961. This book has been written in an attempt to meet this need. Inevitably the compression imposed on the author has obliged him to offer some summary interpretations that he has not enough space to justify; he refers the curious student to the mass of easily available literature on individual subjects. The present study aims at giving the general shape of Soviet history during the years from 1945 to 1961. It has struck the author that in Soviet society each sector of activity must be viewed in relation to the whole, so that the monolithic pattern of totalitarian politics can be appreciated. More than any other major power, the Soviet Union does not lend itself easily to compartmentalized study, since every branch of Soviet life is carefully trimmed to grow toward the Communist society of the future.

CHAPTER I

THE IMPACT OF THE SECOND WORLD WAR

The Second World War had two main consequences for the Soviet Union. At home Soviet industry and agriculture, built up during the Five-Year Plans with such energy and sacrifice, lay in ruins. No other country that took part in the struggle against Hitler suffered so much. Viewed in terms of human lives, the toll was colossal. Those who remained to build Russia's future were stunned by the psychological impact of a whirlwind war that had uprooted the whole of the Soviet economy and to a somewhat lesser extent the social, political, and ideological foundations on which that economy had been constructed.

Abroad lay potential compensation for domestic havoc. Soviet armies occupied Eastern Europe, one of history's greatest political vacuums and a traditional thorn in the side of Russian security. The victory that appeared so Pyrrhic to the Ukrainian peasant deprived of his home heaped incalculable prestige on Stalin as he conferred with Roosevelt and Churchill at Yalta. Even if the Anglo-Saxon leaders had not thought fit to show such deference to the protector of Stalingrad, the wide geographical distribution of Soviet troops would have lent eloquent force to Stalin's opinions. And Stalin was determined to receive his pound of flesh for what Russia had given of herself in the war.

The present chapter is concerned with the Soviet balance sheet of losses and gains as they appeared during the closing stages of the war. It is essential to keep in mind the great contrast between domestic losses and opportunities for diplomatic success abroad, because Stalin's policy from about 1944 onwards, both in its internal and its external aspects, consisted in weighing up the salient factors of the two situations and then fixing the most expedient relationship between them.

SOVIET LOSSES

Human Lives

When Churchill went to Moscow in August 1942 to tell Stalin that the Anglo-American chiefs of staff had agreed to delay the planned invasion of France, Molotov is supposed to have commented in

Churchill's presence: 'The British Prime Minister will once again prove to us that his country is not in a position to sacrifice men.' At that time Molotov could not have known that approximately one person out of every ten in the Soviet Union was to die in the course of the war, but he did know that the Russian effort did not spare human lives as a matter of policy.

There were several contributory reasons for the different policies pursued by the Soviets and the other Allies. The Red Army was led by a totalitarian dictator who had exterminated millions of his own people during the period of agricultural collectivization and again at the time of the Great Purge of the 1930s; he was not the sort of man to shrink from sacrificing Russia's large population to the mechanized power of the German army. Stalin recognized that neither he nor his people could expect any mercy from Hitler, who had proclaimed Bolshevism to be his arch-enemy and the Slav lands the second home of the Germans. The Soviet soldier at the front, unlike his Anglo-Saxon counterpart, was fighting on his own soil, which was occupied by the Nazis for most of the war.

The war claimed nearly 8,000,000 Russian military lives and 11,000,000 civilians. Another 3,000,000 persons were disabled. In the wake of the German retreat 25,000,000 people were rendered homeless. The number of refugees from the western areas of the Soviet Union has not been calculated with any precision, but to take a single example, it is known that more than half the population of Kharkov and Kiev, between 800,000 and 1,000,000 people, was evacuated to the east to provide a labour force for transplanted industries. Because of the enormous drain on manpower into the forces, by 1942 more than 50 per cent of those employed in the armaments industry were women.

Although loss of human life represented the greatest debit on the Soviet balance sheet, it was also the one that was to be remedied, if indeed one can talk of a remedy for death, at the fastest rate of any of the disadvantages with which Russia emerged from the war. Throughout Soviet history there has been a very rapid natural increase of population. The Soviet census of 1939 gave the total population as over 170,000,000, an increase of more than 23,000,000 persons over the census of 1926. By 1959 the population had swollen to more than 208,000,000 inhabitants. Despite the fact that this sum included an extra 20,000,000 or so persons living in the territories acquired by the USSR between 1939 and 1945, the recuperative powers of a nation that was relatively youthful in composition were decidedly strong.

The Economy

It was fortunate for Soviet industry that labour did not remain in short supply for long after the war. Approximately one-quarter of the country's total pre-war stock was wiped out during the war years. In his book *The Economy of the USSR during World War II*, N. A. Voznesensky, the Chairman of the State Planning Commission in the post-war period, tells us that as much as two-thirds of the total wealth existing before the war in areas occupied by the enemy was written off in 1945; these same areas had accounted for much of Russia's industrial and agricultural riches in 1939.

Let us look at individual branches of the economy. The hardest hit were those that formed the core of the heavy industrial base that had been given preferential treatment throughout the period of the Five-Year Plans. During the war production capacity of pig iron receded by 73 per cent as compared with 1940, steel by 55 per cent, and rolled steel by 61 per cent; steel output in 1945 only came to a little over eleven million metric tons. Electric power production, which had been a primary objective of the Soviet economy since Lenin's time, fell by 44 per cent.

The oil industry had made spectacular progress since the 1920s, especially at Baku. New and rich oil deposits between the Volga and the Urals, nicknamed the 'Second Baku', were developed prior to the war, although in 1940 the western areas of the Soviet Union still accounted for 88 per cent of all oil produced. By 1945 output at Baku was only about half that of 1940, while the increased exploitation of the 'Second Baku' area was not sufficient to compensate for the decline further west. Neither area fell to the Germans. This is significant because it shows that the drop in industrial output was due to many other factors besides German devastation. Although oil is a vital commodity, particularly in wartime, the wells at Baku were neglected during a great part of the war. Skilled technicians were drafted into the army, and much equipment, including large quantities of trucks and tractors, was commandeered for military use. All the petroleum machinery factories in Baku were employed in the production of military supplies and armaments.

The war history of the Soviet railway system illustrates both the enormous losses incurred and the rapidity with which these losses were made good. A great deal of restoration took place even before the end of hostilities. According to official reports of the Soviet Government, over 40,000 miles of track, 13,000 railway bridges, 4,100 stations, 317 engine depots, and thousands of engines were destroyed by the Germans. Between 1941 and 1943 40 per cent of

Soviet railway tracks were put out of use. By the end of 1945, however, the total length of tracks exceeded that of 1940. Top military priority was given to the reconstruction of lines in ex-occupied areas.

Three major factors contributed to the disastrous state of the Soviet economy. Without doubt the most important of these was the deliberate wrecking carried out by the Germans as they retreated. Nearly 2,000 towns, 70,000 villages, and factories employing 4,000,000 persons were partially or totally destroyed, according to official Soviet calculations. In the second place, the Russians themselves had begun a similar process in the same areas when they too were on the retreat during the earlier phases of the war. On July 3, 1941, Stalin issued his famous 'scorched earth' decree, in which he said, 'All valuable property, including metals, grain, and fuel, that cannot be withdrawn, must be destroyed without fail. . . .'[1] Finally, occupied Russia was forced to contribute to the Nazi war effort. In the words of an article in the *Deutsche Arbeitsfront*: 'The residents of the conquered areas shall be permitted to consume only a part of their production. The balance shall be left to the Staatsvolk [i.e. the Germans] in compensation for its political leadership.' The impact of the German exploitation policy, however, was the least important of the factors that sucked the life out of the Soviet economy. It has been estimated that the contribution of the occupied eastern parts of Europe to the Reich amounted to only one-seventh of what the Reich obtained from France.

In the course of the war Soviet industrial output was rigidly contained within the armaments branch, to the detriment not only of consumer goods and agriculture but also of other sectors vital to any modern war effort. This was reflected in the sad state of the oil and transport industries. Most of the lorries that carried the Soviet armies into action were imported under lend-lease and were of American, British, and Canadian make. Thanks to such concentration of effort, the production of Soviet armament factories in the provinces that escaped German occupation went up by 500 to 600 per cent.

The adroit transference of Soviet plants to the unoccupied areas and the subsidiary aid of lend-lease had a significant effect on the Soviet weapons industry.

The shift of heavy industries to the east was a continuing one. The movement had already begun prior to 1941, indeed, prior to the Revolution, but it was easier to increase output in areas where industry had been established for a long time; and in 1939 the region of the

[1] Joseph V. Stalin, *War Speeches and Orders of the Day* (London: Progress Pub. Co., 1945), pp. 10–11.

lower Dnieper and the Donbas was still the main centre of iron and steel production, just as Leningrad, Moscow, and Kharkov retained their pre-eminence as engineering centres.

Shortly before the war further factories were built in the eastern areas of the USSR. After Hitler's attack, the shift was continued on a massive scale. The full story of this aspect of the war is not known, but we do know that at least 70 per cent of the total capital equipment of Leningrad industry, other than building structures, was evacuated to the east during 1941-2. In general only goods that were indispensable to the war effort were removed, and rarely as far east as Asiatic Russia. (The lines of communication with the western front were congested quite enough, thanks to German wrecking of the railway system.) It was in the regions of the Volga, the Urals, and Western Siberia that shanty-type buildings, often in wood, were constructed to house evacuated plants. Between 1941 and 1945 ten new blast furnaces with an annual output capacity of 2,500,000 tons were brought into operation in the east. This was the spearhead of the production campaign that turned out an average of 30,000 tanks and fighting vehicles and nearly 40,000 planes each year between 1943 and 1945.

The hardships undergone by those who were recruited to work under such conditions must have been enormous, but the problems caused by inadequate accommodation and hurried adaptation were perhaps no greater than those that had confronted the newly-collectivized peasants of the 1930s or that were to burden the workers on the Virgin Lands scheme in the coming Khrushchev era. Since 1917 the Russian people have been accustomed to totalitarian economic planning, with its scant regard for human comfort.

Unlike the shift of Soviet industry to the east, lend-lease was a temporary phenomenon. It did not lead to any postwar development of Russian trade with America, Britain, or Canada. Yet during the Second World War Russia received $3,000,000,000 worth of goods from her Allies annually, from guns and planes to machinery, boots, and food. Both in quantity and in value, these imports far exceeded the 1931 peak of prewar purchases. Stalin's refusal to allow Czechoslovakia to benefit from the Marshall Plan, the United States' postwar successor to lend-lease, finally slammed down the economic Iron Curtain for Eastern Europe as well as for Russia herself, who, as can be judged by the extent of her war damage, could have used foreign credit to great advantage after 1945.

Outside the privileged sector of heavy industry the position in Russia was much worse by the end of the war. Housing, agriculture, and consumer goods production all suffered terribly. Between 1941 and 1945 there was no time to devote any attention to these branches of the economy. Industrial equipment could be evacuated, but neither homes nor the rich earth of western Russia, which had yielded half of the country's food before the war, could be moved. Factories turning out consumer goods were denied priority in the move to the unoccupied lands.

These three sectors had been in a sorry state even before the outbreak of the war. Inadequate and low-quality housing has always been one of the worst features of the Soviet standard of living. Overcrowding in the cities during the urbanization of the 1930s aggravated the situation. The destruction of over 50 per cent of all urban living accommodation and of roughly a quarter of rural housing in the occupied territories drove millions into dugouts, caves, and other temporary shelters. The plight of those who fled to the east was little better, because an acute shortage of accommodation existed there. Even as late as 1961, as a result of early neglect and wartime devastation, the housing supply lagged far behind the elementary requirements of city inhabitants.

The outlook for agriculture at the end of the war was very depressing. Even the land spared by the Germans or beyond their reach lay neglected, since mobilization for the Red Army had deprived the collective farms of nearly half the labour force devoted to field work. The old people and children who remained to carry on the work were not equal to the task. Most of the technological gains achieved at great expense in the pre-war period were lost. Farm production in 1945 has been estimated at 60 per cent that of 1940 by Dr Naum Jasny, an expert on Soviet agriculture. The same author gives a grim picture in his *Socialized Agriculture of the USSR* (pp. 69-70):

> A marked decline in farm output followed directly upon the first shot; one can even rightly speak of 'collapse'. The decline in the uninvaded territory during the whole war (including 1945) was probably more than three times as large, in percentage terms, as the decline in Russian farm output during the war of 1914-18.

Some branches of agriculture suffered more than others. The decline in valuable technical crops like cotton, flax, sunflower seed, and sugar beets was offset by an increase in the acreage in potatoes and vegetables. Because of the slaughter and removal of sheep and hogs, the supply of meat decreased more rapidly than that of milk. In 1946 the whole range of Soviet agriculture except cotton was struck by the worst drought in fifty years. The derationing of bread and cereals, promised for the end of 1946, had to be delayed for another year. In the period after the war, Soviet authorities concealed the true extent of the damage to agriculture. This was done chiefly in order to cover up another and more serious problem, the overall impracticability of the planned system of agriculture, which retarded the recovery of this sector of the economy.

The output of consumer goods, the 'poor relation' of the Five-Year Plans during the pre-war period, went down in 1945 to little more than two-fifths of the 1940 level, which itself had been a mere trickle. The third Five-Year Plan began in 1938 under the shadow of Munich, so that any rapid expansion of light industry had to be sacrificed to investment in armaments.

In the midst of the general havoc recorded above, while millions wandered homeless and starving throughout western Russia, Stalin announced a long-range target for steel production without even mentioning the urgent need for bread (February 1946). His statement was less frivolous than the famous words of Marie Antoinette, but just as heartless. Yet his order was obeyed. By 1950, as we shall see, total industrial output was 73 per cent higher than in 1946.

THE PSYCHOLOGICAL IMPACT OF THE WAR

At the end of the war, the Soviet nation girded its loins for an economic struggle that was scarcely less taxing than the military campaign that had preceded it. In order to prepare Russia for the new battle, Stalin had to inculcate the right frame of mind into the nation.

By 1945 the debit side of the Soviet balance sheet did not consist of economic damage alone. Figures and percentages, which in any case cannot be given with great precision, tell only half the story. In the course of the war great psychological changes had also occurred in Russia. For a variety of reasons, men's ways of thought, their approach to such fundamental questions as politics, ideology, and relations with the world outside the Soviet Union had been affected. Writers have taken the title of Ehrenburg's novel *The Thaw* to characterize the period following the death of Stalin in 1953, but it is forgotten that another and earlier thaw occurred during the war period. The change in the nation's mood was just as perturbing as the economic chaos. Its effect was more subtle and was all the more dangerous for that reason. Had this change been allowed to develop freely after the end of hostilities, it could well have resulted in lasting damage to the regime.

The first thaw was a direct consequence of the Second World War. In part it arose from changes in Stalin's policy, but it was also stimulated by contact with the outside world—through German occupation, Soviet relations with the Allies, and the movements of Soviet troops abroad. Each of these influences will be examined in turn.

Changes in Stalin's Policy

In 1956 Khrushchev declared in his secret speech to the Twentieth Congress that the German invasion had come as a shock to Stalin. Even a well-prepared and popular leader would have been taken aback by the *blitzkrieg*; Stalin was neither popular nor prepared. In the summer of 1941, when Hitler's troops were advancing more than 450 miles a month and large numbers of Soviet troops were being taken prisoner, Stalin indicated his nervous state of mind by telling Harry L. Hopkins, President Roosevelt's envoy, that he 'would welcome American troops on any part of the Russian front under the complete command of the American army'.[1]

This was a desperate admission from the dictator who spent the rest of the war keeping even Allied observers away from the front. At the outset of hostilities the reaction of the Russian population was uncertain. Only ten years previously the peasants had been resisting collectivization. The hatred of the regime as a result of the purges of the 1930s still rankled, and there were many national minorities with grudges against the government in Moscow.

Stalin had to make a gesture to win over the masses before they defected to the invader. On the theoretical plane he allowed the ideological struggle to abate for the duration of the war. The party's role was made less obtrusive and the population was deliberately nurtured on a diet of ardent nationalism almost devoid of Communist overtones, that would have been considered incompatible with Marxist doctrine in Lenin's time. Of course the new patriotism was partly spontaneous, but it was also deliberately infused by the party. It proved a useful weapon. Internally it helped to unite the people and narrowed the gap between party members and the masses; externally it placated the Allies, who preferred to see Russia fighting on their side as a nation state opposed to the Nazi regime rather than as a hostile class intent on forwarding the proletarian revolution envisaged by Marx. Stalin had the Allies in mind when, in April 1943, he abolished the Comintern, the main instrument of international Communism. In fact Stalin no longer needed the Comintern to ensure the obedience of foreign Communist parties, but the Allies did not know this at the time. They thought that Stalin had made a real concession.

---

[1] See Robert E. Sherwood, *Roosevelt and Hopkins* (New York, Harper & Brothers, 1948), pp. 339–43.

In Soviet schools, the hub of the propaganda network, the example of the patriotic war of 1812 against Napoleon was the main theme of discussion. Pre-revolutionary as well as Soviet history was used as fuel to ignite nationalistic sentiment, and the names of patriotic heroes like Alexander Nevsky, Aleksandr Suvorov, Mikhail Kutuzov, and Ivan the Terrible cropped up regularly in political speeches and cultural work.

On the administrative plane, too, the tight grip of the party was relaxed. Within the party itself standards of admission were lowered for members of the armed forces, especially during the crisis years of 1941 and 1942. The size of the party increased from 3,399,975 in January 1940 to 5,760,369 in January 1945. A particular effort was made to enlist the support of groups of the population that had suffered from the heavy hand of the party in the past. The army was a prime example. In October 1942, a special decree dispensed with the system of dual command, whereby the political commissars had the same authority as the military commanders. The military were given greater freedom of action, and the more brilliant among them were awarded many honours. Slowly the damage caused by the purge of half the officer corps in 1937 and 1938 was repaired.

The peasants were also handled gently during the war. They made up the backbone of the army and had traditional ties with it dating back to revolutionary days, so that to a great extent Stalin killed two birds with one stone by making an appeal to the military. Peasants who remained on the farm were not prevented from taking over uncultivated *kolkhoz* (collective farms) land for private use or from increasing their personal stock of animals over the maximum allowed. Many peasants seriously believed that after the end of the war the whole *kolkhoz* system would be revised and that they would be granted more independence from state control.

Stalin held out inducements to the *muzhik*'s soul as well as to his pocket. In September 1943, he rehabilitated the Greek Orthodox Church, which had not lost its former grip on the peasant population. The Patriarchate was re-established, and the government set up a new Commission on the Affairs of the Orthodox Church. A Communist minister attended the opening ceremony of the Theological Academy in Moscow, thus officially sanctioning an institution that had been hounded out of all positions of influence since 1917.

In the course of his drive for unity in the face of the enemy, Stalin went so far as to reinstate personalities who had been associated with the opposition in the past. Military figures who had suffered from their connections with Mikhail Tukhachevsky, the most prominent military victim of the 1930s purge, were brought into the war effort; intellectuals who had ruined their careers by indiscreet statements were encouraged to use their talents in the crusade against Nazi Germany; and the campaign against Trotskyism and other political deviations was dropped—there was no need for a scapegoat so long as Hitler's armies remained on Russian soil.

Thus in many ways the tight hold of the party over the Soviet peoples was relinquished in the early stages of the war. In the areas of the country occupied by the Germans, Stalin was appalled by the spectacle of passive acceptance of foreign rule and occasional collaboration. He swallowed the bitter pill and took steps to ensure the goodwill of those who were still free. But in his haste Stalin dangerously overstepped the limits of safety. If it had been allowed to continue, the thaw might have grown into a flood that would have carried away the system.

By the end of the war this danger had been heightened by three parallel developments, of which the first lay quite outside Stalin's control, while the other two could only be regulated in a very desultory manner. In the first place Soviet citizens living in occupied Russia were submitted to a regime that was completely different from anything they had been used to since 1917. On the second and third counts, the official ties struck up between the Allies and the Russians, together with the more unofficial contact between Soviet troops and foreign populations in the countries the Red Army crossed on its way to Berlin, provided many glimpses of the outside world that must have had considerable psychological impact.

The German Occupation
That part of Russia which fell under German domination was out of Stalin's control. All he could do was to remove to the east those sectors of the population that threatened to prove disloyal or that did in fact defect to the advancing Nazis. The deportations *en masse* of seven nationalities—the Volga Germans, the Crimean Tartars, the Kalmyks, and four small Caucasian nationalities: the Chechens, the Ingushi, the Karachai, and the Balkars—showed better than anything else the extent of Stalin's preoccupation with the effect of the war on the minds of the Soviet people. Over 1,000,000 persons were uprooted and sent to Siberia and Central Asia, an operation that compared in magnitude with the upheavals caused by collectivization in the 1930s. Actually Stalin had been hypersensitive in this area, because after his death the Soviet government admitted that so far as

five of the nationalities were concerned the deportations were not justified by military or security considerations.

Until about December 1941, pro-German feeling ran quite high in the areas taken over by the Nazis. Under the pressure of the German advance, hordes of Russian soldiers gave themselves up, though many units fought well. Civilians in the territories incorporated into the USSR in 1939–40, including the western Ukraine, western Belorussia, and the Baltic States, had remained hostile to the Soviet regime and welcomed the German armies. The situation was less clear in the rest of the occupied areas, where the attitude of the population varied from passive acceptance of their new masters to careful optimism with regard to the future under German rule.

If the Nazis had treated their subjects with greater tact, Stalin might well have been faced with more opposition in western Russia. In the event, the ruthless policy applied to the *Untermensch* only served to alienate the local population. The aim of the German authorities to exterminate the Bolshevist creed met with little or no dissent, but the record of misconduct in day-to-day administration soon revolted the Russians who bore its brunt. The turn in the fortunes of the war within the Soviet Union persuaded them to look to Communist rather than to Nazi leadership for the future.

Too late, Hitler agreed to the formation of a Committee for the Liberation of the Peoples of Russia, which was to set up 'a new free People's political system without Bolsheviks and exploiters'. It was to terminate forced labour, abolish the collective farms, and bring in real civil liberties and social justice. Furthermore it recognized the equality of all the peoples of Russia, an enticing bait to the occupied areas where a prolonged tug-of-war with great Russian nationalism since 1917 had received additional impetus during the patriotic war.

The committee was not established until September 1944. It was headed by the Soviet General Alexandr Vlasov and other senior Soviet army officers. Vlasov had toured occupied Russia at the end of 1942 and had been well received by his compatriots. High party members figured in the ranks of those who showed enthusiasm for the aims of the committee. Had it succeeded in mobilizing German Russia and the 5,000,000 Soviet nationals in Germany against the Stalin regime at an earlier stage of the war, the movement might well have played a large part in recent European history. The Soviet leaders were seriously alarmed by the affair.

Relations with the Allies
Soviet relations with the Allies probably had a similar disturbing

effect, but they were confined for the most part to the higher echelons of society, whereas every Russian peasant in the armies advancing on Berlin could form his own ideas about capitalist Europe. Stalin could not prevent the desertion of thousands of Red Army men in Rumania in the summer of 1944, but it was possible for him to restrict official contact with the Allies to a minimum. Numerous articles in *Pravda* and in *Red Star*, the press organ of the army, warned the Soviet people against the false glitter of bourgeois culture. Fear of the effect of association between the Soviet and Western armies in Germany led the Russian authorities to break off the fraternization that developed, particularly at the top levels. Allied commanding officers marvelled at the extent of Soviet security, which saw to it that subordinate officers on the Russian side did not even know under whom they were serving.

Despite the care that was taken, psychological damage was done at several points. Bourgeois culture was allowed to penetrate into Russia during the war. English and American films, plays, and music made their appearance; as late as 1945 *Komsomolskaia Pravda* was recommending so 'decadent' an author as Oscar Wilde.

Soviet Troops Abroad

As they advanced through Eastern Europe, the victorious Soviet soldiers could not help noticing the greater measure of freedom enjoyed by their neighbours, who were not afraid of giving vent to their political opinions even though they were in the process of being thrown from German to Soviet totalitarian control, from the frying pan into the fire. The much higher standard of living that still persisted despite the havoc caused by the war also struck the Russians forcibly. General John R. Deane, who spent two years in Moscow during the war as head of the American military mission, noted this impression at the time of the German surrender:

> The entire party was taken to Karlhorst, a little suburb east of Berlin, in a caravan of captured German motor vehicles. The automobiles must have been specially selected, as they were most luxurious. Mine was a long convertible job with deep soft red leather seats. It could not help but think of what the Russian reaction must have been to such automobiles, considering the old and rickety cars one saw in the streets of Moscow.[1]

Although the Russian troops were no doubt deeply affected by their

[1] John R. Deane, *The Strange Alliance* (New York: The Viking Press, 1947), p. 175.

experiences abroad, they did not return to the Soviet Union with the spirit of revolution that had inspired Russian officers during the Napoleonic wars. Soviet minds had been conditioned by propaganda for many years and could not be changed over a short period and, besides, the Europe they saw was only a vestige of its former self. Those Russians who had spent the longest time abroad during the war had been in German concentration camps; their impressions of life under foreign rule were even less encouraging than those of their compatriots in occupied Russia.

At the end of a victorious war the general mood of any nation tends toward relief, relaxation, and hope of better things to come as a reward for winning the fight. This natural reaction was accentuated in the Russia of 1945. Had not the Soviet people won one of the greatest victories of all time, and done so after ten years of non-stop effort to industrialize under conditions little better than those experienced in wartime? Surely they deserved their reward. The Ukrainian maltreated by the invader, the Soviet soldier impressed by the comforts of capitalist Europe, the peasant who stayed at home and was allowed respite from state intervention, all looked to Stalin for an easier life after the war. They were persuaded that Stalin would give it to them, since during the war he had made several moves that seemed to presage a policy of this kind. They were to be cruelly disappointed.

The series of shocks caused by the impact of both German and Allied influences in the war, coupled with Stalin's own relaxed grip over the minds of his people, taught the Russian leaders a lesson they did not forget during the postwar period. Only the tight control of the party over every aspect of national life would be able to hold centrifugal forces together. The party itself would have to be rigidly disciplined or it would break up too. A dangerous gap between the ways of thinking of party members and of the rest of the population had been created.

Russia remained in a state of crisis for some time after 1945. The postwar period, which on the home front witnessed a struggle to overcome weaknesses in the political and economic systems caused by the war, offered undreamt-of opportunities for Communist expansion abroad; but, if these chances were grasped quickly and thoughtlessly, the Soviet Union, the safe and only harbour of Communism since 1917, might overreach itself and fall a prey to the designs of its enemies. Stalin therefore played his hand with a good deal of caution after the war.

Even before 1945 the Soviet Government had begun to reintroduce the old party line. In 1941 Stalin had laid all the stress in his war speeches on the motherland, but in November 1943, when victory was in sight, he claimed that 'during the war, the party has still further cemented its kinship with the people'. Special care was devoted to the liberated areas, whose inhabitants were addressed in the following style:

> During the occupation, the German invaders tried by every method to poison the consciousness of Soviet men and women and to confuse them. . . . It is the duty of party organizations to stimulate tirelessly the political activity of the workers. . . . Particular attention must be paid to the question of instilling in the population a socialist attitude toward labour and public property, strengthening State discipline, and overcoming a liking for private property and a revulsion to collective farms and the State fostered by the German occupants. (*Pravda*, October 17, 1944.)

Throughout the country the propaganda machine began to dwell on traditional ideological themes for the benefit of all sectors of society. On the wider scene of international relations, the death of Roosevelt in 1945 provided a useful though somewhat artificially contrived watershed in Soviet diplomacy. It was maintained that Roosevelt's departure from the political stage marked the end of the 'progressive' ideas that he had introduced and the onset of typical capitalist reaction. It was not long before Nazi Germany was replaced by America as the symbol of imperialist aggression.

These were the mere preludes on the domestic and international fronts to what were later to be known as the 'Iron Curtain' and the 'Cold War' respectively. Both these phrases have made such a deep impression on the popular mind that it is often forgotten that the phenomena they attempted to describe existed long before these convenient tags were invented. They have in fact been with us to a greater or lesser degree since the day in 1917 when the Tsar's Winter Palace was stormed. Marxism-Leninism as a political philosophy calls for unabated antagonism or 'Cold War' against the non-Communist world. In the face of the latter's natural distrust, backed by overwhelmingly superior military force at least until 1945, isolated Russia had erected an 'Iron Curtain' after the Revolution.

The word 'curtain' is apt when applied to Soviet security during the Second World War. For a brief twilight period the curtain was raised, though against Russia's will. The tragi-comedy of inter-Allied courtesies ensued, then the curtain dropped again; but this time it covered all of Eastern Europe as well. The shock caused by the abrupt termination of relations in which Western statesmen had put far too much naïve faith, together with the Soviet envelopment of the territory east of 'Stettin in the Baltic to Trieste in the Adriatic', as Churchill so graphically put it, only served to make crystal-clear an attitude that had long been familiar in international diplomacy.

At Teheran, Yalta, and Potsdam, as will be discussed below, Stalin was able to make the most of Soviet advantages in shaping the postwar world, since he had long been familiar with the Iron Curtain and Cold War images and knew perfectly well that they were ingrained too deeply to disappear during a short, unnatural period of co-operation with non-Communist states. In the glow of optimism brought on by final victory against the Nazis, Roosevelt and, to a much lesser degree, Churchill went through the parody of pretending that wartime relations would blossom into permanent co-operation, and in so doing failed to strike the hard bargain that Stalin fully expected them to make:

> Perhaps you think that just because we are the Allies of the English we have forgotten who they are and who Churchill is. They find nothing sweeter than to trick their allies. And Churchill? Churchill is the kind who, if you don't watch him, will slip a kopeck out of your pocket. Yes, a kopeck out of your pocket! And Roosevelt? Roosevelt is not like that. He dips his hand only for bigger coins.[1]

SOVIET GAINS

Against a background of disaster at home, the Soviet Union emerged from the Second World War with vastly increased power and prestige on the international scene. Since both advantages stemmed directly from naked military conquests, let us now follow in brief outline the movements of Soviet armies both inside and to the west of the USSR before the end of the war.

Soviet Military Expansion

In the autumn of 1942 the buffers of Leningrad, Moscow, and above all Stalingrad held up the Nazi *blitzkrieg*. Soviet victory at Stalingrad was the turning point of the war, but it need not have been, if Hitler had not so obstinately refused to allow Paulus's army to withdraw from the city; the German army in the Caucasus managed to extricate itself from a position that was much further embedded in Russian lines. In the struggle for Kursk, Orel, and Kharkov the Germans lost

---

[1] Milovan Djilas, *Conversations with Stalin* (New York, Harcourt, Brace & World, 1962), p. 73.

6,000 tanks, which could never be replaced by the factories at home, subjected to constant Allied bombing raids. The Soviet artillery gradually triumphed over the Panzer divisions, which in combination with the Luftwaffe had previously proved invincible on every front. Even more than equipment, the German commanders lost the initiative, and the chance of forcing a decision on the enemy. At the beginning of 1943 the Germans invested the maximum in military skill and forces on the Russian front, without success.

In 1944 the advancing Soviet armies crossed Russia's 1939 frontiers. With many divisions held down in Western Europe by the Allied invasion, the German army in the East bore the brunt of Soviet assaults, which were no longer confined to a front of 400 miles but stretched over a distance of 2,000 miles—from the Arctic Ocean to the Black Sea. In winter in the snows of Leningrad, in spring in the mud of the Ukraine, in summer on the plains of Belorussia and Rumania, in autumn in the Carpathian mountains and along the Hungarian plains, the Soviet troops proved their superiority. They had it within their power to capture almost any objective in Eastern Europe.

A main summer offensive was launched by the Russians just two and a half weeks after the Anglo-American invasion of Normandy. On June 23rd they moved forward, not from the great wedge in southern Poland that had been opened up after the Ukrainian victories of 1943, but from the line further east and to the north, in Belorussia. In less than a fortnight the Red Army pushed the Germans out of Belorussia. By the end of the year the main Russian front stood astride the centre of Poland. Meanwhile in the south Soviet armies struck out against Rumania, which then declared war on Nazi Germany.

Besides consolidating the fronts already held, Russian armies spread further afield, moving through Hungary and Yugoslavia in the south and the Baltic states in the north. Thus practically the whole of Eastern Europe was systematically covered by Soviet troops, a factor that had great weight in the diplomatic talks between the Allies. After Roosevelt's insistence on a policy of unconditional surrender for Germany, there was no need for Stalin to rush his armies into Berlin. Vienna, not Berlin, was the strategic centre of Eastern Europe, and by February 1945 Stalin had the Allies' word for it that Berlin would be within the Russian zone of occupation under any circumstances.

In January 1945, the Russians launched an all-out attack on their fronts from the Baltic to the Carpathians. When Hitler's Chief of

General Staff told the Fuehrer that 225 infantry divisions and 22 armoured corps were marshalled against them on the Eastern front, Hitler's incredulous reply showed that even after four years of close combat with the Russians he was still as incapable as the Allies of grasping the significance of Soviet military might and its political consequences. 'It's the biggest imposture since Genghis Khan! Who is responsible for producing all this rubbish?'[1]

By April 30th, a few days after Zhukov's armies had encircled Berlin and Soviet patrols had met up with the American First Army on the Elbe, Hitler was dead. Vienna had been taken by the Russians on April 13th. Prague too was left to Stalin, because Eisenhower obligingly halted his troops on the Elbe a few miles inside Czech territory. Eisenhower believed, wrongly as it turned out, that the Nazis were building up a final defence in the Alps. Thus by the time war in Europe came to an end on May 7, 1945, Soviet armies had spread out over the whole of Eastern and most of Central Europe, thanks to their superior power and their adroit use of the political situation.

The Soviet military achievement was considerable on its own merits; compared to the efforts of her Allies on the continent of Europe it appeared even more remarkable. The failure of the Anglo-Saxon powers to open a second front in 1942, which Stalin had been led to expect, made British and American statesmen feel indebted to the country that had borne the main burden of combat for many months. This gratitude was combined with the fear felt in 1942 that Russia might extricate herself from the war and allow the Germans to throw their whole weight against Britain before the American war machine came into full operation. A general aura of wartime emotionalism enhanced these sentiments and inclined the Anglo-Saxons to an optimistic view of Soviet policies. The Nazi-Soviet Non-aggression Pact of 1939, though of recent date, was quietly ignored.

Stalin, Roosevelt, and Churchill

Against this background of Russian strengths and weaknesses, Stalin met Churchill and Roosevelt for the first time in November 1943, at Teheran. Having directed the course of the Soviet campaign down to the smallest detail, Stalin had a clear view of his nation's balance sheet. All his discussions with the Allied leaders were carried on in the light of what he knew; he ignored the world at large, and was not interested in general plans for postwar international society, as were

[1] H. Guderian, *Erinerungen eines Soldaten* (Heidelberg, 1951), p. 347.

Roosevelt and Churchill. His sole intent was to rebuild shattered Russia as quickly as possible, both for her own sake and so that she would be ensured a predominant influence in the areas through which her troops were to march.

What were the personal attitudes of the two men who met Stalin at Teheran and Yalta? We know something of the problems Stalin had to contend with. To what extent was he likely to get his way with Roosevelt and Churchill?

We have already noted the military debt that Britain and America owed to Russia at the time of the Teheran meeting. This was symbolized by the presentation to Stalin of the encrusted sword sent by George VI for the city of Stalingrad. As early as 1941, at the time of the German attack on Russia, Roosevelt had told Churchill that he would support publicly '*any* announcement that the Prime Minister might make welcoming Russia as an ally'.[1] In his broadcast to the nation in the same year, Churchill expressed no fears about Russian ambitions beyond the Soviet borders. The West in 1941 was too urgently in need of help to express any caution regarding future Soviet intentions, even if Russia did survive the German onslaught.

But at Teheran Churchill took a more sober view of future Allied co-operation. Opinions that he had long held because of his Conservative politics and his aristocratic social background had been reinforced at his unpleasant meeting with Stalin in August 1942, in Moscow, when he had to inform the Soviet leader that the proposed second front would not take place that year. His suspicion had further been roused, as we shall see below, by the attitude of the Russians to the Polish government-in-exile in London.

Roosevelt had had fewer contacts with the Soviets, either during the war or before. His political triumphs lay in the domestic field. Personally, he was an idealist with great charm; he did not see why other men, even Stalin, were incapable of being converted to his way of thinking. Politically, there were two main reasons why Roosevelt was more conciliatory than Churchill. Not only was he bound to be grateful for military co-operation already received, but the United States was also wooing Russia for help in the war against Japan. In addition he saw himself and Stalin as the protagonists of anti-imperialism, with Churchill in the opposite camp.[2]

Out of these differences between Roosevelt and Churchill arose

---

[1] Winston Churchill, *The Second World War*, Vol. 3, *The Grand Alliance* (London: Cassell & Co. Ltd, 1951), p. 369.
[2] W. H. McNeill, *America, Britain, and Russia: Their Co-operation and Conflict, 1941–1946* (Oxford University Press, 1953), p. 345.

frequent opportunities at Teheran and Yalta for Stalin to play off the one against the other, thus weakening the effectiveness of both. When Stalin invited Roosevelt to stay with him in the Russian embassy in Teheran, he was carrying out on a personal level what Soviet foreign policy had tried to do since 1917—split the united capitalist front. Roosevelt occasionally disagreed outright with Churchill's views during the Yalta discussions. This too was on the personal level. But since every word spoken at Teheran and Yalta had enormous repercussions for the postwar world, major items of policy were also affected.

Teheran was the site of the first meeting between the three heads of government. Whereas their subsequent encounter at Yalta was to deal with planning for peace, at Teheran arrangements for the future course of the war took pride of place. At Teheran in 1943, and at Yalta and Potsdam in 1945, the same international problems came up for repeated discussion. They are treated below by subject, rather than chronologically, in order to avoid confusion.

The amicable Allied relations that had prevailed even between Churchill and Stalin at Teheran began to wilt at Yalta in February 1945, and had disappeared altogether by the time of the Potsdam Conference in July. In the winter of 1943 the need for military cooperation bound the Allies together, and although Stalin was extremely reticent on the subject of combined plans for the postwar world, in which he was supposed to take a leading role, he did not comment too adversely on Allied aims. In 1943 sensitive areas like the Polish problem were bypassed. Even at Yalta, the positions of the three statesmen were still fluid, though clouds loomed on the horizon. However, most of the major decisions affecting the postwar world were made at that time. Five months later relations between the West and Russia had deteriorated to such a degree that few positive results were achieved in the course of the Potsdam Conference. At this meeting the American delegation was headed by Truman, a very different man from Roosevelt. It was he who wrote in the *New York Times* two days after the German invasion of Russia: 'If we see that Germany is winning we ought to help Russia, and if Russia is winning we ought to help Germany, and that way let them kill as many as possible.'

Russia in Eastern Europe
Of all the problems discussed at Teheran, Yalta, and Potsdam, the future of Eastern Europe was to have the most significance for postwar relations between the Soviet Union and its ex-Allies. It is

important at this point to make an assessment of Russian aims *as of 1944–5* in this area, and to avoid assigning with the wisdom of hindsight any intentions that simply did not exist or else were only very dimly outlined at the time.

What, then, were Stalin's thoughts on Eastern Europe at the end of the war? While it is impossible to pin them down with certainty, some interesting facts emerge. In the first place Stalin made it quite clear that the territorial objectives of Soviet diplomacy were practically the same as they had been during the period of the Soviet-German Non-aggression Pact. During the whole course of the war Stalin affirmed that the areas Russia had annexed from Poland, Rumania, and Finland in 1939 and 1940 belonged to her on a permanent basis. At Teheran Stalin declared also that the Baltic States of Lithuania, Latvia, and Estonia, which had been annexed in 1940, had become member republics of the USSR by virtue of the free vote of their peoples.

Far less explicit was the nature of Soviet plans for the territories through which the Red Army marched on its way to Berlin. It seems probable that Stalin had no long-term blueprint for Eastern Europe. We must try to put ourselves in his place and consider what this area of the world meant to him at this time. First and foremost, Eastern Europe had to be drawn into the Russian sphere of influence. For the second time in the twentieth century Germany had inflicted devastating losses on Russia, sweeping across the wide plains and defenceless territories of the small nations that separated her from the USSR. In 1944 Stalin was still thinking in terms of pre-nuclear strategy. Even if Germany did not arise from the ashes and attempt to take her revenge, there was always the chance, to Soviet ways of thinking at least, that bourgeois governments would stage another intervention or else secure a ring of pro-capitalist states around Russian borders. Stalin's fear of Germany dominated his ideas on foreign policy at this time. We shall see this fear dominating his plans for Poland, the German gateway to Russia, and his ideas on international co-operation in the postwar world.

Stalin was determined that the East European states should not fall under the control of domestic governments that might be hostile to the Soviet Union. This need was recognized by Russia's allies, and led to the Anglo-Soviet agreement on spheres of influence in the Balkans. It is doubtful whether in 1944 Stalin had any fixed intention of submitting the East European states to uncompromising Soviet rule. When the Soviet Government stated on July 26, 1944, that it did not 'pursue the aim of acquiring any part of Polish territory or of changing the social order in Poland',[1] it was not necessarily indulging in double-talk.

In October of the same year Stalin expressed the opinion in a conversation with Stanislaw Mikolajczyk, the Polish Premier, that Communism did not fit the Poles as a nation. It seems that at first Stalin merely hoped that Communist parties in Eastern Europe would wield sufficient influence to prevent the emergence of anti-Russian tendencies.

It would be rash to rely on Soviet statements as a guide to Soviet policy, but in this case practical Soviet moves lent credence to the opinion given above. These actions revealed a policy of flexibility with regard to the future of the East European states. This is illustrated by wartime relations between Moscow and the Yugoslav and Polish Communists. In 1942 Tito was criticized for allowing his partisan movement to acquire 'a Communist character'. In Poland a heated quarrel ensued between local Communists who maintained a rigid, orthodox view of revolutionary tactics and their more flexible compatriots brought in from Moscow.

Stalin's geographical manipulations in Poland showed that at the beginning he had no precise plans for forcing a Communist government on that country. He annoyed the Poles by refusing to make any concessions about their eastern frontier. Yet if Poland as well as Russia were to be part of a new Communist commonwealth, what need was there for Stalin to be so adamant? Soviet relations with Communist parties in the Axis countries were also strained because of the crippling reparations that Stalin demanded from Hungary, Rumania, and Bulgaria. There would have been little reason to ransack and antagonize Eastern Europe if Stalin had already envisaged the pattern of Soviet economic control that evolved in the area after the war.

At the root of Stalin's behaviour lay his aversion to spontaneous revolutions by any of the foreign Communist parties. George Kennan thinks that the spirit of Trotsky, rather than that of Hitler or of any other capitalist demon, haunted Stalin the most. Having once ousted Trotsky and built up socialism in one country, a policy that ensured his position as the head of the world Communist movement, Stalin would have run counter to his whole previous way of thinking had he deliberately encouraged revolution in Eastern Europe. He had been against revolutions before 1939, when Russian strength was growing rapidly. He was even more cautious in 1944-5, when his own country, the bastion of his personal power, lay in ruins.

[1] *Soviet Foreign Policy During the Patriotic War*. Documents translated by Andrew Rothenstein. Vol. 2 (London: Hutchinson & Co.), p. 93.

The existence of a number of states outside Russia in which Communist rule seemed a likelihood for the future created an entirely new set of problems for Stalin. At the end of the war he directed his attention chiefly to the rehabilitation of Russia, a problem with which he was perfectly familiar, while cautiously watching developments in Eastern Europe. But before long he was to extend Socialism in One Country to Socialism in One Zone on a systematic basis. Stalin was to discover that the only way he could ensure undisputed Soviet influence in Eastern Europe was to apply controlled revolution from above. In the long run totalitarian government is incompatible with flexibility, even when that government is exercised indirectly over foreign states.

The Polish Question
In the East European sphere the Polish problem provided the leitmotiv of inter-Allied diplomacy from Teheran to Potsdam. Russia had established relations with the Polish government-in-exile after the German invasion, but these relations deteriorated rapidly, since the Soviets continued to press for recognition of the Polish eastern frontier set up in 1939 after the fall of Poland. When in the spring of 1943 the Polish government-in-exile tactlessly though understandably demanded an investigation of the Katyn massacre of thousands of Polish officers who had been taken prisoner by the Russians in 1939, the Russian government broke off relations and thereafter supported the Union of Polish Patriots established on Russian soil earlier in the war.

At the time of the Teheran meeting the Polish question was the only sign of the rift that was to grow between Russia and the Anglo-Saxon powers. At Yalta Stalin stressed the supreme importance of establishing a strong Poland to act as a barrier to possible future German aggression. The length and vehemence of his speeches on Poland indicated his interest and also reflected the growing tension between the victors. Indeed the failure to achieve a settlement of the Polish question represented a major turning point in the relations between the war partners.

The quarrel over Poland centred on the delineation of her postwar boundaries and above all on the composition of her government. It was agreed at Yalta that Russia should receive that part of Poland lying east of the Curzon line, so called after the British Foreign Secretary on behalf of whom it had been proposed in 1920, and that Poland should be compensated with land from eastern Germany. A decision was also reached with regard to the government: Stalin agreed to admit representatives of the government-in-exile and of other Polish groups to the Communist regime set up by the Soviets on Polish soil.

In connection with the character of postwar governments in Europe, Roosevelt and Churchill persuaded Stalin to sign the broad statement of policy known as the Yalta Declaration on Liberated Europe. In this document the Big Three decided to aid the freed nations 'to form interim governmental authorities broadly representative of all democratic elements in the population and pledged to the earliest possible establishment through free elections of governments responsive to the will of the people'.

Yet in Poland's case it was already proving difficult to set up an independent and democratic government that was also friendly to Russia. Stalin therefore abused the Western definition of democracy and forced pro-Soviet governments on unwilling peoples. If Roosevelt and Churchill had refreshed their memories of Lenin's writings before arriving at Yalta, they might have realized that the Communist definition of democracy was quite different from theirs.

Roosevelt and Churchill were inviting Poland to put herself under Soviet protection by dislocating her borders and population to the extent they did. Communist domination of the provisional government in Poland survived the efforts of the Western Allies to have their say in it. Although the western frontier of Poland was left undefined at Yalta, Russia ceded to the Poles former German lands up to the Oder and western Neisse rivers without waiting for America and Britain to agree. At the Potsdam Conference, James F. Byrnes, the American Secretary of State, agreed to leave to the Poles the territory that had been assigned to them by Russia, but would not make a final decision regarding the frontiers till the signing of the German peace treaty. The treaty has yet to be signed.

Poland was the test case in the tug-of-war between the Allies. Stalin was so concerned for the security of Russia in Eastern Europe that he was willing to alienate his partners in the war over this question. Better than any other example, it illustrated how the United States and Britain were unable to enforce their point of view concerning a country that lay under Soviet occupation. Russian military might counted for far more than Stalin's subtlest diplomacy. The United States was the economic giant of the immediate post-war world, but Russian armies stayed in the heart of Europe while American armies prepared to withdraw as soon as the war ended. The only European power remaining was Britain, crippled by the long struggle against Germany and no match for Soviet arms.

Soviet interference in other East European states followed a similar pattern. In February 1945, King Michael of Rumania was forced to accept the Soviet nominee for the new government, which was Communist-inspired. As the result of a harsh armistice agreement scant regard was paid to Rumanian independence. It should be remembered, however, that this was the attitude in Western Europe also. The Allied military command in Italy for instance was given very wide powers under the terms of the armistice.

While showing no signs of softening his line with regard to vital areas in Eastern Europe, Stalin did make concessions in other spheres where his position was not quite so strong. He adhered initially to an agreement he made with Churchill over areas of influence in the Balkans, whereby Rumania and Bulgaria were treated as part of the Russian zone and Greece as part of the British. Thus when the British declined to intervene in Bulgarian and Rumanian affairs in 1944–5, the Soviet Union did not dissuade the Greek Communists from joining the Greek Government sponsored by Britain.

The German Problem

The future of Germany was the most important problem occupying the minds of Allied statesmen at the end of the war. On account of her industrial and military potential, and because of her location in the centre of Europe, Germany formed the largest part of the spoils that fell to the Allies. Having learned their lesson after the First World War, however, Britain and the United States eventually decided that Germany should be allowed to regain some of her influence in Europe.

Russia found herself in a dilemma. Of all the Allies she had suffered the most at the hands of the Germans, and her fear of a German revival has remained strong to this day. She wished to make Germany pay dearly for the damage that she had inflicted and to shore up her security against the eastern German frontier. On the other hand it was impossible to ignore the long-term claims of the German nation, and a clear-cut policy of revenge would only throw the whole of Germany into the arms of Western Europe. The ambivalence in Soviet policy stemmed from this dilemma.

None of the Allies was prepared to hand over the whole of Germany to any other, and it was too dangerous to allow Germany to go her own way. Some method of joint control over German territory had therefore to be worked out. At the Moscow Conference in 1943 Molotov told Anthony Eden and Cordell Hull that the Russians had not given much attention to the study of the treatment to be meted out to Germany after the end of the war, and even by the end of the Yalta meeting the Big Three had been unable to work out any definite policy for the administration of the Reich. The European Advisory Commission had recommended zones of occupation, which were adopted, but no method was thought out for ensuring that similar policies would be pursued in the various zones, although an Allied Control Council was set up.

The problem came up again at the Potsdam Conference, an inauspicious occasion for settling any delicate matter, since by this time the Allies could only agree to disagree on points that affected their interests, and among these Germany was the most important subject of all. The political instructions for the Allied occupation forces in Germany prepared by the European Advisory Commission were accepted, but only because they were largely negative. No adequate instrument was provided for supervising the enforcement of democratic political parties, free speech, etc., all of which were subject to 'the necessity of maintaining military security'.

The Allied Control Council was virtually emasculated from the start. Byrnes had tacitly accepted independent Soviet manipulations of the Eastern German frontier; in the Western sector Russia was denied participation in control over the economy of the Ruhr. Inconclusive arrangements were made regarding the rights of the Western Allies in Berlin, which was put under four-power occupation although it was situated deep in the Soviet military zone. As a 'temporary' arrangement, two air corridors, a main highway and a railway line were allotted for Western access to the city. General Lucius Clay left the agreement indefinite because he 'did not want an agreement in writing which established anything less than the right of unrestricted access'.[1]

These fragile, unsatisfactory decisions on the German zones and Berlin were still in force in 1965, frozen into permanence by the winds of controversy that have surrounded the German problem since 1945.

Amidst the euphoria of peacemaking, only Stalin at Yalta brought up the vital question of a central German government. At least he was farsighted or cynical enough to guess that Germany once divided would remain divided. But Stalin's own insistence on the subject of reparations was one of the chief causes of Germany's dismemberment. We have noted his deep fear of a German return to power; the theme ran through his war speeches. 'It would be naïve to think that Germany will not attempt to restore her might and launch new

[1] Lucius D. Clay, *Decision in Germany* (London: William Heinemann Ltd, 1950), p. 26.

aggression. . . . History shows that a short period—some twenty or thirty years—is enough for Germany to recover from defeat and re-establish her might.'[1] In the event ten years sufficed to make even a divided Germany a force to be reckoned with again.

Stalin's fear and his knowledge of what Russia had suffered in economic terms during the war drove him to demand a sum of 20 billion dollars from Germany. His request was refused by the United States and Britain, who argued for an apportionment of reparations on the basis of percentages of surplus German capital. The Western Allies were also unwilling to consent to the Soviet proposal for the tripartite administration of the Ruhr. It became clear in the course of the Potsdam negotiations that the concept of German political unity had foundered over the problem of treating the country as an economic whole.

Toward the close of the conference Byrnes suggested that each power should satisfy its claim to reparations by removing capital equipment from its own zone of occupation. In addition the USSR and Poland were to receive 10 per cent of the military plant from the three Western zones and a further 15 per cent in exchange for food and raw materials. This makeshift plan was adopted. It allowed the Soviet Union to carry out reparations without supervision and, what was more important in the long run, to conduct a simultaneous overhaul of the East German economy on Soviet lines. The Prussian Junkers were expropriated and vital industries nationalized very soon after Potsdam. The political revolution was not slow to follow.

Plans for World Government

Germany preoccupied Stalin to such a degree that he had little time for general postwar planning in the international field. His position with regard to the establishment of the United Nations made this quite clear. The initial plans were left to Roosevelt and Churchill, while Stalin merely vetted them. At Teheran he cut short Roosevelt's grandiose plans for organizing world peace and fixed the attention of his colleagues on the problem of controlling Germany. Stalin wanted United Nations troops to garrison military bases inside and around German territory. For him the main purpose of the United Nations would be to keep Germany and Japan permanently weak. To this end the new organization was to be little more than a continuation of the wartime alliance, from which the smaller powers would be virtually excluded. The United Nations was viewed by Stalin as a front

[1] Joseph V. Stalin, *War Speeches and Orders of the Day* (London: Progress Publishing Co., 1945), pp. 10–11.

organization for covering up world control by the Great Powers. He was not interested in providing for a democratic global forum of all nations, large and small, from which a supranational government might arise in the future.

With this aim in mind the Russians at Dumbarton Oaks in the late summer of 1944 concentrated on the machinery of the Security Council, not of the General Assembly, and insisted on the veto in order to avoid being in a permanent minority among the Great Powers. In the same vein they proposed that the new organization should restrict itself to the task of maintaining security and not attempt to deal with social and economic problems. The Soviet Union was soon supported on the first question, but not with regard to the second. It was also successful in obtaining the acceptance of the Ukraine and Belorussia as independent nations in the organization; Stalin realized that the Communist point of view in the United Nations would almost inevitably be outvoted by a 'mathematical majority' of the capitalist powers, as the Soviet Government sardonically referred to the bloc voting from which it was to suffer later.

Russia in Asia
At the end of the war two areas of crisis existed outside Europe: Asia and the Near East. Before Yalta the apportionment of Allied military effort in Asia was very different from that in Europe. The United States, with British aid, had borne the whole burden of the war against Japan, in which Russia had taken no part. Yet despite this military prominence in Asia, which was relatively greater than that of Russia in Europe, the United States failed to secure the political prize that was within her grasp. By the end of the war in Asia, it was the Soviet Union that had acquired new territories in the area; only in Japan itself did the United States retain a monopoly of power.

How did this come about? When British and American military leaders examined the future strategy of the war against Japan at the second Quebec Conference in September 1944, they concluded that it would take approximately eighteen months after the end of the European war to bring Japan to heel. Even if they could not assess the impact of the atomic bomb at that time, the Combined Chiefs of Staff appeared to discount the psychological effect that the breakdown of the European part of the Axis would have on the Japanese. Their rather narrow military outlook influenced Western political leaders, particularly Roosevelt. In his effort to shorten the war and spare American lives, Roosevelt was prepared to bring Russia into action against Japan at great political expense.

Stalin was not slow to use American anxiety to Soviet advantage. At Teheran he hinted that Russian co-operation in the Far East depended on the early formation of a second front in Europe. No mention of Soviet compensation was made, except for vague references to future Russian privileges in the port of Dairen. Then, in October 1944, Stalin told General John Deane, the head of the United States military mission in Moscow, that it did not matter to him if the United States wished to deal with the Japanese alone. This was a very clever move, because it was already clear that Roosevelt was keen to secure Soviet collaboration. General Deane said that Russian aid was indeed required, especially against Japanese forces in Manchuria. Stalin then proceeded to outline a campaign plan that would put Russia in complete military control of Manchuria and the Kwantung peninsula, thus giving her as free a hand as she had in Eastern Europe. At the same time Stalin mentioned vaguely that 'certain political aspects would have to be taken into consideration'[1] if Russia entered the war against Japan.

Two months later, in December 1944, Stalin listed the 'political aspects' to Averell Harriman, the American ambassador to Russia. He wished to regain for Russia all the territory she had lost to Japan since the end of the Russo-Japanese war of 1904–5, plus the Kurile Islands. At Yalta he achieved his aim in his famous bargain with Roosevelt: Soviet control was to be preserved in Outer Mongolia and over the Manchurian railways in co-operation with China; and in addition Russia won southern Sakhalin and the Kurile Islands, the internationalization of the port of Dairen, and the lease of Port Arthur as a Soviet naval base—this last demand had not been made previous to the Yalta meeting.

In return Stalin promised to enter the Japanese war within two or three months after the surrender of Germany. Thus in spite of the fact that the Atlantic Charter declared that the Big Three sought 'no aggrandisement, territorial or other', Russia was allowed to acquire vast new interests at practically no expense. Stalin himself told General Deane that he thought his troops would have to fight for at most three months in the Far East.

As it happened Russia declared war on Japan on August 8, 1945, two days after the atomic raid on Hiroshima, and ended the campaign eleven days later. It is true that even if the Yalta agreement had never

---

[1] H. Feis, *Churchill, Roosevelt, Stalin: The War They Waged and the Peace They Sought* (Princeton, N.J.: Princeton University Press, 1957), p. 466.

come into existence, Russia would probably have moved into the Asian vacuum without encountering any armed opposition from the United States; but, as a result of Roosevelt's bargain, Russian interests in the Far East acquired an air of respectability that was denied them in Eastern Europe.

It is interesting to observe the nature and extent of Stalin's aims in Asia. As in Europe, his motives were rooted in Russian nationalism more than in Marxist revolutionary principles. He staked a claim to old Tsarist possessions in both areas. For the rest, his ideas were vague. He had to bend to superior American force in Japan itself, where General Douglas MacArthur enjoyed a monopoly of control and neglected the Russian representative at his headquarters. In other areas in Asia he remained blind to opportunities that lay wide open to a crusading Communist power with military force behind it. In China itself the Russians promised to give support only to the National Government, thus expressly repudiating the Chinese Communists. The territorial gains in China won by Stalin at Yalta and confirmed in the Sino-Soviet treaty of August 14, 1945, had to be returned within a few years to the Revolutionary Chinese Government. Stalin's reluctance to co-operate with Mao Tse-tung at the end of the war showed that he was more interested in promoting the cause of nationalist Russia than in fostering world revolution.

In the rest of Asia the reimposition of Western control was being opposed by colonial areas that rejected their old masters after the end of the Japanese occupation. The revolutionary situation would have gladdened the heart of Lenin or Trotsky, but Stalin paid little or no attention to it in 1945. Since the abandonment of the Comintern in 1943 Moscow had not tried to take a leading role in Asia. Having won adequate material possessions in the area, the Soviet Government at first neglected the chance to sponsor revolution.

The fact was that possible Communist successes in Indochina, Indonesia, Malaya and Burma could not have been so easily controlled from above as those in Eastern Europe in the immediate postwar period. Soviet troops did not occupy any Asian territory that was ripe for Communism, with the exception of Manchuria and North Korea. Stalin was naturally chary of inflaming virtually independent movements in one part of the world while carrying out closely directed *coups d'état* in another. The Communist take-over in Eastern Europe was sufficient to tax exhausted Soviet military resources to the utmost, let alone Soviet diplomacy. We shall learn of the great opportunities in Asia that Russia let slip from her hands when we come to consider Soviet foreign policy in the postwar years.

Russia and the Near East

The Near East was the third and last crisis area at the close of the war in which Soviet and Western interests were involved. Just as in the case of Eastern Europe, Stalin's only immediate aim in the Near East was to acquire direct influence in areas named in the Soviet pact with Hitler. The Hitler-Molotov conversations of November 1940 had made specific mention of a security zone for Russia in the region of the Dardanelles and had recognized the area south of Batum and Baku in the general direction of the Persian Gulf as the centre of Soviet aspirations.

At the close of the war it was precisely these two areas that felt the brunt of Russian expansionist diplomacy. On the strength of the ambiguous wording of the agreements negotiated at Potsdam, the Russians, in June 1945, sent a note to the Turkish Government demanding that the Montreux Convention of 1936, which had established Turkey's full right to fortify the Black Sea Straits, should be revised and that Russia should be given bases in the straits plus two areas in eastern Turkey. Pressure was applied until the summer of 1946, without success. A similar aggressive manner was maintained with regard to the stationing of Soviet troops in Iran. Until the full force of world opinion as expressed through the United Nations was applied against her, Russia refused to withdraw the garrison she had placed there in the summer of 1941, with British consent, so as to prevent Axis control of the country.

Both Iran and the Turkish Straits have been traditional targets of Russian expansionist policies since Tsarist times. Stalin too was interested in obtaining a hold on them, not for their revolutionary possibilities, but because the first area offered riches in oil and the second a warm-water port.

Russian demands in the Near East also included a claim for mandatory powers over Tripoli and a base in the Dodecanese. Neither claim was successful. In contrast with her enormous gains in Eastern Europe and Asia, the Soviet Union did not fare at all well in the Near East. Again the clue to this discrepancy lay in the fact that there had been no Soviet military occupation in this area, nor had there been any need for Russian armed support except in Iran. And even in Iran Soviet troops had not been engaged in any action and were not the only Allied force in the country.

Aside from the areas in the Near East mentioned above, Russia behaved with remarkable restraint in 1944-5. A clear gauge of Stalin's nationalist, as opposed to revolutionary, aims was his refusal in 1944 to put pressure on Greece, a country with a Communist party sufficiently strong to take over the reins of power, and his concentration on countries like Turkey and Iran, countries that could offer no hope for a Communist take-over but which possessed material assets that appealed equally to Nicholas II and to Stalin.

When Churchill reminded Stalin at the Teheran Conference that the Bolsheviks had come to power in 1917 proclaiming 'no annexations, no indemnities', a slogan that was the opposite of Stalin's policy from 1943 to 1945, Stalin replied, 'I told you that I am becoming a conservative.'

The attitude of the Bolsheviks at the close of the First World War was strikingly different from Stalin's to the conferences that regulated the postwar scene after the second twentieth-century struggle between the Germans and the Russians. After the Revolution the Bolsheviks viewed the political stage through the prism of world revolution, a drama in which Russia merely happened to play the primary role. At Brest-Litovsk they were forced to give away much of western Russia, but they found solace in their class brothers abroad, who, they believed, would soon join them in the fight against the bourgeoisie. 'Our final negotiations,' Trotsky declared, 'will be with Karl Liebknecht'—the leader of the German Communists. At the end of the Second World War Stalin paid much less attention to instigating uncontrolled revolution and far more to collecting territories that would enhance Russia's national prestige or provide for her security. In addition to the gains that have already been mentioned above, Russia acquired as her own during the period from 1940 to 1946 portions of Finland, Rumania, Czechoslovakia, Afghanistan and the northern part of East Prussia.

By 1965 the only territories that had been occupied by Soviet troops after the war and that had later been released from Soviet control were northern Iran, eastern Austria, the naval base of Porkkala in Finland, and small areas of China. The rest of the vast areas occupied by Stalin's armies were transformed from above in strict accordance with the pattern of Soviet National Communism. Only China and Yugoslavia developed independent Communist revolutions. Soviet pressure exerted abroad without the presence of Soviet troops at one time or another has not succeeded in converting a single state to Communism, unless North Vietnam or Cuba can be put in this category.

Thus a prophecy made by Stalin at a dinner party in the Kremlin on June 5, 1944, came true: 'This war is not as in the past: whoever occupies a territory also imposes on it his own social system. Everyone imposes his own system as far as his army can reach. It cannot be otherwise.'[1]

---

[1] Milovan Djilas, *Conversations with Stalin* (New York: Harcourt, Brace & World, 1962), p. 73.

CHAPTER II

STALINISM AT HOME, 1945-1953

STALIN AND HIS AIDES

The Second World War changed the face of Europe, involved the United States once and for all in international affairs, and sparked off a chain of colonial revolutions in Asia and Africa. The domestic policies of all save one of the participants in the war altered radically, the defeated states were compelled to make a fresh start; the democratic victor nations, with the exception of the United States, voted for new governments and policies; but even the United States had a change of leadership.

Russia alone acted as if the war had never happened. She was a victor nation under totalitarian rule. Roosevelt died at his work, Churchill was voted out of office, but Stalin remained in power, more secure than ever as a result of his military triumphs. The figure of Stalin dominated Soviet history from the time of Trotsky's downfall in 1927 until his own death in 1953, and his memory still casts a long shadow over it even now. Any estimation of Soviet politics in the postwar years must start with an account of the man and those who occupied positions of power under him.

In the preceding chapter no distinction was made between Russian and Stalinist policy, since they coincided. After 1945 Stalin remained at the head of both the party and the government machinery by virtue of his positions as the general secretary of the party and as chairman of the Council of People's Commissars (Ministers, after 1946), respectively. These posts, and his control over the secret police, enabled Stalin to penetrate into any sector of Soviet life, enforce all his designs, and prevent the rise of likely rivals for power. The victorious course of the war merely served to shore up his unassailable position and enabled him to reassert his control over national life with great rapidity after 1945.

Retrenchment and a return to the *status quo* existing before the war were Stalin's aims. By 1945 he was sixty-six years old, an ageing man set in his ways who had been allowed to govern without restriction for nearly twenty years. The sudden threat to his power in the form of the Nazi invasion, together with the great material and psychological damage it caused, frightened him. At the earliest possible moment he reinstated those features of the regime which he knew from experience would provide stability. Both his cautious temperament and the nature of Soviet postwar expansion induced him to act in this way. Experimentation would be suicidal in the ruined fortress of Socialism; it was vital to rebuild the old walls so that they would be strong enough to protect not only the Soviet Union but the newly-won Socialist camp as well.

Stalin's Lieutenants

In the course of describing the political scene in the Soviet Union between the end of the war and Stalin's death, there will be little occasion to mention the work of the dictator's aides. For the most part policies were executed by anonymous party and government machines in Stalin's name. The 'personality cult', which Khrushchev was to criticize so much after his rise to power, was full-blown at this time.

Nevertheless, the activities of Stalin's lieutenants and their relative positions of power during this period deserve our attention for several reasons. These men were to decide the course of Soviet policy in the years after 1953 when they took hold of the reins of effective power. Their reactions after the death of Stalin were governed by the experience they had acquired during long years of work near the summit of power. When the totalitarian edifice built by Stalin appeared to totter after his death, they hastened to salvage, each for himself, the separate bricks upon which their own strength had rested prior to 1953, and to use them in the fierce struggle that went on behind the façade of 'collective leadership'. That struggle can only be understood in the light of their relative positions before Stalin's death.

Stalin's own methods of *divide et impera* are more easily understood if we examine the way in which he controlled the activities of his henchmen in the years from 1945 to 1953. There is a tendency on the part of historians of the USSR to exaggerate the omnipotence of Stalin—a tendency that has grown since Khrushchev's efforts to ascribe all responsibility to the dead dictator, who has come in useful as a scapegoat for the evils that were committed in his name.

Top party leadership in the period 1945–53 was concentrated in the Politburo (Political Bureau). As can be seen from the following table, the composition of the Politburo remained comparatively stable during this period—especially as compared with the fluctuations that affected it both in the pre-war period and in the years from 1953 to 1961:

COMPOSITION OF POLITBURO

1939 (after the Eighteenth Party Congress)	1948	1953 (confirmed on March 6th, after Stalin's death)
Stalin	Stalin	
Molotov	Molotov	Molotov
Voroshilov	Voroshilov	Voroshilov
Kaganovich	Kaganovich	Kaganovich
Mikoyan	Mikoyan	Mikoyan
Andreev	Andreev (excluded 1952)	
Khrushchev	Khrushchev	Khrushchev
Zhdanov (died 1948)	Malenkov (appointed 1941)	Malenkov
Kalinin (died 1946)	Beria (appointed 1946)	Beria
	Voznesensky (appointed 1947, died 1950)	
	Bulganin	Bulganin
		Pervukhin (appointed 1952)
		Saburov (appointed 1952)

Most of the changes occurred as the result of natural deaths. Only Andreev and Voznesensky were disgraced. The situation, like that in domestic policy as a whole except for the economic sphere, was relatively static. Policies that were more dynamic, in industry and in foreign affairs, demonstrated an even, relentless progression that was in marked contrast to the sudden turns of policy that were to characterize the post-Stalin era, especially during the years from 1953 to 1957. This was due to the continuity in leadership and the maintenance of a power structure that had grown up gradually under the same leader since the late 1920s. In this sense the war was only an interlude, catastrophic though its effects had been.

After the end of the war Andrei Zhdanov and Georgi Malenkov appeared to be the foremost of Stalin's lieutenants, although they never really emerged from Stalin's shadow. Unlike Malenkov, Zhdanov was an Old Bolshevik. The son of a Tsarist school inspector and an intellectual, he rose to prominence in 1934 when he was appointed head of the Leningrad party organization after the assassination of Kirov. A passion for ideological purity had led him to take a major part in the propaganda campaign against Trotskyites and other 'enemies of the people'. This was good training for the man who was to conduct a wholesale literary purge inside Russia and in East Europe after 1945. Zhdanov's transfer from Leningrad to Moscow early in 1945 brought him back to the nerve centre of political power, especially since he was given a place in the Secretariat of the Central Committee.[1]

Until then Malenkov had been able to maintain his ascendancy in the Secretariat, where his only serious rival was Andreev; but Andreev only had a tenuous hold over the party apparatus, and even that probably weakened when his agricultural policy was criticized after 1946. Malenkov had been employed in Secretariat work since 1925 and had acquired a wide experience in the cadre department of the apparatus. By 1935 he was the assistant director of the *Otdel Rukovodiashchikh Partiinikh Organov*, the body that supervised the activity of leading party organs throughout the Soviet Union and conducted the purges.

His prolonged employment at the fount of patronage had turned him into one of Stalin's indispensable aides. He learned the value of controlling the organizational side of party life and became adept at imitating the methods that had brought Stalin to supreme power. In the struggle that ensued between Malenkov and Zhdanov from 1945 until the latter's death in 1948, there were faint reminders of an earlier fight between Stalin, the manipulator of men, and Trotsky, the brilliant but often ineffectual theorist who appealed to men's minds.

The exact cause of this struggle is still unknown. It is clear that in this period there was considerable tension between Malenkov and Zhdanov and also a certain amount of friction between Malenkov and Khrushchev, but the pattern of these differences is hard to interpret. Rivalry was bound to grow keen between the potential heirs of an ageing dictator who played off one man against the other in order to maintain his own pre-eminent position. It may be conjectured that the rivalry was more acute than appears from the scant evidence available. When the death of Stalin cleared the air and political issues could be disputed openly between the leaders, the fierceness of the struggle for succession was obvious to all. In comparison the years before 1953 are like a dark age, hard to fathom and hazardous to interpret.

Personal jealousies probably had something to do with the tussle between Malenkov and Zhdanov. In 1941 Malenkov was appointed to the State Committee of Defence over the head of Zhdanov, although Zhdanov, unlike Malenkov, was a full member of the Polit-

---

[1] The Central Committee of the party was in theory the supreme authority in the intervals between party congresses, but in actual fact all power had long since devolved first on the Politburo and then on Stalin. The Secretariat retained some influence even after the war through its power of appointment and dismissal of party members and its effective use of mass propaganda.

buro at that time. In 1944 the Council of the People's Commissars gave Malenkov additional prestige by making him chairman of the reparations committee that supervised the dismantling of German industry. This appeared to pique Zhdanov, who criticized Malenkov's management of the committee and succeeded in getting the system replaced by one whereby Soviet corporations in Germany produced goods for the USSR.

In 1946 Malenkov was no longer on the list of Central Committee secretaries, although it is not known whether there was any direct tie between his demotion and Zhdanov's intervention. There may also have been some connection between the rivalry of the two men and the administrative purges that Zhdanov carried out under the cover of his ideological campaign against the intellectuals. In 1947 G. F. Alexandrov, a close associate of Malenkov, was dismissed from his post as head of *Agitprop*, the Department of Agitation and Propaganda of the Central Committee, and his *History of Western European Philosophy* was attacked by Zhdanov.

The growing rivalry was cut short by Zhdanov's death in August 1948. That the significance of the quarrel was probably greater than appeared on the surface was shown by the subsequent extensive purge of Zhdanov's supporters. The purge centred on the Leningrad party organization, Zhdanov's stronghold, and was carried out by Malenkov among others. By July 1949 all five secretaries of the Leningrad City Committee had lost their posts. The first secretary, P. S. Popkov, was replaced by V. M. Andrianov, one of Malenkov's protégés. Malenkov returned to the Secretariat on July 20, 1948, just before Zhdanov's death, and was thus in a position to carry out the purges with a relatively free hand.

The 'Leningrad Affair', as it came to be called by Khrushchev, was by no means confined to Leningrad alone, nor even to the aftermath of the struggle between Malenkov and Zhdanov. Khrushchev told the Twentieth Party Congress in 1956 in the course of his secret speech that 'those who innocently lost their lives included Comrades Voznesensky, Kuznetsov, Rodionov, ... and others'. M. N. Rodionov, the chairman of the RSFSR Council of Ministers, had no clear connections with the Leningrad organization, but Voznesensky and Kuznetsov were closely associated with Zhdanov; Voznesensky had joined Zhdanov in the attack on Malenkov's administration of the dismantling of German industry.

Voznesensky may well have been the target of Malenkov's wrath; but Stalin, who according to Khrushchev 'personally supervised the "Leningrad Affair"', also had a hand in his fall. In his 'Economic

Problems of Socialism', which appeared in 1952, two years after Voznesensky's death, Stalin criticized planners like Voznesensky who had taken economic voluntarism too far. At the Nineteenth Congress in 1952 Malenkov remarked that 'denial of the objective character of economic laws is the ideological basis of adventurism in economic policy, of complete arbitrariness in economic leadership'. Voznesensky's policy of trying to ensure that producer goods were sold at a price estimated according to the cost of manufacture was dropped after his death.

The 'Leningrad Affair' provided a cover for widespread purges, which in some areas had little to do with Malenkov's original ambitions; he did, however, make use of empty posts to put in his own supporters. Thus Voznesensky's state-planning post was given to Malenkov's protégé Saburov. In the same way Malenkov's new-found predominance in the Secretariat allowed him to consolidate his hold over party cadres throughout the country; in the years before the Nineteenth Congress many changes were made in the party organizations of the republics.

Thus for a variety of reasons the number of those who suffered as a result of the 'Leningrad Affair' increased in snowball fashion. The successive purges were not bloodless by any means. Khrushchev later mentioned by name several men who had lost their lives, and referred indirectly to other deaths. All the leading officials of the Leningrad organization who were dismissed disappeared without trace.

The rivalry between Malenkov and Zhdanov had considerable repercussions, but the less spectacular antagonism between Malenkov and Khrushchev, which had its roots in these years, was to have far more significant consequences after Stalin's death.

Khrushchev's rise between 1945 and 1953 led to several defensive moves on the part of Malenkov—and not of him alone, because other senior members in the party hierarchy noted Khrushchev's growing influence with some trepidation. Since 1938 he had been first secretary of the Ukrainian party, the most important party organization after those of Moscow and Leningrad. At the Eighteenth Party Congress in 1939 the Ukrainian delegation was the largest, forming 17 per cent of the votes. The party organs in the Ukraine were not atrophied to the same extent as the centre of political power: the Central Committee of the Ukrainian party met regularly four times a year during the postwar period, whereas the Central Committee of the CPSU[1] only met after long intervals. In the vital years from 1944 to 1947, when the Ukraine was undergoing feverish economic, social, and

[1] Communist Party of the Soviet Union.

ideological rehabilitation in the effort to wipe out all traces of the German occupation, Khrushchev combined the posts of first secretary and chairman of the Council of Ministers in his particular domain.

Partly out of jealousy, political leaders in Moscow criticized Khrushchev's work in replacing party personnel in the Ukraine, and in March 1947 Lazar Kaganovich was sent to replace him as first secretary, although Khrushchev kept the less important position of chairman of the Ukrainian Council of Ministers. Kaganovich was sent to the Ukraine partly in order to stamp out nationalist tendencies; Khrushchev implied in a speech reported in *Pravda* on July 3, 1957, that his own policy had not been considered sufficiently stringent in this respect. Khrushchev survived the attack and even appeared to thrive on it, for he resumed his position as first secretary in December 1947, and at the end of 1949 was called to Moscow as a Central Committee secretary.

By recalling Khrushchev to Moscow, Stalin redressed the balance of power among his lieutenants. In 1949 Malenkov was at the height of his successful campaign against Zhdanov's supporters. Apart from Stalin himself, Khrushchev was the only figure of great influence in the reorganized Secretariat who could challenge Malenkov's supremacy at the hub of the party apparatus.

Further hints of the incipient rivalry between Khrushchev and Malenkov were forthcoming in the agricultural sphere, which throughout Soviet history has been the testing ground and often the grave of Communists aspiring to power. Khrushchev's plan to amalgamate the collective farms into larger units was put forward and carried out without any criticism from Malenkov as far as is known (by the end of 1952 the number of collective farms had been reduced from 252,000 to 94,800), although there is evidence that Beria thought the programme was carried out too fast.

But Khrushchev's less practical idea of setting up 'agro-towns', in which peasants would live under urban conditions, was directly attacked by Malenkov at the Nineteenth Party Congress in 1952. No doubt Malenkov was encouraged by Stalin's unobtrusive agreement with him on this matter. *Pravda* withdrew its authoritative support for Khrushchev's initial speech on the 'agro-towns', and in an article of 1957 Khrushchev himself revealed that Stalin had not put much confidence in his agricultural schemes.[1] Khrushchev obviously sympathized with Andreev, who was dropped from the Politburo at the Nineteenth Congress for having sponsored the small labour unit system on the collective farms. In his secret speech to the Twentieth

[1] N. S. Khrushchev, in *Kommunist* (No. 12, August 1957).

Congress, Khrushchev said: 'By unilateral decision, Stalin had also separated one other man from the work of the Politburo—Andrei Andreievich Andreev. This was one of the most unbridled acts of wilfulness.'

A brief comparison of Malenkov's and Khrushchev's relative positions of power in the late 1940s tends to show that Malenkov's fear of his rival was not unwarranted.

The whole of Khrushchev's career up to this period had been spent in secretarial jobs in the party apparatus, the centre of nearly all influence by the end of the 1920s. Khrushchev became a member of the Central Committee in 1934, five years before Malenkov, and a full member of the Politburo seven years before him. Khrushchev took an early interest in organizational management; he put this to good use by building up a personal following in the Ukraine and in Moscow—a following that was to prove loyal to him in the years immediately after Stalin's death.

Malenkov's position in the Secretariat furnished him with an unrivalled mine of information on party careers, which he could manipulate at will, but always only with Stalin's approval. He both gained and suffered from his close ties with the dictator. His special position gave him a certain degree of flexibility, reflected in his arbitrary transformation of the cadre machinery in 1948. Men further away from Stalin hardly dared to act independently, though it is significant that Khrushchev's sturdily autocratic leanings in the Ukraine during this period have gone on record,[1] despite the fact that he could be and was called to heel at Stalin's whim.

Malenkov's proximity to Stalin procured him a seat on the State Defence Committee during the war. Khrushchev was not elected and therefore remained his subordinate; but Khrushchev was the undisputed head of the organizations he controlled, whereas Malenkov was only one of the several secretaries in the Central Committee and probably bowed to Zhdanov as well as to Stalin in the Secretariat of 1945. Malenkov's control over men was great, but he dealt with them only through letters and through his research assistants in the Cadres Department—not through the flesh-and-blood contacts that helped Khrushchev to knit so many enthusiastic supporters together. Malenkov was to suffer more than his rival from Stalin's death and the subsequent denigration of Stalin's methods, which Malenkov among others tried to prevent.

Malenkov, Molotov, and Kaganovich, the three men who were to

[1] On this see M. MacDuffie, *The Red Carpet* (New York: W. W. Norton & Co. Inc., 1955), pp. 199–200.

form the core of the 'anti-party group' that opposed Khrushchev after Stalin's death, were all connected much more closely with Stalin in their work than was Khrushchev. Molotov's lack of originality and his capacity for patient labour in the background cast him as a perfect henchman for Stalin; their association dated from pre-revolutionary days. In the 1930s Stalin moved Molotov from party to government work, although he had occupied crucial apparatus posts in the 1920s. His influence remained static and even appeared to decline towards the end of Stalin's life—as seen, for example, by his replacement as Foreign Minister in 1949 and the later threats to his life in the 'Doctors' Plot' of 1952.

Kaganovich had succeeded Molotov as first secretary of the Ukraine and Moscow before veering away from the party apparatus in the 1930s, when Khrushchev replaced him as first secretary in Moscow and Malenkov took over from him in the cadres section of the Secretariat. He then devoted himself increasingly to the building and transport industries.

It is worth noting that once Molotov and Kaganovich left the party apparatus and transferred to posts in the government and the economy respectively, their power appeared to decline. Despite the setback the party received after the war, it never ceased to be the focus of most influence in the Soviet Union. Jockeying for a commanding position immediately after Stalin's death, Malenkov and Molotov were to place their hopes in the new strength of the state as opposed to the party machine and to pit that strength against Khrushchev in the party apparatus; but they were not to succeed.

THE PARTY

In 1945 the party was still the main instrument of Stalin s rule though it was declining in importance beside the growing bureaucracy of the government machine. Party membership had increased very rapidly during the war years, from almost 4,000,000 in 1940 to nearly 6,000,000 by 1945; but quantity did not imply quality, as Malenkov remarked in 1947, and many of those who had been admitted to broaden the party base in a period of crisis only served to harm its efficiency in peacetime. The complexion of the party had changed greatly during the course of the war. Considerations as to the social origin and political soundness of new members had been neglected, and by 1952 the white-collar intelligentsia formed the largest section of the party. The age pattern had also altered significantly within the ranks of the party. It has been estimated that by

1952 roughly three-quarters of the members had joined the party since the start of the war in June 1941; nearly half were under the age of thirty-five and three-quarters under forty-five.

These changes brought to the fore a new type of party man, whose approach to politics was to have some effect on party leaders after the death of Stalin. At least half of the new members had undergone military service, but had little knowledge of Communist doctrine. For them the Revolution of 1917 lay in the mists of history, together with the violent idealism that had accompanied it. A party member aged thirty-five in 1952 had been born in the year of the Revolution but had matured in the late 1930s, in the flush of industrialization and some years after all political controversy had ceased within the party. Unlike the Old Bolsheviks,[1] who on the whole had spent a great deal of their lives in danger and obscurity, the younger members had been able to profit from the relative stability of the Soviet regime and acquire some sort of technical education. They came to occupy responsible positions in the large bureaucracy made necessary by the economic transformation of the country, and took their privileges more for granted than did their elders.

In spirit as well as in age they were nearer to technocrats like Mikhail Pervukhin and Maxim Saburov, elected to the Central Committee of the party in 1939 and 1952 respectively, than to Anastas Mikoyan and Lazar Kaganovich, old Bolsheviks who had joined the committee in the early 1920s. All four men worked in the economic sphere in the postwar years and sat on the Politburo in 1952, but their backgrounds were very different. Mikoyan and Kaganovich had been trained as revolutionaries and were already acting as Jacks-of-all-trades in the Soviet government at the time when Pervukhin and Saburov were undergoing intensive technical studies that took them nearly ten years to complete. In the period after 1945 the two younger men worked as experts on the State Planning Commission, while Mikoyan and Kaganovich dealt with less technical matters and occasionally played leading roles in top party politics.

In one significant respect, however, the younger generation of party members was of one mind with Stalin. Like him they had had little contact with the world outside the Soviet Union, and had come to view their country with a patriotic pride amounting to nationalism —which ran counter to the ideas of the majority of Old Bolsheviks, who combined cosmopolitan experience with theories of world revolution. Since their birth the younger men had been carefully wrapped in Soviet propaganda and kept in ignorance with regard to

[1] Members who joined the party before 1917.

the rest of the world. Although they were better educated, they were scarcely less narrow-minded than earlier party generations. Any impressions they may have gained of the non-Soviet world during the war were ignored after 1945.

After the war it was necessary to put the administrative machine of the party in order. The great influx of new recruits had made it unwieldy and of unreliable quality. After 1945 far fewer new members were allowed into the party, which only increased by just over a million in the years from 1945 to 1952. Opportunities for rapid promotion were not as frequent as had been the case prior to and during the war. In July 1946, the Central Committee of the party decided to increase the efficiency of party organizations and shortly afterward issued a decree designed to reinforce established procedures that had been dispensed with during the war years, especially at the grass roots level; for although the State Committee of Defence had been given absolute power over all party, government, military, and other organizations in the country, pressure of business had hindered it from exercising close control over local party secretaries. As a result the latter had been able to build up quasi-independent organizations full of their own supporters. Immediately after the end of the war they were subjected to attacks from the party centre accusing them of apathy and of a tendency to obstruct the rise of younger officials. Purges followed on a considerable scale, but did not have the violent character associated with the 1930s. In the USSR as a whole, 27·5 per cent of the district party secretaries were changed at conferences held late in 1947.

The proportion of dismissals was much higher in those areas that had been occupied in the war. In the Ukraine and Belorussia the party machines had seriously deteriorated. Two-thirds of the party membership of the Ukraine was composed of ex-soldiers, many of whom were not qualified for the posts that they held. The Central Committee took radical measures; by the middle of 1946, 38 per cent of district party secretaries and 64 per cent of district executive committee chairmen had been changed.

On the eve of the Second World War the Soviet Communist Party still kept its unique position under Stalin as the spearhead of political control over all sectors of life except the secret police, which obeyed Stalin alone. After 1945 it was essential for the party, if it was to maintain its dominant role, to reassert its influence over such areas as the state bureaucracy, the economy, and the armed forces. By tradition party organization was not confined to its own ranks, but attached itself like a leech to the bodies of these other groups. We shall trace the fortunes of renewed party control over each interest group in turn.

The State Bureaucracy

The party did not meet with great success in its efforts to regain control of the state bureaucracy, which had already been slipping gradually from its grasp before the war. Since the inauguration of the Five-Year Plans in 1928 the governmental machine had been growing in size and importance, and in 1939 new regulations were introduced to facilitate the entrance of its members into the party. The central bureaucracy had also forged close ties with the new technical élite, another group that was becoming increasingly important. The men in both sectors had often received a similar education and were acquainted with each other's spheres of work. On the technical level they began to connive in an attempt to resist the pressure of central party organs for increased production. Although the omniscient presence of Stalin until 1953 precluded any chance of the two groups obtaining much say in the political area, their combined strength after Stalin's death was to be pitted against the party in a struggle for political power.

The rise of the government bureaucracy coincided with the atrophy of the party organs. By refusing to call an All-Union Congress or Conference between 1945 and October 1952, and rarely gathering together the Plenum of the Central Committee, Stalin converted the party into just one more instrument of individual rule, on a par with the government bureaucracy. This adjustment of power relations was reflected in the increasing number of laws issued by the Council of Ministers, the government equivalent of the Politburo. Petty bickering between the lower levels of the two hierarchies occurred with more frequency after the war.

The balance of power was influenced by other factors in the period under review. The party, seriously weakened by the Great Purge of the 1930s, submitted to the Leningrad purge in 1948 and was still unsettled at the time of the 'Doctors' Plot' in 1952. The government, on the other hand, was strengthened by further centralization of its administrative authority after the end of the war. The co-operative movement was also brought under the supervision of the government at this time.

The Party and the Economy

In other areas of national life the party did succeed in reasserting its influence, though this often went hand in hand with penetration by governmental organs. After the war the wrecked economy had to be harnessed to central control in order to fulfil the targets of the fourth Five-Year Plan, initiated in 1946.[1] The growing international tension lent a sense of urgency to the operation. During the summer of 1946 many complaints were registered in the Soviet press with regard to the 'anti-Soviet' activities of officials in industry. Abuses were ascribed to the slackness of factory managers and trade union officials, whose irregular behaviour was widely commented upon. An article in *Trud*, the organ of the trade unions, noted at the end of August that in the important Krivoi Rog iron-ore mines organization was bad, the Stakhanovite movement was inactive, and production was low. In order to remedy this and thousands of other similar cases, labour laws retained their wartime stringency. Workers could not quit their jobs unless they were ill or wished to take up advanced studies. Very harsh punishment was meted out for absence from work. Conscription of labour, established in 1940, was extended.

Although the Party Control Commission and the party-directed Trade Union organization continued to ensure vigilance in industry after the war, the role of the government was enhanced. A new Ministry of Labour Reserve was formed in May 1946, and in June 1947 a decree authorized the Council of Ministers to mobilize boys from the ages of fourteen to seventeen for training in the Trade and Railway schools, youths and girls from the ages of sixteen to eighteen for training in Factory Apprentice schools, and men over nineteen for underground and steel-mill work. More important still, the wartime tendency of the party to take over direct supervision of economic operations and supplant the professionals responsible for them was counteracted after 1945. In the words of an article which appeared in *Bolshevik*, the theoretical journal of the party: 'The party has firmly and consistently abided by the principle that the direct administration of the economy must be in the hands of the *state* agencies, [author's italics] and the party, as the directing and guiding force of the proletarian dictatorship, carries out the management of the economy through the economic agencies; in this connection, confusing the functions of the party and economic agencies, driving the latter from management of the economy, or, above all, replacing them by party bodies is not permitted.'[2]

The disorganization of Soviet agriculture was even worse than that of industry. To remedy the situation a resolution of September 19, 1946, significantly issued jointly by the Council of Ministers and the

[1] The first Five-Year Plan had come into operation in October 1928.
[2] See *Bolshevik* (No. 2, January 1951), pp. 47–55.

Central Committee, aimed at retrieving for the collectives the land and equipment that had been taken by the peasants for their personal use. Charges were made concerning speculation among officials, the excessive employment of able-bodied workers in administrative posts, and the falsification of returns for grain deliveries to the state.

A Council on Collective Farm Affairs was set up in October 1946, to carry out the reforms and to step up party representation in the collective farms. The first half of the council's programme was fulfilled, but not the second. Until 1950 the traditional picture of an agricultural system relatively free from party infiltration remained in force. The failure to extend party supervision to the local levels entailed more reliance on central direction, which included governmental as well as party agencies; the Ministry of Agriculture played a considerable role in this way, working through the agricultural committees of the executive committees of the local soviets, i.e. through the state as opposed to the party pyramid.

Economic Reconstruction
The task of redeeming wartime losses in the economy was enormous. At the beginning of 1946 Stalin announced long-term targets for three or more new Five-Year Plans, requiring at least fifteen years of hard effort. By March 1946, the draft of the fourth Five-Year Plan had been adopted by the Supreme Soviet.

The disorganized state of the economy hardly allowed for long-term planning. The haste with which the plan was put into effect pointed to considerations of a political rather than of an economic nature; international tension was already rising. Although it was impossible to estimate accurately the cost of postwar investment or the size of the labour force, detailed targets were set for increased output over the five-year period. Iron and steel were set at 35 per cent above the pre-war level, coal at 51 per cent, electricity at 70 per cent, etc.

The plan was the first of its kind to be issued on time. It was like its predecessors, however, in that priority was given to heavy industry, thus shattering the hopes of a deprived nation that had looked for some recompense for the war effort. The Soviet government was not willing to cut off the roots of its armaments industry. The targets for consumer goods production were not nearly so high as those for heavy industry, nor were they stated with any precision. In fact they were to be underfulfilled by a wide margin. Agricultural targets were also unambitious: the grain harvest for 1950 was only scheduled to show a 7 per cent increase over that of 1940, which had yielded 119 million metric tons.

Nevertheless the achievement of the fourth Five-Year Plan was truly amazing and was the most dynamic feature of the domestic Soviet scene in the period 1945–53. Despite the wartime devastation and loss of life, by 1950 the 1940 level of industrial production had been exceeded by over 40 per cent. How was the miracle accomplished? Several factors that worked upon each other were involved, but the most important of them was undoubtedly the great sacrifices made by the Soviet population, under the whip of the party, in terms of long working hours, intensive effort, and scanty rewards for its labour. These elements had played a large role in all the previous Five-Year Plans.

Another boost was given to the economy through the utilization of productive capacities that could not be tapped in 1940 due to the effect of the purges of the 1930s. This factor had a large though imponderable influence on the economy. For instance, steel output capacity for the period 1937–40 was estimated at three and a half million tons, but the actual output of steel only went up by just over half a million tons during these years. Any comparison of industrial output in 1940 and in the postwar period must take this into account.

Productive stimulus was created during the war through the introduction of new industrial plants in the eastern zones of the USSR. Although special emphasis in the plan was put on the task of restoration in the wrecked western regions, and industrial production as a whole in these areas was designed to increase by 15 per cent above the pre-war level, higher rates of growth were laid down for the eastern zones, which made a significant contribution to the economy after the war. Iron and steel production in the Urals and Siberia, as well as in the Far East, Transcaucasia and Kazakhstan, rose at a very fast rate; new textile mills in Central Asia supplemented the output of older plants in the Moscow area; Turkmenistan was scheduled to increase its total industrial output by 76 per cent during the time limits of the plan; and the Kirghiz Republic intended to double its production.

The reparations Russia received from the defeated nations, including Germany, Hungary, Rumania and Finland, also helped to speed up the Soviet recovery. It has been calculated that in terms of payments and other benefits Russia's income from the start of 1945 to the end of October 1956 amounted to five billion roubles annually, which probably represented more than 10 per cent of the total fixed investment of the state. Soviet seizures of capital equipment and other resources in occupied Manchuria, a rich mine of booty, were also considerable. Joint stock companies giving great advantages to the Soviet Union were formed in most of these areas.

Although in the long run the economic benefits resulting from these sources may not have contributed to Soviet industry as much as was thought at the time, especially by the anti-Soviet press, there is no doubt that they gave a valuable initial boost to the Russian economy immediately after the war, when they provided a quick means of injecting life into an exhausted industry. German prisoners of war in Russia supplemented the sparse labour force. If, as has been calculated, there were approximately 2,000,000 of them in Soviet territory in 1945, they represented about 10 per cent of the total hired labour employed in material production. Many of them did not leave Russia until 1955 or 1956.

The discrepancies between the amounts invested in heavy industry, consumer goods production, and agriculture soon began to have their effect on the corresponding sectors of the economy. Whereas overall industrial production had already exceeded the level of 1940 by 1948, some sectors lagged far behind the general index. Housing suffered enormously during the war, and despite the fact that by January 1946 two and a half million people had been transferred from dug-outs and caves to proper dwellings, nine-tenths of those deprived of their homes were still unaccommodated. American visitors to Stalingrad in 1947 were taken aback by the aspect of the city, which still lay in ruins—although many of the former inhabitants had returned to the bombed-out shells of their homes. The standard of living of the great majority of the Soviet people remained lamentably low, thanks to the lack of interest in consumer goods output: by 1952 production in this sector had only increased by just over one and a half times in comparison to 1940, whereas capital goods production had risen by two and a half times.

The prostrate agricultural sector was further hampered by the continuation of pre-war policies that acted as a brake on production. Compulsory deliveries by the collective farms to the state at low prices, combined with meagre pay to the peasants for their labour, dried up most sources of initiative. Ambitious peasants spent more time on their private plots, which yielded higher profits, but after the war items produced in this way were subject to extremely heavy taxation. The small amount of consumer goods the peasants bought in the co-operative stores was also subject to high sales taxes.

In agriculture the party was faced with a dilemma that still exists, and which has changed but little in character throughout the period covered by this book; either Communist doctrine could be thrown to the winds, as was the case in the 1920s during the New Economic Policy, leading to a substantial increase in agricultural output as the result of private capitalist ventures on the part of the peasants; or else ideological orthodoxy and strict discipline could be reimposed at the cost of economic prosperity.

There appeared to be no issue from this dilemma. In the periods when considerable licence was granted to the peasants, the latter interpreted their economic freedom too liberally, as was seen during the war years when well over two million acts of illegal misappropriation of public land were perpetrated. Even long periods of enforced discipline and close party supervision did not succeed in stamping out the individualistic bent of the Russian peasant. By 1957 privately-owned animals were still producing roughly 55 per cent of the milk and meat of the Soviet Union.

So long as insufficient attention was paid to improving the situation in agriculture the economic situation went from bad to worse. The irreconcilable nature of the tussle between the central administration and the peasants was further illustrated between 1940 and 1950, when the total labour force employed in agriculture was reduced by about 11 per cent and investment in farm machinery and fertilizers was very low. Such a disastrous combination of policies inevitably produced poor results, which were concealed by various methods. An attempt was made to divert public attention from mournful realities by a display of propaganda pyrotechnics. Stalin announced a gigantic plan to change the climate of Russia from within ten to twenty years. Belts of trees were to be planted to shelter the dry lands in the south of the country exposed to winds coming off the deserts of Asia. A law of October 1948 provided for nearly 15,000,000 acres of new forests. The grandiose plan came to nothing. The southern steppes stayed dry and no information was forthcoming on what had happened to the tree belts.

At the Nineteenth Party Congress, Malenkov made optimistic statements on the condition of agriculture that were not corroborated by the facts, and which Malenkov himself was to contradict in his report of August 1953, after Stalin's death. The number of cattle at the beginning of 1953 was still below the total recorded for 1928, and grain production two years before the convening of the Nineteenth Congress did not equal that of a good pre-war year. Such a dismal situation could not be ascribed only to the ravages of the war, from which industry quickly recovered. The deadlock in central policy and the neglect of agricultural problems were just as much to blame. No thorough-going new solutions were tried out, with the result that

E

agriculture not only did not recover from the war, but manifestly decayed.

The Party and the Army

It was perhaps more vital to achieve political control over the army than over any other group after the war. The immense prestige of the armed forces and the mass entry of their members into the ranks of the party presented a threat to the predominant position of the party and state organs under Stalin's manipulation. It was precisely this group of the population that had been most subject to extraneous influences in the course of the war. Also, the Soviet army had always had close ties with the peasants, who formed a vast recruitment pool for it. The peasants in the years after the war, as indeed throughout Soviet history, were the most dissatisfied sector of the population. If the latent combination of the armed forces and the peasants had materialized, it might have proved fatal to the regime.

Prophylactic action against the army took place on two levels. The system of party control over the army, which had been tested and perfected during hostilities, was left in force: military officers were assisted by deputy commanders for political matters. The main body of soldiers was submitted to a purge, which reached its height in 1947. Soviet troops who had been prisoners of war were treated very severely. Special attention was paid to military forces abroad, and large numbers of men were recalled for interrogation. One Soviet defector estimated that at least 20 per cent of the Soviet administration in East Germany was arrested over a period of three years.[1] At the same time the general cleaning-up of party ranks within the Soviet Union included a high proportion of military personnel who had been recruited hurriedly during the war.

At the top level, highly popular military leaders were reduced to obscurity, while Stalin took care to build up an image of himself as the real hero. During the war Zhukov, the conqueror of Berlin, was given due credit for his prowess, but afterward his role as the 'Saviour of Russia' was played down by party propaganda and by Stalin in person. He was relegated to a minor post in the provinces. In contrast, Bulganin, the professional party man with whom Zhukov had quarrelled in 1944, when the former was posted as political commissar on the Belorussian front, became a Marshal of the Soviet Union together with other political leaders.

---

[1] Harvard Project No. 532, p. 27 (quoted in Z. Brzezinski, *The Permanent Purge*, Cambridge, Mass.: Harvard University Press, 1956).

The Occupied Areas

The critical situation in western Russia after 1945 was due partly to the havoc left by the German occupation and partly to discontent among the national minorities. Disciplinary measures that were applied throughout the USSR had to be applied with particular severity in this region. After the end of hostilities the state of war was declared to be still applicable in the Baltic republics and in those western provinces of the Ukraine and the Belorussian Soviet Socialist republics that had been under Polish sovereignty. Military courts of the Ministry of the Interior (the secret police) continued to apply criminal law in these areas. Armed resistance to the Soviet regime went on long after the Red Army had occupied the western Ukraine, and there were official references to fighting by underground groups as late as 1954 in the Ukraine, and well into 1956 in Lithuania. Wartime dislocation and apathy or outright hatred on the part of the local population hampered the work of the party and the government.

A mixed policy of coercion and persuasion was applied in the western areas. Deportation on a large scale took place in the three Baltic states after their reincorporation into the USSR when the German armies were driven out. By 1949 nearly one quarter of the population of these three countries had been removed to the interior of Russia. Great Russians were dispatched to fill their place. Although the central Soviet organs were not so tactless as to put Russians in top positions of authority, most of the deputy jobs were filled by them, including key places in the security service. There was resistance to the collectivization of agriculture in the new areas won at the end of the war, and the programme was forced through in Galicia and the Baltic states only in 1949-50.

Methods of persuasion were used in the attempt to build up the strength of party organizations in these territories. The turnover of party jobs was much higher in western Russia than elsewhere. Yet even here the purge could not compare with that of the 1930s either in intensity or in the nature of its consequences. Dismissed officials no longer feared for their lives but were often merely demoted or transferred to less important positions. The average sentence for some of the worst offences connected with infringements of the collective farm statute was ten years' imprisonment, a lenient punishment by previous Soviet standards. The shift from reliance on violence to more gentle methods was reflected in the redrafting of the Soviet Codes of Law. In the months after the end of the war the drafting committees recommended the elimination of the emergency provisions in the Criminal and Civil Codes, which had been used with such drastic effect by Ezhov in the 1930s. A decree of 1947 abolished the death penalty in peacetime, substituting twenty-five-year prison terms for the most serious crimes.

Thus although the party still relied on both persuasion and repression to gather support and to crush opposition, the holocaust of the 1930s was not repeated—though the political climate probably warranted it even more after 1945 than in the earlier period. The fact that the whole of organized life was in need of revision after the war, together with the great shortage of trained manpower, probably acted as a brake on central policy, though violence was used where it could be used to effect, as was clear from the case of the Leningrad purge after Zhdanov's death in 1948.

The Secret Police[1]

The iron fist of Soviet rule was still strongly represented by the security machine, though in the immediate postwar years it played a less obvious role than the gloved hand of ideological propaganda. It is necessary, however, to stress its importance before Stalin's death in order to show the size of the power vacuum that its decline created thereafter. The expanded role of the police in the campaigns for collectivization and the development of industry, not to mention the witch-hunting that accompanied Stalin's rise to supreme power, had led to the acquisition of great economic and psychological influence.

The Ministry of the Interior under Beria's control still retained its own army after 1945, together with its own factories, railways, and an incalculable pool of labour in the penal camps.

After the war the secret police was assigned some special tasks, including the progressive communization of the annexed countries, the development of atomic weapons, and the supervision of irrigation projects. The police also supplemented the party as an instrument with which Stalin could reassert his control over all sectors of Soviet life. It helped to impose the strict labour laws in industry, restrained peasants who tried to abandon the collective farm system, and dealt summarily with the bands of partisans who continued to oppose Soviet rule in the western republics after the war. It continued to intervene in the private and spiritual lives of Soviet citizens, endeavouring to stamp out all religious and local nationalist sentiment. The ubiquitous presence of the security machine in Soviet life

[1] The secret police, which changed its title several times before the end of the Second World War, was officially organized through the Commissariat for Internal Affairs. The Commissariat was also restyled as the Ministry of the Interior by an amendment of March 15, 1946.

was one of the hallmarks of the Stalinist era that impressed itself on all who came in contact with it—and even on those who did not, for everyone lived in fear of its hidden power.

The security network was administered solely by the People's Commissariat for Internal Affairs until April 1943, when a separate Commissariat for State Security was established. Beria controlled both organs, and after the war gathered many fellow-Georgians around him. Together with Malenkov he had a hand in the Leningrad purge, but his adversaries struck back by getting his henchman, V. S. Abakumov, replaced by S. D. Ignatiev as head of the Ministry of State Security in 1951. Beria's Georgian associates were also attacked in the following year.

Until after Stalin's death, however, it proved difficult to shake off the subtle grasp of the police over all sectors of Soviet life. Its hold was even firmer than that of the party, for it was not responsible to the party, but to Stalin alone. Although it seems that the security machine had passed the peak of its influence by 1938, when Ezhov was relieved of his post as People's Commissar for Internal Affairs, it cannot be omitted from any consideration of the Stalinist era, since it was an imponderable factor in the system of totalitarian control that Stalin reimposed on Russia after the war.

THE DRIVE FOR IDEOLOGICAL PURITY

The tightening of the administrative structure was accompanied by a campaign to cleanse Soviet minds of wartime influences and to reaffirm Marxist doctrine. At the end of the war other factors besides the dangerous departures from the party line and military and civilian contacts with the capitalist world put considerable strain on the regime. The Soviet people believed that the pressures that had been temporarily relaxed during the war would remain so after 1945. They expected considerable reforms, both political and economic. It was generally thought that the concentration camps would be abolished, that the harsh collective farm system would be modified, and that labour laws would be revised in the workers' favour. Expectations of a continuous 'thaw' were firmly held by the 5,000,000 Soviet citizens who were repatriated to the USSR after the war. Although some of them had passed the war years in foreign concentration camps, others had tasted freedom and found it sweet; indeed many of them had to be repatriated by force.

Soviet education, the main prop of Marxist teaching, was in a sorry state at the end of the war. In 1941 there had been 1,222,805 teachers in the Soviet Union; at the start of the school year 1943–4 only 774,795 were available. The postwar scarcity was especially acute in the western regions, which was precisely where bourgeois German indoctrination had taken root. Altogether eight universities and nearly 200 other institutes of higher learning were wiped out during the hostilities.

In view of the political disorganization that had affected men's minds, it was vital for the regime to take drastic measures. If Russia was to be rebuilt at the rate specified by the fourth Five-Year Plan, a disciplinary atmosphere reminiscent of the industrialization drive of the 1930s had to be kept up after the war. It is possible that Stalin and his lieutenants seriously believed in 1945–6 that the capitalists were about to attack Russia. In any case it was a convenient excuse for justifying the renewed demands upon the Russian population for hard work and a correct political attitude. As early as August 1945, Mikhail Kalinin, the President of the Supreme Soviet, was proclaiming the revised line:

> But even now, after the greatest victory known to history, we cannot for one minute forget the basic fact that our country remains the one socialist state in the world.... The victory achieved does not mean that all dangers to our state structure and social order have disappeared. Only the most concrete, most immediate danger, which threatened us from Hitlerite Germany, has disappeared.[1]

In a speech on February 9, 1946, Stalin stressed the possibility of future conflict between capitalism and Communism. This and other hints preceded the all-out ideological campaign that was begun in the second half of 1946 and continued without pause until 1950. One year after the war the propaganda machine for the entire country was once more completely under Stalin's control. Its efficiency, dating from pre-war years, was proved yet again by the speed and effectiveness of the campaign.

A major part of the attack was directed at Western influences that had seeped into the country as a result of the war. Party control was reasserted over a wide area of intellectual activity but, as in the case of the administrative reforms, the impact of the war years left a permanent mark. A strong admixture of patriotism and national sentiment was instilled into the revised 'line'. The synthesis of new and old was typified by the catchword, 'Soviet patriotism', which appeared very frequently in the course of the propaganda campaign.

[1] *Propaganda i Agitatsiia* (No. 18, Leningrad, 1945), p. 3.

The great Russian traditions evoked during the course of the war were given less emphasis; but the Soviet way of life, including its composite national feeling, as well as its ideology, was heralded as being superior to capitalism.

Perhaps Stalin believed that the appeal of the party and its doctrine was not sufficient to spur the population on at a time when party links with the masses were insecure; certainly Stalin himself was apt to think more along national than Marxist lines at the end of the war.

Soviet Literature
Much attention was given to the correct approach to literature in the postwar period. In general the Soviet regime has wavered between two rather different attitudes toward literary creation. In some periods very strict supervision has been imposed in the belief that the arts can be drilled to order and yet produce work of great talent; when this theory has been disproved by a high tide of mediocrity, various liberal elements have been introduced. Up to the present time, some relaxation of control has allowed genuine works of art to appear, but writers have pushed their freedom beyond the limits which the State finds tolerable. The aftermath has inevitably been a subsequent period of close supervision and poor literary results. The postwar period was one of reimposed controls.

The campaign was led by Zhdanov, who after March 1946 ranked third in the Secretariat of the Central Committee after Stalin and Malenkov. His power appeared to increase as a result of his activity in the ideological field. Following on a decision of the Central Committee of August 2, 1946, regarding the tightening-up of ideological discipline among leading party workers, a decree of August 14th contained an attack on two Leningrad magazines, *Zvezda* and *Leningrad*. Although it was confined to these two journals, the decree was intended as a general assault on the whole literary world inside the Soviet Union.

Leningrad was chosen because it has always been the centre of culture in Soviet times, and also because Zhdanov's influence carried special weight there in view of the fact that he had been the first secretary of the Leningrad party organization until 1944. The journals were accused of publishing works full of 'servile adulation of contemporary bourgeois Western culture' and denigration of the Soviet people. Subsequently the same theme was enlarged upon in speeches by Zhdanov and A. Fadeev, the secretary of the Union of Soviet Writers.

Writers who came in for heavy criticism included Michael Zoshchenko and Anna Akhmatova. Zoshchenko was an outstanding Soviet humorist whose short stories were aimed at the foibles of Soviet bureaucrats. In the period before the war his satires had been hailed as a valuable spur to self-improvement, but in the tense atmosphere of the late 1940s they were viewed in quite a different light. His work was now seen as an attack on party morals, and lacking in a sense of patriotic enthusiasm. Zoshchenko had spent the war years away from the front, in peaceful Kazakhstan. He was expelled from the Union of Soviet Writers. Akhmatova's downfall was caused by her lack of interest in the new themes that had come to be the stock-in-trade of all writers, rather than for opinions contrary to the party line. Her contemplative love poems in lyrical mood were considered out of tune with Zhdanov's hearty call to arms: 'Soviet literature neither has nor can have any other interests except those of the people and of the State. Its aim is to help the State to educate youth . . . to make the new generation cheerful, inspired by faith in its task, unafraid of obstacles and ready to overcome them all.'

All literary work had to be actively involved in the ideological struggle. Typical approved novels of the new climate included Konstantin Semonov's *The Smoke of the Fatherland*, which compared the American and Russian ways of life to the advantage of the latter; Semion Babaevsky's *The Knight of the Golden Star*, a plea for incentive on the collective farms; and Nicholas Virta's *Battle of Stalingrad*, a breviary of Soviet patriotism that interpreted the war as the triumph of the regime and the party rather than of the army. Party demands on the intellectuals became more burdensome as time went on. In 1945 *The Young Guard*, a novel by Fadeev about the youth resistance movement against the Germans, received very favourable critical reviews, but two years later the secretary of the Union of Soviet Writers upbraided him for not having laid sufficient emphasis on the role of the party in the movement.

Stalin and the Intellectuals

All fields of intellectual endeavour from music to biology, philosophy, and physiology, came in for stringent party criticism. Propaganda was relayed at two levels: on a comparatively sophisticated plane for consumption by the students and the intellectuals themselves, and in vulgarized form for the rest of the population. Thus Zhdanov's *ex cathedra* speeches to the intellectuals were accompanied by preposterous assertions that deprived the non-Soviet world of many of its claims to original inventions—for example that radio was invented by Popov, not Marconi—and these provided the European and American press with many a humorous article.

Occasionally Soviet efforts on the higher level seeped down to the popular one. The best-known example of this was the Lysenko controversy, which came to a climax in the summer of 1948. After an open struggle in which Stalin intervened on the side of the biologist Lysenko, the Soviet Academy of Agricultural Sciences confirmed Lysenko's theory that acquired characteristics could be transmitted genetically to succeeding generations, a proposition that was impossible to prove. It was a useful claim for the party to make, however, since it served a triple purpose. It implied that the children of good Communists would be born good Communists, and that the classless society could be created despite fallible human nature. The doctrine was also applicable to agriculture, which might conceivably benefit from higher production. The immediate and only lasting result of the controversy was the expulsion of twelve members of the Academy of Agricultural Sciences who resisted Lysenko's (and Stalin's) bizarre ideas.

This purge was by no means an incidental outcome of the theoretical struggle. Some aspects of the *Zhdanovschina*, as it came to be called, were less concerned with ideology than with administrative problems of the type that have been noted above in connection with Stalin's reassertion of control over the nation. During the war years, when ideological control was not so effective, some of the top posts of the Soviet intellectual bureaucracy had been taken over by men whose allegiance to the regime was not absolutely certain. In June 1947, several philosophers were criticized and subsequently dismissed from the Central Committee Directorate of Propaganda, although they did not lose their university posts. This was because the directorate was an essential tool for exercising ideological control over the country, whereas real or fictitious heresies pronounced in individual universities did not have such a harmful influence.

A similar campaign to oust powerful groups of intellectuals was directly linked with a discussion on the Marxist interpretation of linguistics in the summer of 1950. Stalin's attack on the views of N. Marr, the eminent philologist who died in 1934, led to the removal of his followers, many of whom occupied important university posts. In addition, however, Stalin's obscure and often inconsistent statements appeared to have two purposes of a theoretical nature. In denouncing Marr, Stalin put forward the thesis that the future 'language of socialism' would not be an amalgam of existing languages, as Marr had postulated, but one pure idiom, which, it was hinted, would be Russian. A corollary to this theory was the assertion that political action took precedence over economic development and that the state was able to manipulate the economic base and to transform society. This ran counter to Marx's proposition that the superstructure, including the state, was merely the reflection of the base.

Both of Stalin's propositions expressed in ideological terms the political situation that existed not only in Russia, but also in the emerging socialist camp in Eastern Europe. The first proposition was an attempt to clarify the new structure of international Communism, which, in Eastern Europe at least, represented the first stage, not of supranational, stateless world Communism on Marxist lines, but of a Russified world state based very closely on the Soviet Communist model.

The second proposition was not new; it had been expressed by Stalin in the 1930s, at a time when the economic base of the Soviet Union was being built up through political direction from above. The economic effort of the postwar years inside Russia was carried out in a similar climate of political coercion. Furthermore, Stalin's notion now applied with particular force to the situation in Eastern Europe. By the end of 1948 the new People's Democracies all relied on the strength of their political superstructure, represented by the ruling Communist parties, for their strength and guidance; it was only after that date that the economic base was fully transformed from above on Communist lines as the result of political pressure. Seen from the international angle, Russia's ties with the countries of Eastern Europe under her control at the time when Stalin spoke out against Marr were almost entirely political in nature. The official economic equivalent of the Cominform, the Council for Mutual Economic Aid, was not formed until January 1949, and its aims remained a dead letter until after Stalin's death.

Related ideological issues of genuine significance in their own right were brought up by Stalin in his *Economic Problems of Socialism in the USSR*, which appeared on the eve of the Nineteenth Party Congress in 1952. It seems as though Stalin wished to restrain those Communist theoreticians and economic planners who had taken his message of 1950 too much to heart and were neglecting the essential doctrine of Marxism.

'They are amazed by the colossal achievements of the Soviet regime, their heads are turned by extraordinary successes of the Soviet system and they begin to imagine that the Soviet regime "can do anything", that "everything is child's play" to it, that it can negate scientific laws and fashion new ones. What is to be done with these comrades? I think that systematic repetition and patient explanation of so-called "commonly known" truths is one of the best means of Marxist education of these comrades.'[1]

Stalin denied that political action from above could radically change the historical development of the economic base in the long run, though he did not retreat from his previous position, but merely uttered words of caution. He feared that his own voluntaristic interpretation of Marx might induce his lieutenants in Russia and Eastern Europe to take independent and increasingly uncontrolled measures.

Economic Problems of Socialism also dwelt on another matter, the situation of world capitalism. As early as 1946 the prominent Hungarian economist Varga had put forward the idea in his book *Changes in the Economy of Capitalism Resulting from the Second World War* that capitalism would escape a fundamental economic crisis for at least a decade after the end of the war. He defended his thesis with a mass of facts that could be observed by any Communist, but his view was heretical in that it implied that war between the socialist and capitalist camps was not inevitable.

If Varga was right in thinking that capitalism had made concessions to the working class and was reforming itself without resorting to the overthrow of existing systems, then it was in Russia's interests to co-operate with the non-Soviet world rather than to continue the Leninist policy of revolution. But a policy of this nature did not accord with the image of a divided world that Stalin was so rigorously enforcing immediately after the war. Therefore a campaign parallel to Zhdanov's in the cultural sphere was waged from 1946 onward against Varga's view on international economics.

Varga's opinions, together with their political implications, were eventually accepted by Khrushchev at the Twentieth Party Congress in 1956. After Stalin's death in 1953 a policy of peaceful coexistence was followed in practice by some Soviet foreign-policy makers, although the theory was only formulated in public in 1956. Even in 1952 Stalin shifted slightly from the orthodox view: he agreed with Varga's opponents that the crisis of world capitalism was imminent, but he affirmed that in view of the increased power of Russia and the new 'socialist camp of peace', war was more likely to break out among the capitalist states than between them and the USSR.

The great ideological campaigns between 1945 and Stalin's death

[1] J. V. Stalin, *Economic Problems of Socialism in the USSR*, published in *Bolshevik* (September 1952), p. 89.

demonstrated the continuing importance of ideological issues in the Soviet system. This does not mean that after the end of the war pure Marxist-Leninist doctrine was instilled into the masses merely for the good of their Communist souls. Postwar Stalinist ideology was a strange mixture of original Marxist-Leninist thought and many diverse accretions that had clung to the doctrinal core since the days of the Revolution. As had been the case with Christian ideology, the impact with reality had in time changed the face of the belief. What happened to the Communist theory when the Bolsheviks finally captured governmental power was not dissimilar to the transformation of Christian theory after the rise of the mediaeval papacy, except that the change was more rapid and profound in the case of Communism, since its struggle was entirely with the harsh facts of this world and it could look to no other world for final truths and the realization of its tenets.

The burden of the existing situation—a Russian nation that could not entirely ignore its historical course before 1917, nor change its geographical contours with their political implications; the hostility of the rest of the world, which denied the new revelation and prevented its application; the subsequent need to construct a safe home base for the struggling infant state, a base whose national foundations of necessity contradicted much of the international ideology it was supposed to promote—all combined to modify the theory. Thus Trotsky, the greatest prophet after Lenin, was muzzled, and had to make way for more realistic and worldly-successful men like Stalin, who postponed the millennium of total Communism and was accused of practising old-fashioned power politics, just like bourgeois statesmen in the capitalist countries.

We have seen Stalin as the head of the Russian nation in action at Yalta and in the diplomatic negotiations near the end of the Second World War, when he was interested in obtaining territorial acquisitions for his country rather than in looking for opportunities to extend the Communist revolution. But in the next chapter we shall see him carefully imposing Communism on those same acquisitions with a fanatical thoroughness that went beyond, and occasionally harmed, Russian national aspirations. Stalin's notions on foreign policy were a strange mixture of Communist ideology and traditional power politics; at one moment the Communist side would be more prominent, at another the national side, according to the nature of the situation.

The same was true in domestic politics. The Soviet leaders no doubt believed for the most part in the ideology that they reimposed on their people after the war—though there was an occasional echo of Dostoevsky's Grand Inquisitor, who upheld the tenets of a faith in which he no longer believed, but which gave him all the material power he possessed over the superstitious masses. Indeed the timing of the reimposition of ideological orthodoxy was governed by considerations that had little or nothing to do with Communist theory. It has been pointed out how the campaign was used to cut the Soviet Union off from the outside world and to reassert totalitarian control over a nation in chaos. The two aims were interconnected, because the retention of the dictatorship could be justified by stressing the menace of hostile capitalism.

In the same way that the scholastic philosophers of the Middle Ages interpreted the world around them in terms of the authoritative doctrines the church fathers had handed down to them, so Stalin and Zhdanov preferred to interpret intellectual matters in terms of the doctrines received from Marx and Lenin. Thus Varga was crying in the dark when he tried to explain the real nature of postwar capitalism: 'I think too many comrades say too mechanically: either—or. *Either* planned economy *or* complete anarchy. That is not how the matter stands. . . . With the either-or method we cannot understand the very complex new phenomena of contemporary capitalism.'[1]

For Varga's opponents capitalism and Communism had to be as distinct as black and white, as heaven and hell—there was no limbo in between. Lysenko had to be right because his views fitted in with Marxist doctrine. No other justification was needed. Ideology again triumphed over the facts in the revised version of the *History of the USSR*, which had been criticized in 1947 for giving too much space to the 'factual' presentation of history and lacking sufficient interest in 'questions of theory and generalization'.

It is vital to understand the peculiar Stalinist approach to ideology because there is no doubt that it had great influence on the formation of Soviet policies, not to mention the mental conditioning of a whole generation. The climate was to change perceptibly after Stalin's death. Even more than Stalin, Khrushchev liked to think of himself as a practical politician with his feet firmly planted on the ground, as is clear from these words of his aimed at Stalin and his adherents:

'I know men who are taken for theorists, yet their whole theoretical wisdom is essentially based on their ability to juggle with quotations from Marxist-Leninist classics on every apt and inapt occasion. These pseudo-scholars, who pretend to be theorists,

[1] Varga in *World Economy and World Politics* (Moscow, November 1947).

are unable to comprehend such an important detail of Marxist wisdom as the fact that people must above all eat, drink, live and be clothed if they want to be in a position to occupy themselves with politics, science and art.'[1]

THE NINETEENTH PARTY CONGRESS

The Nineteenth Party Congress, which met in Moscow in October 1952, was the first to be held for over thirteen years. The delay in calling it could be ascribed in large part to Stalin's neglect of constitutional normality, but the themes of the congresses in the individual Union republics that preceded the All-Union Congress pointed to other reasons for the delay. The individual republic meetings had laid great stress on the need to improve political education among party members and to deepen their understanding of the role they were expected to play in the country. The party rank and file had been recruited so haphazardly during the war that there was little point in assembling a nation-wide congress to lay down a co-ordinated policy until these new members had received some preparation in their jobs at the local level.

At the Nineteenth Party Congress Malenkov was acclaimed more than any other leader except Stalin, who naturally received the greatest ovation. Stalin's *Economic Problems of Socialism*, published just before the opening of the meeting, formed the centre of much of the discussion. Stalin favoured Malenkov by allowing him to present the main report of the Central Committee, but as usual he took care to maintain a balance between his lieutenants by letting Khrushchev give the report on the new Party Rules. Similarly four of the new Central Committee secretaries appointed at the congress were associated with Khrushchev, but the other two were Malenkov men.

Organizational changes made at the congress definitely benefited Khrushchev. The old Orgburo, a sub-committee of the Central Committee for executing policy, was disbanded. The party Politburo was replaced by a larger body now called the Presidium. Malenkov had been a member of the Orgburo, but Khrushchev had not. The enlarged Central Committee now contained many more regional party secretaries with experience similar to Khrushchev's; indeed he had many associates among them, especially from the Ukraine, and was to build up his power with their support in the struggle against Malenkov after 1953.

The new Presidium of the party, consisting of twenty-five full mem-

[1] N. S. Khrushchev, in *Kommunist* (No. 12, August 1957).

bers and eleven candidate members, included a larger proportion of the leaders in the government administration than had been the case in the old Politburo. The new influx of government officials into the highest party organ reflected the growing prestige of the state interest group as opposed to that of the party.

An inner bureau was secretly established. Given the almost complete continuity of persons and responsibilities from the Politburo to the Presidium (only Andreev was dropped), this smaller body probably consisted of the men who had previously formed the old Politburo. The fact that the new inner bureau of the Presidium was more informal in nature, and fluctuated in its composition according to the subject treated, enabled Stalin to swamp the influence of his more experienced aides with new voters. Apparently he was preparing to make changes among the leaders. Khrushchev later avowed that the new reshuffle 'was aimed at the removal of the old Political Bureau members and the bringing in of less experienced persons so that these would extol him [Stalin] in all sorts of ways'.[1]

The main themes of the congress were contained in Stalin's thesis on economics, Malenkov's presentation of the main report of the Central Committee, and Khrushchev's statement on the new Party Rules. The Congress adopted a fifth Five-Year Plan for the period 1951–5. It was traditional in tone: the accent still lay on heavy industry and the Soviet nuclear programme was obviously due to receive increased support. Much of Malenkov's report described the upsurge of the Soviet economy in glowing terms, and Mikoyan went on to outline a policy of offering unconditional assistance to the less-developed countries. By 1952 industrial output within the USSR had risen to a level at which it was already possible to contemplate such a scheme. Mikoyan's speech was one of the first signs of the swing of Soviet foreign policy in the years from 1952 to 1956 from an attitude of outright hostility toward the non-Communist world to a stance of peaceful coexistence. Even Stalin gave some attention to this novel topic, for in his thesis he referred to the prospect of surpluses in the East European countries.

THE 'DOCTORS' PLOT' AND STALIN'S DEATH

Both Malenkov and Khrushchev stressed the need for discipline within party organizations in their reports to the congress. The new

[1] *The Anti-Stalin Campaign and International Communism*, a selection of documents edited by the Russian Institute, Columbia University (New York: Columbia University Press, 1956), pp. 84–5.

Party Rules provided for the maintenance of a strict hierarchy in the party ranks, together with close supervision by the higher echelons. Article 13 of the Rules gave the secret police a firmer grip over party members. The political atmosphere, which had been relatively tense since the 'Leningrad Affair', was tightening up even more. The purge of Beria's supporters in Georgia took place in 1951, and the same year witnessed a new wave of purges in Eastern Europe.

On October 15th, the day after the end of the congress, the newly-elected Central Committee was summoned to hear Stalin accuse Molotov and Mikoyan and suggest that 'these old workers of our party were guilty on some baseless charges. It is not excluded that had Stalin remained at the helm for several more months Comrades Molotov and Mikoyan would probably have not delivered any speeches at this [the Twentieth] Congress'.[1] Mikoyan later confirmed in conversation with the American journalist Louis Fischer that he and Molotov were in danger at this time; in 1949 both men had already been deprived of their respective posts as Minister of Foreign Trade and Minister of Foreign Affairs.

Definite signs of an approaching purge were evident by January 1953, when *Pravda* announced that nine doctors, seven of them Jewish, had been accused of killing a number of high Soviet leaders, including Zhdanov. These charges were refuted in the Soviet press directly after Stalin's death, but their significance at the time was ominous. The linking of anti-Semitism with Zhdanov's name suggested that Stalin intended to revive Zhdanov's campaign against 'rootless cosmopolitans' and all that this campaign entailed in the ideological sphere. Anti-Jewish tendencies were evident in the trial, which was taking place in Prague at this same time, of Rudolf Slansky, the general secretary of the Czechoslovak party.

The Soviet police was accused of inefficiency for having failed to uncover the 'Doctors' Plot' in good time. Beria was involved as head of the Ministry of Internal Affairs. In retrospect it now appears as if the Georgian purge had been intended to sweep the ground from under Beria's feet prior to attacking him in person. After his fall in 1953 he was never accused of instigating the 'Doctors' Plot', although he was charged with a long list of other crimes.

Stalin's manipulation of the reformed Presidium and the renewed interest of the Press in promoting junior men to top positions suggest that the dictator was planning a large-scale purge of senior officials.

[1] *The Anti-Stalin Campaign and International Communism*, a selection of documents edited by the Russian Institute, Columbia University (New York: Columbia University Press, 1956), p. 84.

Malenkov's future might also have been involved, since his connection with Beria had been close in the 'Leningrad Affair' and remained so until after Stalin's death. After Stalin's creation of the 'Doctors' Plot' Malenkov's name figured far less frequently in the Soviet newspapers. It later became clear that Stalin was also intending to carry out a purge among the economic élite.

None of the top Soviet leaders except Stalin appeared to have a direct hand in the scheme, though the subsequent disappearance of Poskrebyshev, Stalin's personal secretary and chief of the Special Section of the Secretariat, pointed to his complicity. Stalin's death soon afterward left the purge hanging in mid-air, but in 1954 a number of security police officials were executed for having fabricated the charges involved in the 'Doctors' Plot'. No other plans were implemented. A full-scale purge in the wake of Stalin's death, which in itself was sufficient to upset the monolithic political structure, was probably felt to be too dangerous a move by the surviving party leaders, even in the unlikely event that they had agreed to a purge from which some of them would have suffered.

On March 6, 1953, it was announced that Stalin had had a stroke two days before and that he had died on March 5th. It is not known for sure that he did in fact succumb to a brain haemorrhage. It was only clear that the Stalinist era in Soviet politics had ended on an undertone of violence, a violence that had characterized it ever since the Georgian's rise to supreme power in the later 1920s.

In a perverse way the last eight years of Stalin's life were the most remarkable of his long rule. By the time of the Second World War the period of innovation on the domestic scene had come to an end. There were no new departures in the ideological sphere or in the realm of practical policy during the postwar period. Only in foreign affairs was Stalin compelled to face new problems, and we shall see that he dealt with them in very conservative terms, pursuing lines that had long been familiar to him whenever it was possible to apply them. When this was not possible, Stalin compensated for the steps he had to make into the unknown abroad by retrogressive policies at home.

Inside Russia the will of a hardened dictator was matched against the strivings of a whole society and prevailed. We have seen the methods Stalin used to maintain both his own position and the characteristics of the pre-war Soviet state. We know that for the most part he succeeded. Far less is known of the silent resistance from below to this twentieth-century Metternich. It is clear from the mood of the Soviet nation at the end of the war that political changes of a liberal nature were widely expected. The Soviet nation, more than any other people, had good reason to demand and hope for reform, but other nations realized their wishes, and the Soviet Union did not. As soon as the war was over, the Soviet people were submitted to the same repressive system that had weighed on them since the 1920s. After 1945 a veil was drawn over their true feelings. Only after Stalin's death, with Khrushchev's denunciation of the dead leader in 1956 and the subsequent revelations of the nature of everyday life in the totalitarian state before 1953, was this veil torn aside.

What is remarkable about Stalin's last years of rule is that he succeeded so completely in holding back the reins of history's chariot against the inclinations of a great and victorious nation at a time when, as is known from repeated experience through the ages, the political atmosphere was most congenial for reform. His eventual triumph proved three things. It showed once more how the Russian people as a body was capable of acquiescence in conditions that were an almost intolerable burden on the individual conscience, though allowances must be made for the sheer exhaustion of the nation in 1945. It also demonstrated the ruthless efficacy of Stalin's political machine, which survived the war to serve yet another day, despite the fact that it was already outworn. Finally it proved that for the Soviet people Stalin was the hero of the war and the saviour of the Communist homeland, however bitter it may have been to live there after 1945.

By his defiance of the national will and the force of progress, Stalin managed to transplant the Russia of 1939 into the postwar world. Only after his death did the monolithic structure slowly break up, a process that would have begun between 1945 and 1953 except for the stubbornness of one man. Perhaps the most impressive token of Stalin's strength came after his death, when it proved so difficult to reform a political system that had seemed ripe for demolition at the end of the Second World War.

CHAPTER III

STALINISM ABROAD

In the period between the end of the war and Stalin's death in March 1953, the most dynamic changes affecting Russia occurred in the sphere of foreign policy. Apart from the dramatic upsurge of the Soviet economy, the domestic scene was static, merely witnessing the reaffirmation of the Stalinist policy that had characterized it before the war—although some new developments as a result of the upheaval were woven into the old pattern. Domestic policy has been treated first, however, because it served as a prototype for Communist governments in the emergent Soviet bloc, especially after 1947. An understanding of the internal situation in Russia during these years helps to illuminate the system that was imposed on the territories occupied by Soviet troops during the war. It is often said that a country's foreign policy is merely the extension of its domestic policy. This was certainly the case with regard to the Soviet bloc, since it was shielded from the reaction of the outside world and was unusually susceptible to Russian control.

In this chapter we shall deal in turn with the three world crisis areas as they appeared at the close of the war—Europe, Asia, and the Near East. In addition Soviet behaviour in the United Nations, the embryo focal point of world politics, will have to be considered. Most of our attention will be directed toward the scene in Eastern Europe, since it remained the centre of Soviet interest until Stalin's death. This was the case for two reasons. The presence of Soviet troops in Eastern Europe permitted active intervention that would have been more dangerous in other areas of crisis. Secondly, Stalin's dichotomic view of the world prevented Soviet diplomacy from making any headway in the emerging countries of Asia and the Middle East, which, despite their newly-won freedom from the imperialist yoke, were still put in the same category as their old capitalist masters in Western Europe. Only after the death of Stalin and the great upsurge of the Soviet economy, buttressed by a Sovietized Eastern Europe, did Russian interest in Asia and the Middle East come to life under the banner of peaceful coexistence. Some scholars have argued recently that a major shift in Soviet foreign policy took place in the last year or so of Stalin's life. It is true that there were signs of resistance from below to the dictator's outdated methods shortly before his death, but the author is inclined to agree with those scholars who interpret the mainstream of Soviet policy in traditional terms, viewing it as the product of a tired, rigid mind that still dominated the conduct of government.

EASTERN EUROPE

During the period from 1945 to 1953 Stalin had to deal with a problem that was entirely new in terms of Soviet practice but had been at or near the centre of theoretical discussion since 1917—the extension of the Revolution beyond the frontiers of the USSR.

We have noted Stalin's aversion to the idea of independent revolutions outside the Soviet Union, especially at a time when his own country was passing through an unsettled stage. The conservative tenor of Stalin's domestic policy after 1945 was evident in his foreign policy also. In the years from 1945 to 1953 no genuine political revolutions were permitted by Stalin in the areas under the control of his armies; spontaneous revolutions outside those areas were frowned upon, except perhaps in China, although even there the exact nature and extent of Soviet co-operation remains a matter of conjecture.

The enormous changes that took place in Eastern Europe after the war did not come about in the wake of the 'complete overthrow of the established government in any country or state by those who were previously subject to it', which is the dictionary definition of political revolution.[1] In Poland and in Czechoslovakia the expatriate bourgeois governments were scarcely 'established' in the true sense of the word; and in no state except Yugoslavia was a government overthrown 'by those who were previously subject to it'. In Poland, Czechoslovakia, Hungary, and Rumania external Soviet pressure was applied over a relatively short period in successful attempts to change the composition of the governments, but these manoeuvres can no more be called revolutionary than can the packing of eighteenth-century English Parliaments with Whig or Tory supporters.

It is a fact that after 1947 social and economic revolutions followed on the political conversion to Communism in Eastern Europe. In the course of a few years Soviet methods that had evolved over the long period of collectivization and industrialization in Russia were applied with savage disregard to prevailing conditions, but with typical caution Stalin ensured the establishment of sound Communist

[1] *Shorter Oxford Dictionary*, 1959, pp. 1729–30.

political bases before embarking on the 'Second Revolution'. In 1917 Lenin had scarcely achieved political supremacy before announcing sweeping economic reforms.

The gradual Soviet take-over in Eastern Europe may be divided into three main periods. Up till the end of the war quasi-independent Communist factions backed by Moscow strove to gain strength in each country. From 1945 until 1947 these factions achieved sufficient power to take over their respective governments, and in this second period they came much more under the Soviet heel. Finally, with the hardening of the Cold War and signs of unrest in Eastern Europe, Stalin imposed the 'Second Revolution' between 1947 and 1953.

Up to the End of the War

The foundations of Soviet influence in Eastern Europe had already been built before Soviet troops actually appeared in the area toward the close of the war. Moscow-inspired Communists had set up strong underground regimes supported by partisan forces. Although their immediate aim was to rid their countries of the German invader, their long-term purpose remained what it had always been—the seizure of political power. During the war Moscow harboured many Communist leaders from Eastern Europe who were later to take over the government of their own countries.

The activity of Communist partisans, especially in the Balkans, aroused the suspicions of the exiled governments at an early stage in the war: fighting broke out between nationalists and Communists in Yugoslavia in 1941, and in Greece and Albania in 1943. Yugoslavia presented a special case in that Marshal Tito had managed to take over most of the country on his own before Soviet troops entered in September 1944; the Russians agreed not to occupy the western part of Yugoslavia, and by March 1945 Tito had secured their total withdrawal. The unique significance of Tito's independent effort was to take on much greater proportions in the following years.

In Allied Poland and Czechoslovakia Soviet influence was more tenacious, although it encountered difficulties in spreading because these countries were under close observation from the West, which resisted Soviet pressure by remonstration, but not by force. The struggle between the Allies over the political hue of the Polish Government at the end of the war was exacerbated by traditional anti-Russian feeling in Poland and sympathy for the Anglo-Saxon cause. Furthermore a non-Communist resistance movement had been formed in Poland during the period when the Soviet Union was still on friendly terms with Germany; it was scarcely less radical than the

Communist movement and was not hampered by the need to look continually to Moscow for instructions.

In both Poland and Czechoslovakia the Communists carved out enclaves from border areas (in the lands east of the Oder-Neisse line and in Bohemia respectively) in which they succeeded in enforcing rigidly totalitarian control, later used by the Soviets as a model for extension to the whole of the country. In Czechoslovakia the Soviet Union could trade on pro-Russian sentiment and the pliability of President Eduard Beneš, who agreed to the formation of a People's Front Government at Kosice in March 1945. Its tragic fate will be recorded below.

Less caution in the furtherance of Soviet aims was necessary in the Axis satellites, which could not complain about rough treatment by the victor and were of less interest to the West due to their geographical position and historical ties. Bulgaria's pan-slavism helped to speed up the process in that country. In September 1944, the underground Fatherland Front took over the Bulgarian Government in the presence of Soviet military power, and by the spring of 1945 the Communists had ousted the strong Agrarian National Union under Dr Georgi Dimitrov, which had competed for supremacy with the Communists under cover of the Fatherland Front. The shift to Communist dominance was nearly as fast in Rumania, where Andrei Vyshinsky delivered an ultimatum to King Michael in March 1945, prior to the installation of Petru Groza as Prime Minister of a National Democratic Front Government, in which all the key posts were held by Communists.

Soviet mishandling of Hungarian political parties presented an interesting case. A provisional government was formed from a genuine coalition in December 1944. The Communists were overshadowed at first by the Small Farmers' Party, which led the opposition to Soviet acts of brutality in the country. But the Communists held the Police, Agriculture, and other ministries. They swept caution to the winds in the autumn of 1945 by offering to hold free elections in the city of Budapest, and were defeated by an absolute majority of the Small Farmers. In the free national elections that were allowed to follow, the Communists only gained 17 per cent of the popular vote against the Small Farmers' 57 per cent. Zoltan Tildy and Ferenc Nagy, the leaders of the victorious party, came into power, while Stalin's henchman Rákosi had to abide by the nation's decision and wait for his cue at a later date. Apart from elections in Czechoslovakia and the Soviet-occupied zone of Austria, this was the only case of free voting in the Eastern European countries under Soviet control.

Its disastrous results taught the Soviet Union a lesson that it was not to forget in the years from 1945 to 1953. In order to be efficacious, Soviet influence had to be total and binding.

From 1945 to 1947
Soviet policy in occupied Eastern Europe during this period was motivated by three main objectives. First there was the urgent need to deny the area to Germany, not only for the present, but for the future as well. National security was the predominant factor in the minds of those who fashioned Soviet foreign policy. This obsession resulted in two subsidiary aims—the establishment of domestic governments in Eastern Europe that would be friendly to the Soviet Union, and the free use of the area as an economic mine from which materials and capital could be extracted for the benefit of crippled Soviet industry. There is no doubt that Stalin feared that world capitalism would eventually attempt to wrest Eastern Europe from the Soviet sphere of influence. The hardening of international relations in the years 1946–7 confirmed him in this belief, as did growing signs of unrest within Eastern Europe at the same time.

Stalin's answer to the problem was to impose rigid totalitarian patterns on all the East European countries under his control after 1947. This involved a second long-term aim, which only gained positive impulse some time after the end of the war—the Sovietization of Eastern Europe. Politically this was achieved throughout the area by 1947 except in Czechoslovakia, but the enormous social and economic revolutions which alone spelt fully-fledged Communism in conformity with the Soviet pattern, were effected after 1947 only.

The process of political alignment with the Soviet Union, which as we have seen was already under way before the end of hostilities in some countries of Eastern Europe, continued in Hungary, Rumania, Bulgaria, and Czechoslovakia on similar lines after the end of the war. These four countries still conserved most of their pre-war class patterns in 1945.

In his book *The East European Revolution* (pp. 169–71), Professor Hugh Seton-Watson has given us a clear picture of the Soviet-guided Communist take-over in the first four countries. Three stages were involved.

> The first stage was the genuine coalition. Several political parties, differing in social basis, and possessing each its own party organization, combined on a common short-term programme, which nominally included a purge of fascists, fairly radical social reforms,

political freedom and a foreign policy friendly to both the USSR and the Western Powers. Real freedom of speech and meeting existed, and there was little political censorship except on one subject—the USSR. Not only might Soviet policy not be criticized, but it was hardly possible to write anything about any aspect of Russia which did not coincide with the official Soviet line. But this seemed a small price to pay. Apart from this, a wide variety of opinions, representing various political views and social categories, could be freely expressed. Nevertheless already during the first stage the Communists seized control of most of the 'levers of power'—in particular the security police, the army general staff and the publicity machine. . . .

The second stage may be described as the bogus coalition. The governments still contain non-Communist parties, but these are represented by men chosen no longer by the party membership but by the Communists. The essential feature of this stage is that the peasant parties, and any bourgeois parties who may have been tolerated at the beginning, are driven into opposition. In this stage opposition is still tolerated, but becomes increasingly difficult. Opposition newspapers may be published, but their distribution becomes dangerous in the capital and almost impossible outside it. Censorship is exercised not only by the government but also by the Communist-controlled printers' trade unions, which 'indignantly refuse to print reactionary calumnies against the people's authorities'. Opposition meetings are broken up by lorryloads of Communist toughs, while the police 'objectively' take no action against aggressors or aggressed. . . .

The third stage is the 'monolithic' regime. There is a single Communist-managed 'front', with one hierarchy, one centralized discipline and one organization. An important feature of this stage is the enforced fusion of the well-purged social democrats with the Communists in a United Workers' Party. . . . In the third stage all open opposition is suppressed, and its leaders either escape abroad or are arrested as 'spies of the Western imperialists' and either executed or sentenced to long prison terms.

In Yugoslavia and Albania civil wars had swept away the old political and social structure that still held in Hungary, Rumania, Bulgaria, and Czechoslovakia at the end of the war. In Poland too the Nazis had uprooted the existing regime, and on its entry into the country the Red Army effectively stamped out the remnants of the old political structure in the form of the Polish resistance movement.

As a result these three countries did not conform to the pattern outlined by Professor Seton-Watson. Yugoslavia and Albania passed directly to the third stage in 1945 without ever experiencing the first two. Poland omitted the first stage and slipped into totalitarianism in the autumn of 1947 after the flight of Mikolajczyk, the sole remaining force amongst the Polish democrats. We have already traced the course of the first stage which came to an end in the spring of 1945 in Bulgaria and Rumania; by the autumn of 1947 they were in the grips of the last stage. Hungary and especially Czechoslovakia were the laggards in this evolutionary process. The first country remained in the initial stage until May 1947, the second right up to the coup by Moscow's puppet, Klement Gottwald, in February 1948.

The timing of the changes in the various countries was closely tied to the Soviet military position. For example in Hungary, which the Red Army was due to leave in 1947 on account of the impending peace treaty between Hungary and the Soviet Union, political terrorism was stepped up as of December 1946, since the Soviet Union feared that without Russian military influence inside the country the Moscow-controlled Communists would lose their hold over political life. The parliamentary regime in Hungary fell just four weeks before the Soviet troops had to leave the country.

The extension of Soviet influence in Eastern Europe not only caused an upheaval in the world balance of power; it also called for a complete reappraisal of Communist theory with regard to world revolution on Marxist lines. According to orthodox Marxism-Leninism, revolutions outside the USSR resulting in the overthrow of the bourgeois state structure would be followed by a dictatorship of the proletariat. This was not the case in actual fact in the countries of Eastern Europe. No political revolutions were forthcoming, and the somewhat hesitant process of political transformation that took place in the countries subject to Soviet influence did not allow for the early establishment of a dictatorship of the proletariat. How could the position be described in an anomalous regime like that of Czechoslovakia after the war?

The Soviet answer was provided in the title of the People's Democracy, a phrase first used by Tito in 1945 at the Congress of the Yugoslav Fatherland Front. The People's Democracy was neither a Soviet Republic (the very idea of this analogy would have been enough to arouse panic in Western statesmen after the war) nor a bourgeois state; it was a mongrel form lying somewhere between the two. It was not a clear-cut definition of a static phenomenon. Rather it was intended as a temporary guide to and description of the existing reality, for use by Communists whose duty it was to understand the political structures they were working on and constantly changing by their own action. As an article of dogma it was in the adaptable Leninist tradition rather than in that of more rigid Marxism.

The concept altered as the Soviet grip tightened over Eastern Europe. In November 1946, Wadyslaw Gomulka, the Secretary of the Polish Workers' Party, echoed the contemporary Soviet line by asserting that 'our democracy is also not similar to Soviet democracy, just as our social system is not similar to the Soviet system'.[1] But by 1947 the economist Varga was in trouble with the theorists for having laid too much stress in his book of 1946 on the bourgeois elements in the economic structure of the People's Democracies; he was not keeping up with the times. By December 1948, after the onset of the new hard line in Soviet foreign policy, Georgi Dimitrov, the Premier of Bulgaria, was contradicting Gomulka's statement of 1946:

> 'The Soviet regime and the Popular Democratic regime are two forms of one and the same system of government, based on the union between the town and agricultural workers. Soviet experience is the only and the best pattern for the building of socialism in our country as well as in other countries of Popular Democracy.'[2]

We shall see how after 1947 the transitional period was considered to be at an end, and rigid conformity to the Soviet pattern was enforced in all spheres of life.

SOVIET INFLUENCE IN CENTRAL AND WESTERN EUROPE: 1945-8

At the end of the war the twin threats of victorious Soviet armies in the heart of Europe and of violent social upheaval expressed in sharp political turns to the left faced opponents of Communism throughout the continent. To many political observers it seemed as if Stalin's armies might continue their march westward from Berlin and impose Communism on countries whose populations were by no means uniformly hostile to the creed. Soviet troops occupied the eastern zones of Germany and Austria as completely as they did the rest of Eastern Europe, while the Communist Parties of France and Italy commanded a wide popular following. As it turned out, Communist

---
[1] *Glos Ludu* (No. 330, 1946).
[2] Speech by Dimitrov to the Fifth Congress of the Bulgarian Communist Party on December 25, 1948.

influence in all these areas except for Eastern Germany had waned considerably by 1948.

Both the eastern zone of Germany and eastern Austria were occupied by Soviet armies and may conceivably have formed parts of Russia's intended *cordon sanitaire*, but for different reasons they did not in this period undergo the transformation that befell most of Eastern Europe. Eastern Germany was a near miss, however, and it was not for want of trying that it had not conformed to the usual pattern by 1948. Soviet policy in this area was ambivalent. On the one hand the Germans in the eastern zone were punished for their wartime role by territorial deprivations and a severe reparations policy; on the other hand the Soviet leaders realized that an alienated Germany would create a formidable opponent for the future in the heart of Europe. Consequently, during the meetings of the Council of Foreign Ministers after the war the Russians posed as the protector of a future united Germany.

At the same time the Soviet zone was submitted to political, social, and economic manipulations that were not unlike those in the rest of Eastern Europe. Russia was the first Allied Power to recognize political parties after the German surrender. The weak Communist Party was merged with the Social Democratic Party in February 1946, but for a long time the resulting Socialist Unity Party was not strong enough to become the typical mass party of an East European People's Democracy; municipal elections due to be held in the autumn of 1948 were indefinitely postponed. The influence of the old professional classes was still strong in politics as well as in social life. The Socialist Unity Party included not a few of them in its ranks, while the Communist cadre of officials lay very thin on the ground. Although the peasants had benefited from agrarian reforms carried out as early as September 1945, they remained conservative in their attitude and struggled against the imposition of collective farming.

Initial Soviet efforts in Eastern Germany were above all directed toward extracting reparations. The silence of the Yalta and Potsdam agreements on the subject of the acquisition of capital within Germany was taken by the Russians to mean tacit approval, though the Western Allies interpreted the agreements in the opposite sense. The thorough and ruthless Soviet methods employed in gathering reparations from Eastern Germany spelled economic advantages on a huge scale for domestic Soviet industry, but politically they were disastrous, sacrificing Allied goodwill and any chances of eventual reconciliation with Germany.

Communism in Austria was even less successful than in East

Germany at the end of the war. The harsh character of the Russian occupation succeeded in alienating the local population, which voiced its opposition to Communist rule by denying the party all but 5 per cent of the total vote in the free elections held in 1945. The Communist Ministers of the Interior and Propaganda were ousted from the provisional government, and a parliamentary government was set up from which the Communists were excluded for lack of popular support.

In Western Europe Soviet foreign policy fared no better than in Austria, although in France and Italy the Communists had had a real chance of taking over both governments after 1945. France was the most important country for Communist policy among the Western European democracies. In October 1945, the French Communist Party polled five million votes, thus acquiring a dominating position in the electorate. De Gaulle's government was compelled to offer five posts to Communists, but they were not allowed to take over the key Ministries of Foreign Affairs, of the Interior, or of War.

Stalin's hands were full with problems inside the USSR and in Eastern Europe; also, his penchant for sly caution and his apparent desire, at least at this stage of international relations, not to arouse the suspicion of his wartime allies, bade him abandon any scheme for armed uprising in Western Europe and rely on the considerable strength of the French and Italian Communist Parties in the hope that they would be able to gain supremacy by legal means. In 1945 Stalin was not being over-optimistic. In France the Communist Party was the only one capable of organizing a mass following; the other parties of the left were insignificant by comparison. But as Soviet intentions in East Europe became increasingly clear and the Cold War grew in intensity, it became futile for the French Communist Party still to cling to the outworn policy of the Popular Front and claim patriotically that its only intention was to give wholehearted support to the republican majority in the National Assembly. Even in August 1947, after the announcement of the Truman Doctrine—that proclamation of American mistrust of Soviet foreign policy in Europe—and the dismissal of the Communist ministers from the French Government, the press organ of the French Communists insisted that they were 'the indispensable rampart of the Republic. . . .'

The wolf in sheep's clothing was no longer listened to with such enthusiasm by workers in either France or Italy. In the spring of 1947 the Communist vote declined considerably in France; in Italy the party leader, Palmiro Togliatti, launched an attack on the Roman Catholic Church at the same time, thus revealing the true face of

Communist aims. The remaining Communists resigned from the Italian Government in May of the same year. The spectre of a Soviet Europe extending from Moscow to the English Channel was banished, though it has never ceased to haunt the NATO powers to this day.

THE DEVELOPMENT OF THE COLD WAR

In the first chapter of this book we had cause to describe the early rumblings of inter-Allied mistrust over questions of international policy; by 1947 these rumblings had developed into a steady flow of protest on both sides. Since the changes in East Europe were at the centre of the quarrel, the growth of the Cold War is treated at this point, although it should not be forgotten that the disagreement of the West with the USSR also concerned problems in Asia and the Middle East.

The Cold War increased in intensity after 1945 as the result of two sets of factors. In the first place the legacy from the pre-war period, which has been discussed in connection with the coining of the phrase the 'Cold War', remained to cloud the international political scene. Neither long-standing Soviet Communist hatred of the West, nor Russian nationalist territorial ambitions were altered one jot by the war; no more was Stalin's personal character. If anything the Soviet leader became even more xenophobic and security-minded than before. In the second place the deep-seated mistrust between the Allies was amply nourished after 1945 through a series of events that convinced each side that it could not afford to maintain any confidence in the other.

Early Western suspicions over Soviet policy toward Poland were quickly reinforced by Soviet pressure on Bulgaria and Rumania and the Soviet handling of the reparations issue in Germany. For their part, the Russians viewed the disclosure of America's monopoly possession of the atom bomb, the abrupt ending in August 1945 of lend-lease aid, and Russia's virtual exclusion from any influence over the future of Japan or Italy as omens of renewed capitalist threats directed against the weakened defences of socialism.

Past memories and contemporary experience awakened a common neurosis in the two camps. This found expression in phenomena like the *Zhdanovshchina* in Russia and, at a later date, McCarthyism in the United States. On the Russian side constant fear was no doubt heightened by the inferiority complex from which the USSR had suffered since 1917 in her relations with the West. Typical expressions of this mutual fear were revealed in two speeches made by Stalin and

Churchill on February 9 and March 5, 1946, respectively. They reflected the growing tension in the international arena and perhaps more than anything else drew the attention of statesmen throughout the world to the serious nature of the situation.

Stalin's speech reasserted Lenin's theory that the uneven development of capitalism leads to universal war. Stalin's pessimistic view of future relations with the West was probably coloured by the consideration that his vision of a hostile world would act as a stimulant on the Russian people to rebuild their shattered state with added vigour. Churchill's speech at Fulton, Missouri, was likewise inspired by mistrust and fear. Calling the attention of his distinguished audience (which included the President of the United States) to the fact that 'from Stettin in the Baltic to Trieste in the Adriatic, an Iron Curtain had descended across the Continent', Churchill urged American statesmen to join with the British Commonwealth in a joint effort to ward off the threat of Communist aggression. At the time many of his listeners thought that his appeal was premature and would only serve to increase Soviet suspicions. The British loan proposed in the American Congress on December 6, 1945, was considered to be sufficient evidence of Anglo-American political solidarity, and there seemed to be no necessity for using the fear of Russia as an additional welding force.

In the light of later events, Churchill's comments on Soviet moves in Eastern Europe appear to be relatively mild in nature, but at the time they came as a shock to some of his listeners. In March 1946, except for Poland, concrete evidence of open Soviet pressure existed in Bulgaria and Rumania only, both of them ex-enemy powers. On the subject of Poland, Stalin had already admitted to Churchill and Roosevelt at Yalta that Russia could not afford to allow a government hostile to herself to be established in an area of such vital strategic importance.

From the Soviet point of view a parallel might have been drawn between methods used in ex-enemy countries occupied by the USSR and those used in Japan, where MacArthur had a strong military control over Japanese politics and industry. Although MacArthur did not in fact resort to such heavy-handed methods as were used in the European ex-Axis countries, his authority was such that he might have acted in a similar manner, and Japanese government and industry were actually reorganized after the war solely according to American designs. This parallel has been expressed in terms of the Soviet viewpoint in order to estimate the effect of Churchill's Fulton speech on the Russian leaders.

Another galling element in Churchill's speech was his scarcely-veiled comparison of Communist to Fascist rule and political techniques.[1] His catching phrase 'the Iron Curtain' came from Goebbels' repertoire, according to the Soviets, and must have stung the nation that had borne the brunt of the Fascist whip. Stalin returned the insult in kind by referring to the 'resemblance' of 'Mr Churchill and his friends' to 'Hitler and his friends'.[2] The content of Churchill's appeal provided a heaven-sent opportunity for Stalin to justify his exaggerated theory that the capitalist powers were intent on invading Russia again, as they had done after 1917 and in 1941. He told the American ambassador in Moscow that he expected another intervention.[3]

In the long run, however, most of Churchill's forebodings were proved right. From the West's point of view, the speech had the beneficial effect of drawing the United States into the growing international contest, for, if Churchill was apt to dramatize the Soviet menace, some of the American leaders in 1946 tended to play it down or to ignore it. In the tense atmosphere of the postwar world both attitudes were dangerous; a compromise between the two eventually proved to be the most effective weapon against Soviet aggression.

The entry of the United States on to the European political scene was slow even after the Fulton speech. In 1946 the number of British forces overseas was only just below the United States figure, in spite of England's sorry economic plight. For September 13, 1946, the diary entry of the American Secretary of Defence, James V. Forrestal, mentioned a plan for the quick removal of United States troops from Germany in the event of Russian aggression; there was little thought of defending Europe.[4] But the situation changed after England's severe economic crisis in the winter of 1946 and her plea of February 1947 for American support in the armed struggle against Communist guerrillas in Greece.

President Truman's Message to Congress in March 1947 called for American military aid to Greece and Turkey. The Truman

---

[1] For instance, referring to the atom bomb, Churchill said: 'I do not believe we should all have slept so soundly . . . if some Communist or neo-Fascist state monopolized for the time being these dread agencies.' He also compared the Nazi threat of the inter-war years to the postwar Soviet menace and talked of 'Communist fifth columns', thus fusing Nazi and Communist techniques.
[2] *Pravda* (March 13, 1946).
[3] Walter Bedell Smith, *My Three Years in Moscow* (Philadelphia: J. B. Lippincott Co., 1950), p. 52.
[4] *The Forrestal Diaries*, ed. by Walter Millis (New York: Viking Press, 1951), p. 198.

Doctrine marked the adoption of George Kennan's containment policy toward Russia; it was also the prelude to a speech made in June 1947, by the American Secretary of State, General George Marshall, in which economic aid was offered to Europe. Although Marshall let it be known that his proposals might also apply to Russia, Dean Acheson revealed that the professed aim of the Marshall Plan was to 'preserve democratic institutions and human freedoms from totalitarian pressures'. The plan was formulated in the belief that Communism would thrive if European economic chaos were allowed to continue.

In Eastern Europe the Polish and Czech political leaders expressed an interest in the American offer, but were ordered by Stalin to reject it outright. The ideology by which the Soviet Union lived clearly taught it the eloquence of economic persuasion; in its crippled condition it would find it difficult to rival the economic influence of the richest country in the world. Even if American dollars did not succeed in undermining Soviet influence in Eastern Europe, Marshall's scheme for integrating American aid into a single plan meant that each nation would have to produce what it was best fitted for. The effect of this might be to retain Eastern Europe as the traditional granary of the West and thus bypass Soviet plans for industrialization in the area. Also the scheme would entail some measure of intrusion behind the veils of Russian security, which was a very powerful weapon in the Cold War.

EASTERN EUROPE: 1947–53

The Czech and Polish attempts to follow an independent line over the question of Marshall aid in 1947 were among several signs that the East European governments were becoming too preoccupied with their own national problems and not paying sufficient heed to Soviet designs for the area as a whole. At this time relations were strained between the Hungarian and Rumanian parties over the territorial issue of Transylvania; this was also true of Poland and Czechoslovakia over the issue of areas on their adjoining frontiers. The most blatant example of national selfishness (as opposed to devotion to the Communist and Soviet cause) came significantly from Yugoslavia, which seemed to think that the Communist camp should be ready to fight the West for the possession of the city of Trieste, which Tito coveted.

Renascent nationalism of this kind, coinciding with the direct entry of the United States on to the European stage, induced Stalin to harden his policy with regard to East Europe. By the end of 1947 the return to Communist orthodoxy inside Russia itself had progressed sufficiently to provide a convenient model for enforcement on the countries under Soviet influence. Stalin's change of policy led to the creation of the Cominform in September 1947, the Soviet rift with Yugoslavia, the Czech political coup, and the dispute with the Western Allies over Berlin—all of which took place in the first half of 1948.

The Cominform (Communist Information Bureau) was the ideological spearhead of the new line. Its headquarters were placed in Belgrade, which for reasons given below was rapidly becoming the centre of nationalist opposition to Soviet domination—although ironically enough it was the Yugoslavs who in 1945 had proposed the re-establishment of some sort of international Communist organization to promote the exchange of views between the various parties. At the opening session of the Cominform in south-west Poland in September 1947, it was again the Yugoslavs who were the most persistent in asserting their ideological orthodoxy.

The chief Soviet spokesman was Zhdanov. This was significant, since it might have been supposed that Molotov or some other member of the Politburo more familiar with questions of foreign policy would be the one to pronounce the diatribe against American aggression and the call to Communist unity. But the imposition of Soviet practice in Eastern Europe after 1947, not only in politics, but in the economic and social spheres as well, was merely an extension of the domestic campaign for conformity headed by Zhdanov. The main activities of the Communist Information Bureau centred on the publication of its organ, *For a Lasting Peace*, which laid down the broad lines of policy to be followed by the People's Democracies in all spheres of national life.

The Cominform's denunciation of Tito in June 1948 represented the climax of a deep-seated maladjustment between Yugoslavia and Russia. More clearly than any other event in the period from 1945 to 1953, the Soviet-Yugoslav quarrel revealed the true nature of long-term Soviet designs in Eastern Europe, at least as they had been moulded by the end of 1947. The dispute coincided with the high tide of Russian nationalism, as opposed to Soviet Communism, and although the quarrel, like that between Henry VIII and the Pope, was clothed in ideological language and dwelt on theoretical subjects, the real core of the struggle lay in the clash over national ambitions. Stalin, as the founder of socialism in one country, had met his match at last.

This does not mean to say that the Soviet leaders were hypocritical. Like the French Republicans engaged in exporting the benefits of revolution abroad:

'... they believed themselves to be cosmopolitans, they were that only in their speeches; they felt, they thought, they acted, they interpreted their universal ideas and their abstract principles in accordance with the traditions of a conquering monarchy. . . . They identified humanity with their homeland, their national cause with the cause of all the nations. Consequently and entirely naturally, they confused the propagation of new doctrines with the extension of French power, the emancipation of humanity with the grandeur of the Republic, the reign of reason with that of France, the liberation of peoples with the conquest of states, the European revolution with the domination of the French Revolution in Europe. . . . They established subservient and subordinate republics which they held in a sort of tutelage. . . . The Revolution degenerated into an armed propaganda, then into conquest. . . .'[1]

In 1945 the Yugoslav regime was more pro-Russian and more prepared to adopt Soviet Communist methods than any other Communist-infiltrated government in Eastern Europe. It was Yugoslavia that first suggested the resurrection of the Comintern or a similar organization. It was also Yugoslavia that collectivized her agriculture at a faster rate than any other People's Democracy except Bulgaria in the period from 1945 to 1948. The ideological purity of Tito's regime was marred in Soviet eyes, however, by the fact that the Yugoslav Communist partisans had won control over their country on their own initiative and had managed to build up a political hierarchy independent of Soviet influence. In the other East European states the Communist regimes were composed of a motley collection of leaders; some of them had been sent from Moscow, others had risen through the underground movements. The amazing solidarity of the Yugoslav band of partisans was without parallel. The career of the famous rebel Djilas was a good instance of this. In 1945 he criticized the behaviour of Russian troops in Yugoslavia and provoked Stalin into demanding an apology, but Tito left his wartime comrade in a position of power. Even after Djilas's later break with Tito, and the publication in the United States of his critique of Communism, *The New Class*, Tito mitigated his old friend's prison sentence until

---

[1] Albert Sorel, *L'Europe et la Révolution Française*, 3rd ed. (Paris, 1893), Part I, pp. 541–2.

the appearance of a new manuscript, *Conversations with Stalin*, made him change his mind. Regardless of whether their directives were obeyed or not by Tito, the Soviet leaders in 1948 could no longer tolerate a system in Eastern Europe that they were unable to supervise from the inside, and in which the army, the police, and the party cadres were all in the hands of Tito's own men. The mainspring of the new conformity that was imposed after 1947 lay in a rigid hierarchy whose summit was Moscow.

Significantly the Soviet-Yugoslav quarrel grew over issues of power, not of ideology. In January 1948, *Pravda* attacked Tito's scheme for a Balkan federation, not primarily on ideological grounds, since Stalin had at first egged Tito on in his plans, but because Tito's hold over the reins of power inside Yugoslavia could not be weakened despite the attempts of Soviet agents. If Tito could manage both to prevent the Soviet military and economic mission in Yugoslavia from infiltrating into Yugoslav domestic affairs and to dominate a Yugoslav-Bulgarian federation that eventually aimed at including Rumania, Albania, and Hungary, a new independent nexus might be created in south-east Europe that could elude Soviet domination. The Soviet propaganda war against Tito was accompanied by more practical measures. Soviet agents in the Belgrade Cominform office attempted to establish a Stalinist group within the Yugoslav party, while other East European Communist parties were ordered to isolate Tito.

Efforts to contain the quarrel broke down after the failure of Edward Kardelj, the Yugoslav Deputy Premier, to appease the Soviet leader during a visit to Moscow. A rift followed immediately in March 1948, when the Soviet Union withdrew its military mission from Belgrade. The Soviet party complained that the Yugoslavs were holding back information regarding their internal affairs. Much of the dispute continued along these petty lines, touching on Soviet control in a joint Soviet-Yugoslav trading company or on Yugoslav reluctance to dismiss an official who was not liked by the Russians. This section of the debate may seem of trifling importance, but in fact it dealt with the many hinges on which Soviet power rested in the other East European countries. The quarrel was peppered with Soviet complaints of an ideological nature, but their very hollowness proved that they did not form the real basis of Soviet grudges. Tito was accused of running his party on dictatorial lines, of concentrating key positions in the hands of a few favourites, and of co-opting new members for the Central Committee instead of electing them—this from a ruler who held the whole of the Soviet Government and the

Communist Party in his grasp and had not called a Party Congress for nine years!

Stalin's final blow fell at the end of June, when Yugoslavia was expelled from the Soviet Communist camp by the Cominform. Since the Cominform officially voiced the opinion of all the East European Communist parties, Tito's isolation was complete. The headquarters of the Cominform was transferred to Bucharest.

The polite debate between Yugoslavia and Russia had deteriorated into an open clash of power. At first the opponents argued through diplomatic notes, but when Stalin took practical steps at the beginning of 1948, they were countered by Tito. The final break seemingly left Yugoslavia without a genuine political ally in the world. Russia appeared to be on the brink of employing armed force against her. Tito parried once again, this time by an even more daring move: he re-established contact with the capitalist West.

Tito resolved to hold fast. If he had not, he would surely have suffered the fate of other East European leaders who were purged in the wake of the Yugoslav quarrel; and his party would have dissolved at the touch of Soviet intrusion. Apart from Andrija Hebrang and one or two other party leaders, the Yugoslavs once again demonstrated their solidarity by backing up their leader in what appeared to be a foolhardy gesture. Luckily for Tito the spine of his supporters was composed of young idealists and nationalists who had followed him through the war, and whose views on political affairs, and in particular on foreign affairs, were too naïve and narrow-minded to allow for any second thoughts.

Stalin met with more success in his efforts to consolidate Soviet power in Czechoslovakia during the same year (1948). In view both of her strategic position on the western fringe of Soviet-dominated Europe, and of her industrial might, which came second to that of Russia in Eastern Europe, Czechoslovakia was of vital importance to the nascent Soviet bloc. She also happened to be the East European laggard in following the three stages of Soviet Communist infiltration outlined earlier in this chapter. The first stage, a genuine coalition between Communists and other parties, was achieved in March 1945, with the formation of a People's Front under Beneš, but the second stage of a bogus coalition only ensued in February 1948.

This was preceded by a Soviet ultimatum in the summer of 1947 forbidding Czechoslovakia to apply for Marshall aid, a move which filled the non-Communist parties with foreboding. The crisis was used by the Communist Minister of the Interior, Jiri Nosek, to pack the police with his own men as a prelude to new governmental elections under Communist pressure. In February 1948, all the non-Communist ministers except the hesitant Social Democrats resigned in protest, but their gesture was in vain since it did not rest on any solid basis of power. After only four days Beneš gave in to the Communist demand for a new government in which the non-Communist ministers would be selected exclusively by the Communists. The third stage of monolithic Communist rule was in sight. In February armed workers appeared on the streets and militant committees under Communist control took over the factories and the Czech radio. The Soviet Union sent Valerian Zorin, a former ambassador to Czechoslovakia and at that time Deputy Foreign Minister of the Soviet Government, to supervise the Communist coup in Prague. The most tragic victim of the affair was Jan Masaryk, the son of the founder of the Czechoslovak state. He did not resign with the other ministers, but after only fourteen days grasped the full implications of Communist totalitarian rule and then apparently committed suicide, although he may have been killed by the Communists. Beneš resigned from the government in June, and Gottwald, one of Moscow's most faithful henchmen, became President.

The new Communist take-over in Eastern Europe came as a profound shock to the West. Stalin's *coup de grace* against democracy in Czechoslovakia was more swift and brutal than in any other country. Its consequences were easy to foresee after what had already happened in the rest of the area. Czechoslovakia, like Poland, had enjoyed especially friendly relations with the Western democracies during the war, and even at the end of 1947 three-quarters of her foreign trade was still carried on with the West.

Western suspicions aroused by the Czech coup and the Soviet-Yugoslav quarrel were galvanized by the Soviet imposition, in June 1948, of a blockade on the non-Russian sectors of Berlin that lay far inside the Soviet zone of Germany. This followed on the Soviet Union's final departure from the Allied Control Command in March, thus ending four-power government in Germany. Stalin's first act of overt aggression against the West was motivated by an old malady of his, a deep-seated fear of German power. At this time the Western Allies were intending to integrate West Germany into their group, thus anchoring great industrial potential on their side. The introduction of a reformed currency in the western zones of Germany and also in the western Allied sectors in Berlin provided the Soviets with an argument similar to the one they had used against the Marshall Plan; economic pressure was being put on the western part of Germany, while the reform could only create monetary troubles in the Soviet zone.

There may have been some sense in Stalin's reasoning, but there was little in the steps he took to act on it. No doubt he counted on both previous Western softness and non-interference in East European affairs (the Czech coup had provided a very recent instance of this) and on Berlin's delicate geographical position. He was disappointed. The Western Allies swiftly organized an airlift of vital supplies from West Germany into Berlin. A peaceful settlement was not reached until May 1949. Stalin's aggressive action led directly to the formation of the West German Federal Republic on May 23, 1949. This was preceded by the definitive establishment of American forces in Europe through the instrument of the North Atlantic Treaty Organization, signed in March 1949. Stalin retaliated in October of the same year by setting up a German Democratic Republic in the Soviet zone, although the Communist equivalent of NATO, the Warsaw Pact, was not agreed upon until 1955. These parrying moves on the part of Russia and the West overclouded three Soviet attempts —in the spring of 1949, in the summer of 1951, and in March 1952— to prepare for German reunification through nation-wide elections and an eventual peace treaty. The West insisted on free elections throughout Germany, to which Russia could not agree.

The failure of Soviet policies in Berlin and Yugoslavia taught Stalin and the West a sound lesson. Until 1948 Soviet influence in Eastern Europe had gone from strength to strength, protected by the might of the Red Army. But as soon as Stalin became so bold as to encroach on territory controlled by the West—or even for that matter on Yugoslavia, an area that was ideologically but not militarily a part of the recognized Soviet sphere of influence—he met with no success.

Stalin's double failure to force his opponents' hands either in Berlin or in Yugoslavia affected his policies in Europe. The solidarity of the Allies convinced him that he could go no farther in Western Europe at that time, while Yugoslavia's stubborn resistance within the Communist camp forewarned him that other national Communist leaders might imitate Tito. The Soviet Union now began to concentrate on cementing its hold on the rest of East Europe; from this time on a quicker pace was set and more drastic methods were employed.

The purges in East Europe following on Tito's excommunication were the clearest indication of the shock Moscow had received. Although the liquidation of some of the top leaders in East Europe cannot be wholly explained by the phenomenon of Titoism—for there were other reasons springing from changing conditions in the individual countries and on the world scene—there is no doubt that Stalin's new apprehension and the convenience of labelling unwanted

Communists as Titoists speeded up the process. Now that both protagonists in the Cold War had thrown down the gauntlet it was necessary to steel themselves for open struggle. The last gap in the Iron Curtain had been closed by the Communist coup in Czechoslovakia, but there was as yet little homogeneity within party ranks. After the war many opportunists and former members of pro-German parties had climbed on to the Communist Party band-wagon in East Europe. Not a few had reached very high positions in the state. It was obvious that some of them would have to go.

Less evident but equally important was the need to purge the type of person who had risen to influence during the war in the Communist resistance movements and had subsequently inclined to national rather than to purely Communist or rather pro-Soviet Communist policies. Finally, the drive after 1948 to implement far-reaching economic and social plans on Soviet lines called for leaders of a new kind in East Europe. Just as Stalin, the careful organizer and bureaucrat, had replaced Trotsky at the helm of the Soviet state in the 1920s, so now Moscow-trained administrators took precedence over the men who had led the Communist cause to victory in the heroic early days.

Victims of these policies fell thick and fast in 1949: Koci Xoxe in Albania, Traicho Kostov in Bulgaria, and Laszlo Rajk in Hungary were executed for non-compliance with the Soviet line. In Poland the imprisonment of Wladyslaw Gomulka came in the wake of the movement inside the People's Democracies towards national Communism in opposition to the Soviet prototype. Gomulka had been the only East European leader to object to the formulation of the Cominform. Again in 1949 he tried to stem the mounting tide of Soviet control over Polish affairs, but his protests, unlike those of Tito, were not founded on any solid power basis independent of Soviet manipulation. Also in contrast to Tito, the source of Gomulka's grievances was ideological in nature from the start. As a result, he was bound to lose against the country that had a monopoly of both power and Stalinist ideology.

The purges in the higher reaches of the states concerned were accompanied by the increasing use of terror at all levels. The secret police acquired more power in East Europe and became largely independent of national party control, while remaining subservient to Soviet designs. A regular system of concentration camps developed in the various countries and forced labour was recruited on the Soviet pattern. Especial blame was attached to persons convicted of crimes of negligence in the fulfilment of state economic plans; highly-placed members of the Roman Catholic Church became the target of frequent attacks. The timing of the major purges shows yet another tie between internal and external Soviet policy in these years. The 'Leningrad Affair' on the home front preceded the first wave of East European trials, while the case of the Jew, Rudolf Slansky, the General Secretary of the Czech party, was connected with Stalin's initiation of the 'Doctors' Plot' in 1952.

The figure of Stalin dominated the Soviet and East European scene to such an extent that the ties between domestic and foreign policy were exceedingly close, even for a totalitarian regime that from 1948 onward was treating other states under its supervision almost as if they formed part of the Russian national inheritance. The advent of more rapidly enforced collectivization and industrialization in East Europe after 1948 was characterized by the application of methods that Stalin had himself put through in Russia in the late 1920s and the 1930s.

The marked conservatism and reliance on past experience that we have noted in other spheres, and particularly in connection with the reassertion of party control over the Soviet nation after the war, was again apparent in the Second Revolution in East Europe. In industry Five-Year Plans were carried out on well-tried Soviet lines: the Russians were so slavishly copied that in this period no regard was paid to economic interdependence between the countries. Autarchy prevailed, and there was a dangerous repetition of almost identical schemes, overstressing the role of heavy industry within each country and leaving no room for inter-state collaboration. The collectivization campaign likewise relied on such familiar procedures as high taxes, forced state deliveries, party pressure, and some measure of violence. By 1953 collectives and state farms in Bulgaria took up a maximum for East Europe of 62·7 per cent of the arable land compared with a minimum of 20 per cent in Rumania. These were relatively low percentages when one considers that in the non-agricultural sphere the nationalized sector of the labour force in 1948 amounted to 63·9 per cent in Czechoslovakia.

The *Zhdanovshchina* in Russia was the prelude to similar campaigns in Eastern Europe after the formation of the Cominform. The Soviet example in the arts was frequently referred to as a model to be followed; there was no lack of material for study. By the time of Stalin's death one half of the entire production of books in Poland consisted of translations from the Russian. Writers who agreed to conform were said to be progressive, and in time the combined weight of censorship and persuasion resulted in work that was only slightly less cowed and monotonous than Soviet productions. Only a few

Catholic publications in Poland escaped the new uniformity. Just as the *Zhdanovshchina* in the Soviet Union was concerned as much with the central control of administration as with ideological questions, so the Polish and other East European campaigns dealt with the organization of intellectual life. In 1947 new regulations did away with the last vestiges of university autonomy in Poland, and in 1951 all previously existing scholarly institutions were replaced by the centralized Communist Academy of Science. By the same year private publishers had been squeezed out of all but a 3 per cent slice of the general book market.

Political and ideological expression was given to the accelerated changes after 1948 by Soviet propaganda, which emphasized the gradual fusion of the concept of the People's Democracy with its Soviet prototype. In this period all the East European states under Russian control adopted new constitutions reflecting the new and closer relationship between each individual country and the USSR. The outward forms of independence were retained, however, in order not to antagonize the states concerned, nor to provoke the West more than was necessary. Yugoslavia and Communist China kept a watchful eye on Soviet methods in the area. It was in Moscow's interest to ensure that the ties between Russia and any one country in Eastern Europe were stronger than contacts among the countries themselves. Freedom of movement inside Eastern Europe was very restricted, and Communist leaders only met at gatherings in the Soviet Union; political separatism was as rigid as economic isolation—all roads led to Moscow.

Direct consultation between the Soviet leaders and their East European counterparts was part of the informal scheme of Soviet control that underlay the more official governmental relations. The party organs carried the life-blood of uniformity to the whole Communist body. The operation was so successful that even as early as three or four years before Stalin's death many of the fundamental decisions in East Europe were being put into effect, not on explicit instructions from Moscow, but in accordance with the general political atmosphere that emanated from the Soviet centre. The climate had indeed changed since the days when free elections in Hungary had unexpectedly turned the wrong way for Stalin.

Stalin's continuous aim from about 1944 onward was to ensure that Eastern Europe would remain permanently in the Soviet sphere, but the precise extent to which he at first intended to sovietize the area is open to dispute. The pressures exerted by the Cold War, the inexorable tendency of totalitarian rule to stick at no half-measures, and the national Communist proselytizing impulse spurred on the creation of what is now known as the Soviet bloc. By 1953 the Russian giant had set up six embryo puppet states in its own Stalinist image in Eastern Europe. Until the death of the Soviet dictator they all danced to the Russian tune; but after the ascendancy of Khrushchev three of them, Poland, Hungary, and Albania, were to jib at Moscow's string-pulling and like Pinocchio take on a life of their own.

ASIA

From 1945 to 1948

Stalin's chief interests after 1945 are related in this and the preceding chapter in order of descending importance. The rehabilitation of the Soviet homeland occupied the first place in Stalin's mind, followed by a guarantee for its security in the form of a Soviet-controlled Eastern Europe. Russia's Asian frontiers were protected by the generous concessions Stalin obtained at Yalta. Until 1949 and the rise to power of the Chinese Communists Stalin had his hands full with problems in Russia and Eastern Europe.

In Asia (and also in the Near East) Stalin restricted his activities at first to 'a fluid resilient policy directed at the achievement of maximum power with the minimum responsibility on portions of the Asiatic continent lying beyond the Soviet border ... the exertion of pressure in various areas in direct proportion to their strategic importance and their proximity to the Soviet frontier'.[1] The Soviet Union in the years after 1945 was still a land power, and therefore exercised regional rather than global influence outside its own borders; the strong connection that has been noted above between the presence of the Red Army and the successful imposition of Soviet controls abroad only served to underline this regionalism, since the Red Army's moves were circumscribed by the need to maintain overland communications with its home base.

The only parts of Asia that fell under direct Soviet control after 1945 were those areas occupied by Soviet troops in August 1945 (Manchuria and North Korea), and the territories allotted to Stalin at Yalta (southern Sakhalin, the Kurile Islands, interests in Outer Mongolia and the naval bases of Dairen and Port Arthur). The two crucial areas were North Korea and Manchuria. After the failure of the Moscow Council of Foreign Ministers' Conference in December

[1] This remarkable prognostication of Soviet policy in Asia was written just before the Allied victory over Nazi Germany by George Kennan, at that time US Chargé d'Affaires in Moscow, to Ambassador Harriman. See *United States Relations with China* (Washington: Department of State, 1949), p. 97.

1945, the Soviet Union proceeded to set up a puppet provisional government in North Korea on lines similar to those employed in Eastern Europe. Headed by Kim Il Sung, a Moscow-trained Communist, the 'Provisional People's Committee of North Korea' carried out political and economic reforms of the type that were put through in Europe.

Manchuria was the biggest prize of Russia's Asian loot. Industrially it was more advanced than any other part of Asia except Japan, which had been, during its occupation of the country, responsible for the progress made there. As in Eastern Europe, Russia carried out large-scale removals of equipment, under the guise of reparations, to strengthen her home base. In view of the fact that Manchuria would have to be returned to China, and a China soon to fall under Communist rule, Stalin's policy appears to have been even more shortsighted (and also more Russian nationalist as opposed to Soviet Communist) in Manchuria than in Eastern Europe. But Stalin was no more able than American observers to foresee the rapid deterioration of the Chinese Nationalist forces under Chiang Kai-shek from 1946 to 1948; what he *could* see was the desperate state of Soviet industry.

In the period immediately after the war, Stalin's nationalist side was certainly to the fore in the Asian arena. On September 2, 1945, he declared that the Japanese defeat in Manchuria had been wished for by Russians of the older generation ever since the Russo-Japanese War of 1904–5. Three years later, in 1948, Stalin admitted to the Yugoslav Communist Djilas that he had been wrong in recognizing the Kuomintang regime at the end of the war, thus temporarily abandoning the Chinese Communists: 'True, we too can make a mistake. Here, when the war with Japan ended, we invited the Chinese comrades to reach an agreement as to how a *modus vivendi* with Chiang Kai-shek might be found. They agreed with us in word, but in deed they did it their own way when they got home: they mustered their forces and struck. It has been shown that they were right, and not we.'[1]

Russia's chameleon-like attitude to the Chinese Communists was shown in her treatment of Manchuria. Having completed half of the stripping operation in the area, the Soviet command offered Chiang Kai-shek joint Sino-Soviet management of the remaining industrial plant, but Chiang refused. Subsequently, in the process of withdrawing from Manchuria in the autumn of 1945 according to the terms of the Sino-Soviet pact arranged at Yalta, the Russians duly handed

[1] Milovan Djilas, *Conversations with Stalin* (New York: Harcourt, Brace & World, 1962), p. 182.

over the cities to the Kuomintang, but permitted the Communists to occupy the rural zones and gave them large supplies of Japanese arms. In the course of the scramble to take over Manchuria before the Communists, Chiang dangerously over-extended his military communications—later in the civil war his most efficient troops were cornered in Manchuria and had to be supplied by air—and it may be that the Soviet Union had deliberately lured him into the trap.

Stalin's Chinese policy at this time and indeed up to the victory of the Chinese Communists in 1949 remains obscure, probably because it was a hesitant, undetermined policy that hung on events. Cautious by nature, Stalin was also inclined to such a course by various other factors, two of which were personal. First, he appeared to dislike the Chinese as a race and was apt to decry their capabilities.[1] Secondly, once before in 1926-7 he had advocated a policy of wait-and-see in the struggle between the Chinese Communists and their opponents and had brushed aside Trotsky's call for aid to the Communist side. Here again, as in so many other fields, the ageing Stalin was leaning heavily on past experience in his dealings with China after 1945.

If he had openly supported the Chinese Communists in 1945, Stalin would have run counter to his policy of initial restraint—a policy demonstrated by Soviet non-interference in Greece and by Soviet pressure on Yugoslavia to prevent her antagonizing the West too much over the question of Trieste. There was no point in carving up the wartime alliance of the Big Three while it was still offering surprising advantages to Russia, of which one of the most significant included the postwar concessions to her in Asia. A more deep-seated reason was probably Stalin's old mistrust of independently-inspired Communist revolutions, which was renewed by his experience with Yugoslavia in 1947-8. China, with her vast potential in manpower, could present a far more serious problem than Yugoslavia unless she was carefully assigned to her proper place in the Communist hierarchy of nations.

The upshot of Stalin's policy—or lack of one—was that the Kuomintang forces lost the Chinese civil war mainly because of their own weakness and corruption, and not because the Soviet Union offered substantial aid to the Communists. Stalin insured Russia against an overwhelming victory by either Chinese side through his action in Manchuria, and also through infiltration into other critical border regions between the Soviet Union and China. In 1930 Mao

---

[1] Stalin told James Byrnes, the United States Secretary of State, '... all Chinese are boasters.' See James F. Byrnes, *Speaking Frankly* (New York: Harper & Bros, 1947), p. 228.

Tse-tung declared that 'when the people's revolution has been victorious in China the Outer Mongolian Republic will automatically become a part of the Chinese federation, at their own will'.[1] He was perhaps being over-optimistic, because Outer Mongolia is the oldest satellite of the Soviet Union. Close Russian control began in 1924; subsequently, under the terms of a secret clause of the Yalta agreement, the Chinese Nationalist Government recognized the independence of Outer Mongolia after a unanimous plebiscite in the area, and in 1946 a treaty of friendship and alliance was signed between the USSR and the Mongolian People's Republic. Soviet control, which had been strong for a long time due to the geographical situation and backwardness of the area, grew considerably after the war through the influx of economic aid and Russian advisers.

Sinkiang, a vital frontier zone to the south-west of Mongolia, was also more dependent on Soviet Central Asia than on Peking or Nanking—for similar reasons. Subject nationalities in the area revolted against Chinese rule in 1944 and received aid from Russia; in 1947 the Soviet Union took over almost complete control. By the late 1940s many of the key posts in Sinkiang were held by Soviet citizens from Central Asia.

The spring of 1946 happened to be a major turning point in Asian as well as in European affairs. Stalin's pre-election speech and Churchill's Fulton speech were followed on April 15, 1946, by the breaking of the truce in China by the Communists, who attacked and took the city of Changchun in Manchuria. On May 16th, a British White Paper proposed that India should receive her independence as soon as possible. India's break with the Mother Country marked the end of an era in colonial policy. Smaller dependencies were quick to follow suit, especially those European colonial territories that had submitted to Japanese rule. The upheavals caused by the war, and the loss of face that the European authorities had suffered through Japanese victories accelerated the process.

Turbulent South-East Asia seemed to present an ideal opportunity, of the kind that Lenin had foreseen in his time, for Soviet intervention in muddy colonial waters. In the event, great chances for Communist expansion in South-East Asia between 1945 and 1948 were hopelessly lost. Why was this so? Stalin was more concerned with internal affairs and with the delicate situation in Eastern Europe, which was easier to supervise due to the presence of the Red Army. Eastern Europe offered a much more convenient field for the imposition of Soviet Communism as developed by Stalin. The area had size-

[1] Edgar Snow, *Red Star Over China* (New York: Modern Library, 1944), p. 96.

able industries and scope for economic expansion, together with a growing proletariat susceptible to Communist propaganda. In Asia Stalin was confronted by lethargic peasant economies to which the Soviet export model would have great difficulty in adapting itself without considerable modification; Stalin had neither the right character nor the right age for indulging in experimentation.

Furthermore, it was events in Europe that first set the Communist and capitalist powers against one another after the war, and although this antagonism was eventually to have great repercussions in China and in the Far East, in these areas it was not initially of the kind that urged Stalin to speed up the communization process in Eastern Europe. The mere proximity of Soviet and British armies in Europe, where Bonn, the capital city of West Germany, was only a little over 120 miles from Soviet-controlled Thuringia, increased the tension that led to the Cold War. The postwar struggle between the two political systems came into focus much more slowly in Asia. During the war period the United States had often been critical of British imperialism, and for their part the British and not the Russians were the first to lead the campaign against the American assumption of sole authority in Japan. At Yalta Roosevelt and Stalin had apparently come to an amicable agreement over the future of China; only at the end of 1945 did Russia and the United States clash over the situation in that country.

Soviet political ideas on the introduction of Communism in Asia remained extremely scholastic in nature. Theoretical wrangles over the various stages of Marxist development in Asian countries were bereft of any relevance to actual conditions in the area. The existence of the many multi-racial societies in South-East Asia was ignored, and no new solution was put forward with regard to the economic problems connected with under-development. By preserving his over-simple view of the world, Stalin lumped together the capitalist nations and their ex-colonies in the same camp and thus failed to grasp the opportunity of wooing the infant governments in Asia at the time when colonial passions were most heated.

Once again the economist Varga viewed the Asian scene with more foresight than his political masters; he reasoned that the great accumulation of sterling credits by a free country like India demonstrated that political and economic independence could be achieved gradually in ex-colonial territories; for Stalin, India always remained a lackey of imperialism.

The result of Moscow's incapacity, lack of interest, and rigidity was that Communism remained a virtually irrelevant factor in South-East

Asia in the vital years 1944–8. Independence was achieved in India and Pakistan in August 1947, and in Burma in February 1948. The dissolution of the Comintern in 1943 was not followed by any indication from Moscow as to whether the line of the United Front should be continued or not. The Comintern's direct successor with ties in Asia, the World Federation of Trade Unions, established in February 1945, gave no substantial aid to Asian Communists. A trickle of confused guidance came from the Communist parties of Europe, which was all there was to go on except for scattered Soviet press and radio statements. The dithering attitude of national Communist parties in Asia was in sharp contrast to that of the nationalist leaders, who were quite sure that independence was their aim and rose to power on their convictions.

Communist lack of initiative was evident in all areas except Vietnam. In Indonesia the Communist Party found itself taking part in a coalition supporting the moderate Sjahrir Government against the more strongly anti-Dutch nationalists. Burma presented a pretty picture of Communist disarray. Three political groups considered themselves Marxists: one of them put forward a variant of the heretical policy advocated by the American Communist Earl Browder, to the effect that there was no need to attack the imperialist power, since it had joined in the revolutionary movement of its own accord.

The Malayan Communist Party got off to a better start by organizing the most efficient resistance movement to Japanese occupation in all Asia. It was permeated by fierce Chinese nationalism and was virtually an extension of the Chinese Communist Party. After the Japanese surrender, however, the party dissipated its efforts in attempting to dominate the labour movement in Malaya instead of continuing with the guerrilla struggle that might have carried it on to victory in 1945.

Indochina provided the only bright Communist hope in the immediate post-war years. The brilliant Communist leader Ho-Chi-Minh proclaimed the 'Democratic People's Republic of Vietnam' in September 1945. In May 1946, he signed an agreement with the French for the inclusion of an independent Vietnam within the French Union, but the incompatibility of his regime with French rule resulted in the outbreak of open war in December 1946. Ho-Chi-Minh was the only resolute Communist leader thrown up by the Asian nationalist movement. He owed nothing to support from Moscow; indeed he came to victory on the strength of his independence from the Kremlin line, which originally played down his achievements because they were embarrassing to the French Communists, who occupied a more central position in Soviet foreign policy. Ho-Chi-Minh embarked on open resistance about one year before Russia finally made her intentions in Asia clearer with the proclamation of a renewed 'hard' line.

From 1948 to 1953
Stalin's decision to accelerate the creeping advance of Communist influence in Europe through the creation of the Cominform in September 1947, and his subsequent power thrusts in Czechoslovakia, Berlin and Yugoslavia, had their counterparts in Asia. The onset of open civil war and the repeated victories of the Communist forces in China after the early months of 1947 gave him encouragement. But whereas the continued momentum of the Chinese Communist effort over many years bore fruit with the establishment of the People's Republic of China in 1949, Russia's late start in Asia on an active militant basis paid far lower dividends.

The chief forum for the new line, the Youth Conference held in Calcutta in February 1948, had been arranged in Prague as early as August 1947, a month before the formation of the Cominform; but it came too late to have much impact. This was illustrated by the presence of two rival Burmese delegations to the conference. The smaller one was Communist-inspired and dedicated to the overthrow of the newly-independent Burmese Government, which, however, was represented by the larger delegation. Nationalist groups had already won the ascendancy in the majority of Asian countries and for the most part remained impervious to armed Communist uprisings after 1948.

Moscow changed its strategy, but hopelessly outmoded theory still prevailed. In the course of one of the main addresses to the conference, Rajani Palme Dutt of the British Communist Party referred to the 'veiled imperialism under the form of slave-controlled "independence"' by which India and other ex-colonial territories were still supposed to be bound to their mother countries.

Only after 1952 did the Soviet leaders realize the true strength of non-Communist nationalist governments in Asia and turn to their third postwar policy: wooing them with gifts instead of ignoring or openly attacking them. But even this more realistic line was to achieve only mediocre success by 1961. The golden opportunities existing in the period immediately after 1945 had gone, perhaps for ever.

Direction of Asian uprisings from Moscow began by being as

indecisive as the previous policy had been. In his report to the first Cominform meeting Zhdanov had little to say on the subject of Asia, and until the end of 1948 the Communist party of India, the most important in Asia after the Chinese party, was unsure as to whether its new 'left' strategy met with Moscow's approval. Co-ordination of the Communist movements in the area was finally handed over to the Permanent Liaison Bureau of the World Federation of Trade Unions, established at the conference of Trade Unions of Asia and Australasia held in Peking in November 1949. The Chinese, not the Russian, member of the Bureau apparently directed its activities. After the Communist victory in China, Chinese influence over Communist movements in South-East Asia increased substantially, mainly among Chinese minorities in the area.

Insurrections broke out in Burma, Malaya, and Indonesia within six months of the Calcutta conference. None of them was successful, although those in Burma and Malaya caused considerable trouble. Only in Indochina did Ho-Chi-Minh move on from strength to strength. In January 1950, the Peking regime accorded Communist Vietnam diplomatic recognition, and Moscow followed suit shortly afterwards.

Although the Communist victory in China was won, as in Yugoslavia, independently of direct Soviet aid and the guiding hand of Soviet ideology, nevertheless it increased Soviet prestige greatly. In the elated phrase of Marshal Voroshilov: 'For the first time in all its history, our Socialist Motherland has common borders of vast length with fraternal peoples who are friendly to us.'[1]

The Sino-Soviet Treaty of February 14, 1950, sealed the new bond. By this treaty China and Russia agreed to consult each other on all important international problems of common interest, to participate in action designed to keep the peace, and to establish close economic and cultural ties. The questions of the Chinese Changkun railway, Port Arthur, and Dairen were also settled in China's favour and an agreement for economic assistance was signed. The Chinese Communist leaders made it clear from the start, however, that their party was in no way subordinate to Stalin's party. Little reference was made to the assistance of the Soviet Union, and Mao did not adapt his peculiar variation of Marxism-Leninism to the Soviet prototype when carrying out his initial political and economic reforms. The slavish methods employed in Eastern Europe after 1948 were not repeated in China. Neither did Mao wish to follow Yugoslavia's

[1] Address by Marshal Voroshilov to his constituents in Minsk on March 7, 1950.

example; his crippled country relied too heavily on Soviet political and economic aid to indulge in dangerous arguments.

China's direct participation in the Korean War, which represented the climax of Soviet efforts in Asia to enforce the new hard line after 1948, added to her stature within the Communist world. Korea had been divided into two areas at the end of the Second World War: the North Korean Government was recognized by the Soviet Union in October 1948, and the South Korean Republic by the United States in January 1949. Both powers withdrew their troops from the peninsula, but in June 1950 the North Korean army, trained and equipped by the Soviet Union, attacked South Korea by advancing over the thirty-eighth parallel.

It is highly probable that the USSR encouraged this intervention. The Korean War appeared as the natural climax to aggressive Soviet action in Asia. Although Stalin thought initially that the North Koreans would win without any Western intervention taking place, the war turned out to be advantageous from the strategic point of view in that it tied down large Western forces in a remote area of the world. Politically it confirmed the fresh bonds between Communist China and the Soviet Union; if the Korean peninsula was won, it would provide a valuable indirect asset to Russia, a land-locked power that had previously engaged in long struggles, with Britain for the control of the Turkish Straits, and with Japan for Korea itself. Finally, the peninsula pointed like a dagger at southern Japan. Success in Korea might easily lead to the rise of Communism in Japan. Left to her own devices, Japan would probably re-emerge as a major power in the Far East, thus discouraging Chinese aggression in the area and also offering China trading opportunities that could pull her away from economic dependence on the USSR. Efforts on the part of the Japanese Communists to disrupt political life in Japan during the Korean War met with little success. In September 1951, the United States signed a peace treaty with Japan, but was not followed in this by the Soviet Union, Communist China, or other Asian powers.

Russian and Chinese hopes in Korea were dashed by the swift intervention of American and eventually United Nations troops under General Douglas MacArthur. No Soviet veto was cast against this action because the Soviet delegate had quit the United Nations Security Council in January 1950, in protest at the rejection of Communist China as a member of the United Nations, and had not returned. After initial difficulties, the United Nations forces repulsed the North Koreans and in October 1950 advanced over the thirty-eighth parallel, approaching the Soviet and Chinese borders. This move provoked an attack by Chinese 'volunteers', who in their turn threw back MacArthur's troops. Truce negotiations began in July 1951, and went on for two years, until after Stalin's death.

The effective resistance that the Soviet Union encountered in Berlin and Korea was eventually to persuade its leaders that their hard line, following upon the formation of the Cominform in 1947, had run them into a blind alley. Yet the lethargic manner in which the Korean War was allowed to drag out showed that no new positive policy lay ready at hand, and it was not until after the death of Stalin that a fundamental change came about in Soviet foreign policy.

THE MIDDLE EAST

Soviet influence and interest in the Middle East in the years from 1945 to 1953 was slight, for much the same reasons that restricted Soviet activities in Asia. In addition, there was no indigenous revolution in the Middle East on the scale of that in China. Significantly, the highlight of Soviet interest in the area lay on northern Iran, from which the USSR was reluctant to withdraw its troops, which had been stationed there during the war to protect the supply line from the Persian Gulf. Apart from this zone, no Soviet armies occupied territory in the Middle East at the close of the war. This fact, coupled with the same short-sighted attitude to national liberation movements that characterized Soviet policy in Asia, barred the way to Russian expansion in the Middle East. There was, however, no lack of trying, especially in 1945-6, when Russia laid a claim to a mandate over Tripolitania and also put considerable pressure on Turkey to grant the Soviet Union wider rights over the Dardanelles. Freer access to the Mediterranean and a stake in North Africa opposite the Dardanelles could lead to much greater Soviet influence in the area. Turkey continued to remain the principal target of Soviet propaganda in the Middle East after 1946. Her positive alliance with the West, and her acceptance of Marshall aid, vexed the Soviet Union.

In the early postwar years the Soviet Union espoused the cause of the Jews in the Middle East and turned its back on the Arabs, although this policy was to be reversed during the era of peaceful coexistence after 1953. When the Arab League countries invaded Palestine after the inauguration of the Jewish state of Israel on May 14, 1948, the Soviet Union called upon the Arab governments to restrain their nationals. By 1953, however, Soviet-Israeli relations had reached a very low point. It may be that the Russians had at first underestimated the strength of the ties that bound Israel to the West; certainly the new state acted as a rallying point for Jewish nationalism within the Soviet Union and thus was regarded as a harmful influence. Soviet policy toward the Arab League in these years repeated mistakes made in Asia with regard to the nationalist movements there. The Arab League was dubbed a tool of British imperialism, and even Nasser's anti-British campaign in Egypt was given little support—most of which was reserved for the Egyptian Communists.

The question of the withdrawal of Soviet troops from northern Iran was the occasion for the first major clash between the Soviet Union and the West in the United Nations Organization. In the early months of 1946, it seemed as though the Soviet Union intended to turn the area into a satellite like Outer Mongolia. Stalin claimed a stake in the region on the grounds of Soviet security, in view of the proximity of the vital Baku oilfields.[1] His motive, if it was a sincere one, was akin to the defensive reaction underlying his early postwar policy in East Europe. The USSR attempted to set up a local Communist Front Government in Iranian Azerbaijan, but the Red Army eventually evacuated the area under continued pressure from the Western states in the United Nations.

THE UNITED NATIONS

During the years 1945–53 the United Nations debates mirrored the deteriorating international climate. The many wrangles in the organization between the Soviet Union and the West focused the attention of the world on the incipient struggle between capitalism and Communism. Stalin's interest in the organization was minimal; he viewed it as a weapon with which the three great powers could check the other nations. Disputes between the major powers should be settled outside the framework of the United Nations, and work within the organization should be concerned only with political questions and not with the promotion of other objectives, either cultural, economic, or scientific in nature.

A cursory review of four incidents selected from an embarrassing abundance of episodes in the United Nations during the first five years of its existence will show how Stalin's hopes were soon crushed.

As early as January 1946, Russia found herself opposed by the other major powers on the question of her claims to northern Iran, not in a private meeting between those concerned, which would at

---

[1] Walter Bedell Smith, *My Three Years in Moscow* (Philadelphia: J. B. Lippincott Co., 1950), p. 52.

least have been according to the methods proposed by the USSR, but inside the United Nations, in full view of a chorus of small nations in the General Assembly. So much for Russia's dreams of 'great power' dominance. In 1948, the United Nations threat to go to the aid of Czechoslovakia convinced the Soviet Union that the international organization was being used as a tool for prying into its valued internal security, although it dared not claim as much with regard to a foreign country like Czechoslovakia. So much for Stalin's pre-war notions of spheres of influence and rigid preservation of sovereignty —meaning Russian sovereignty, though not necessarily Iranian or Czech sovereignty.

The low ebb of Soviet interest in the United Nations was touched in 1949, when Yugoslavia was voted into the Security Council. This body had become Russia's inner defence line, whither she retreated soon after the formation of the United Nations to wield her veto as best she could against the overwhelming majority of non-Communist nations ranged against her in the General Assembly. In 1949 this line was stormed, and a seat given to her most bitter antagonist of that time. During the same period Nationalist China retained her seat in the organization despite the Communist coup in mainland China, and a United Nations army in Korea was fighting against troops armed with Soviet equipment. During these years too, the business of the Economic and Social Council of the United Nations was growing and becoming increasingly popular with the under-developed nations. Molotov had not even mentioned ECOSOC at San Francisco; ECOSOC meetings were now winning the West golden opinions, while Russia still refused to contribute 'one red rouble' to its technical assistance activities.

Why, after seeing her hopes wrecked, did Russia stay in the United Nations? In the first place, her position in the United Nations was different from what it had been in the League of Nations. Russia was a founder member of the organization. She had arrived socially on the international scene. The son of a Georgian serf had been photographed at Yalta with the English aristocrat and the American patrician, discussing the future of the world. Secondly, Russia's continued membership in the United Nations was at least better than self-exclusion from it, with the spectre of an anti-Soviet coalition being formed there in her absence. Within the United Nations she could at least dilute anti-Soviet resolutions and use delaying tactics through her use of the veto. The organization also provided a useful testing ground for the Soviet art of political propaganda, especially in a body like the Trusteeship Council—although the temerity of much Soviet action in the world often caused the propaganda to have a boomerang effect: this was the period of Soviet expansion, frequently undertaken with scant regard for world opinion. The subtler phase of peaceful coexistence was not begun until after Stalin's death.

If we stand back from the international scene as it evolved between 1945 and 1953, we can trace the emergence of three main political zones in the world. The first area to define itself clearly was the Soviet camp of Communist nations in East Europe and Asia. The second zone was that of the NATO powers; partly on their own initiative, but chiefly in the face of the threat from the new Soviet bloc, the NATO powers in Western Europe and the United States grew steadily closer together politically. Outside these two zones lay a host of previously dependent territories that soon began to release themselves from their former masters. Most of the resulting political vacuum was not filled by either Soviet or non-colonial Western influences between 1945 and 1953; independent nationalist movements arose to replace the old regimes.

Political initiative at the international level was conditioned by the three spheres of influence that emerged. Russia had a free hand in the Communist bloc, though China and particularly Yugoslavia, neither of them occupied by Soviet troops, kept their distance. The Western democracies successfully excluded Soviet influence in France, Italy, West Germany, and Berlin, although in contrast to the Communist states under Soviet domination they were not centrally directed by the United States, the strongest power in their midst. In the third political zone, as the protracted struggles over Indochina and Korea demonstrated, the influence of Communist and capitalist countries was almost evenly matched.

We have noted that Stalin's primary aim in taking the initiative in areas bordering on the Soviet Union was to throw a geographical security belt around his country. Communist governments in Eastern Europe in 1945–6 were more a reflection of Stalin's anxiety to protect national Russian interests than to spread world revolution. Yet this secondary aim always seemed to remain at the back of his mind, just as it had throughout the years of socialism in one country; and once his primary aim was achieved, the second one was pursued. Not, it is true, in the full-blooded style that Trotsky would have advocated, but by the carefully engineered political, social, and economic manipulation of Eastern Europe after 1947.

Marx's pristine vision of a Communist world-brotherhood, like so many of his utopian projects, had been reduced to human proportions and distorted in the process. The supranational, egalitarian, Communist alliance of his dreams had been reduced in real life to Russian national domination of small neighbouring states. Communist principles had not been suffocated, but they came as an afterthought.

CHAPTER IV

THE INTERREGNUM: MARCH 1953–FEBRUARY 1956

Outside the Communist camp the great majority of the general public today is still apt to view the Soviet scene in terms that may have approached the reality at the time of Stalin's death, but have since become outmoded and need to be replaced by something different. It is our aim to try to catch the essence of the considerable modifications that have changed the face of Russia since the Stalinist era, and to present them in the pattern in which they slowly unfolded.

Let us recall the main outlines of Stalin's legacy as they appeared at his death in March 1953. They were relatively clear-cut, since they represented nearly thirty years of detailed, energetic planning by one man, whose will had only rarely been thwarted during that whole period. This book began with an examination of one such occasion, the Second World War. We have seen how, after initial setbacks, Stalin contrived to turn even the war interlude to his own advantage by reattaching the Soviet state even more firmly than before to his own purpose—and acquiring a foreign empire in the process.

Both the Soviet homeland and the newly-conquered areas of influence abroad were ruled with the rod of totalitarianism between 1945 and 1953; Stalin had no other yardstick. Centrally-controlled force directed every conceivable sector of life; it was impossible to imagine any kind of apolitical activity. The party probed into every corner, equipped with a variety of tools, while the secret police and the ideological machine exerted even more delicate control over the private lives and thoughts of Soviet citizens.

Long years of this kind of rule had made the Soviet state structure rigid and resistant to change. In the hands of an old and stubborn tyrant this trend was intensified after 1945. Outworn dogmatism led to great political blunders—especially in foreign affairs, where practical knowledge was slight and heavily overweighted by theoretical pontification.

To what end did Stalin apply his instruments of rule in the postwar years? His aim had scarcely changed since the launching of rapid industrialization and the slogan of 'socialism in one country' a generation earlier. Internally, Russia was to be a strong, self-sufficient nation, thriving on a growing industrial base. Externally, she represented by her new might the centre of Communist power in the world; she cast herself as the undisputed leader of all Communist movements and revolutions. A third aim, which grew in importance toward the end of Stalin's rule, consisted in the self-perpetuation and preservation of the regime in general and of its leader's unique position in particular.

THE SIGNIFICANCE OF STALIN'S DEATH

The death of the Soviet dictator ushered in a period of frequent policy changes accompanied by fluctuations in the relative power positions of the members of the 'collective leadership' that ran the state for a short time. The years from 1953 to 1961 cannot be treated as a single phase of Soviet development in the way that it is possible to deal with the period from 1945 to 1953. With Stalin's death the Soviet state awakened out of a political coma; each month brought with it new signs of life.

The long-term significance of Stalin's demise cannot yet be estimated with any precision since the Soviet Union is still divesting itself of the remnants of his work; but the relation of events up to 1961 tells a tale that rarely escapes from the burden of the past, the legacy of the Stalinist regime.

We shall see how the enormous gap left by Stalin's departure from the political scene took four years to fill, involved the sacrifice of over half the Presidium members in 1957, and threw open to dispute, in some cases, revered Stalinist policies that had long gone uncontested. The struggle between those who wanted to pursue the pre-1953 line and those who were determined to jettison part of their political inheritance was bitter and prolonged. The fight was conducted in terms of personal power, but political issues arising between 1953 and 1957 were naturally manipulated by the Soviet leaders wherever they could serve as instruments with which to bludgeon opponents into submission.

The greater part of this chapter is taken up with an examination of this far-reaching struggle. Because of the overriding importance of the succession problem, industrial, agricultural, foreign-policy, and even cultural issues were approached by the Soviet leaders in this period with one eye on Stalin's vacant throne. There was no time to work out carefully-prepared plans for the distant future during the breathless battle for power. It took three years from the time of Stalin's death for one of his lieutenants to produce a coherent political programme for the future. When Khrushchev stood up at the

Twentieth Party Congress, decried Stalin for his domestic policies, and helped to publicize a new line in foreign policy (the theory of peaceful coexistence), it was as good an omen as any pointing to the man who was likely to succeed Stalin. Khrushchev was the first Soviet leader after 1953 who was in a secure enough position to raise his head above water and look to the future with boldness, shaking off much of the Stalinist past as he did so. Stalin's exit from the political stage had very wide repercussions, but they should not be overestimated; Khrushchev's denunciation of Stalin three years after his death marked a greater turning point in Soviet history.

In his book *The Role of the Individual in History*, Georgi Plekhanov maintains that an individual can act as a potent force only when all the other factors in history permit him to do so: a strong-willed man can change isolated aspects of events and some of their particular consequences, but he cannot alter their general trend, which is determined by economic and social forces. On the strength of this Marxist analysis it may be conjectured that, even if Stalin had remained alive, he would not have been able to hold back forces that presaged the future.

By 1952 the Soviet economy had staged an astonishing recovery, which may have influenced even Stalin to relax the pace slightly in heavy industry, as Malenkov and subsequently Khrushchev did after him. Abroad it was clear that with the Korean War Soviet foreign policy had run into a blind alley offering few chances of further progress. In his *Economic Problems of Socialism*, Stalin veered slightly from the orthodox ideological point of view by stating that future wars were more likely to break out among the capitalist states than between them and the USSR.

The other, non-Marxist side of the coin presents us with a different set of facts. Soviet centralism as conceived by Lenin had led to the concentration of power in the hands of a few extraordinary people. After Lenin's death the nature of totalitarian rule in Russia threw up the figure of Stalin, for whom adulation grew to a pitch that surpassed even the cult of Napoleon. The end of Stalin's long rule augured changes of the scope of those following Stalin's succession to Lenin, which cost twelve years to consolidate, involved the lives of millions, and shook the foundations of the young Soviet state. The personality of Stalin was such that he mistrusted all his subordinates and made no provision for a peaceful succession of power after his death. There was neither a party system to establish legal succession by election, nor any constitutional provision for one-man rule. Lenin had at least left a 'will' giving his opinion of his lieutenants.

As a result the Soviet state in March 1953 was in a precarious position.[1] Stalin's successors, experienced in their particular jobs, had no notion of how to take decisions on a national scale—although, as has been noted, Khrushchev's responsibilities in the Ukraine, the second-largest Soviet republic, had afforded him wide scope. The appeal of the leaders to the Soviet people not to panic reflected the sense of inadequacy at the political centre more than the feelings of the population in general, which at first remained bewildered but otherwise unaffected by the death of Stalin. The period from Stalin's death in March 1953 to the meeting of the Twentieth Party Congress in February 1956 is treated as a whole in this chapter because the congress represents a convenient watershed in the post-Stalin era. Inside Russia the opposition to Khrushchev had reached a low ebb just before the convocation of the congress, and it never succeeded in making a decisive recovery. The congress itself set in motion a chain reaction of events connected with the disavowal of the Stalinist past that is still having its effects within and outside the Soviet Union. In the sphere of foreign policy the ideological changes announced at the congress were merely the formal expression of pragmatic innovations that had taken place since 1953.

DOMESTIC POLICY

The New Government

A collective leadership was formed immediately after Stalin's death. Although this type of rule acted as a convenient and comforting façade behind which the power struggle could be waged, it was a reality in the first year or so of post-Stalinist rule to the extent that questions of major import were often discussed by the whole Presidium.[2] But in the long run collective leadership could not be maintained; even in a democracy this form of rule is precarious, and in a country with a long tradition of authoritarian government it was soon found to be more convenient and efficient to revert to one-man rule.

The battle among Stalin's heirs took place on two fronts during this period. On the first, there was a scramble for the seats of power.

---

[1] See Sulzberger's interview with the Czech President A. Zapotocky in the *New York Times*, March 12, 1956. Zapotocky told Sulzberger, 'The necessity for collective leadership and the cult of the individual had already been discussed in Moscow at the Nineteenth Congress in 1952'.

[2] An East German delegation in Moscow in August 1953 dealt with the whole Presidium except Voroshilov and Pervukhin.

Immediately upon the dictator's death the top leaders began to look for key posts in the party and state pyramids. The latent rivalry between the party and the state machines came out into the open as soon as the man who had commanded the two strongholds disappeared. Leading members of other interest groups like the economic élite, the army, and the secret police aligned themselves with one or the other of the two machines.

On the second front individual leaders, and especially Malenkov and Khrushchev, staked their reputations on new policies advocated in their own names.

In March 1953 the Soviet leaders were too preoccupied on the first front to pay much attention to the second. At the start no new political programme or ideas were thrown up, although an atmosphere of general domestic relaxation after the tension of the 'Doctors' Plot' was induced through such measures as an amnesty at home and the release of the defendants in the plot; abroad, the acceptance of the Western principle of voluntary repatriation of Korean War prisoners had the same effect.

Two vital decisions were made with regard to the composition of the government in the days after Stalin's death. First, Malenkov for ten days held both of the key posts, that is chairman of the Council of Ministers (the state machine) and the senior place in the Secretariat of the Central Committee (the party machine). Evidently he arranged the main outline of the new government in conjunction with Beria before a meeting of the party Presidium was called. Thus the joint decision of the Plenum of the Central Committee, the Council of Ministers, and the Presidium of the Supreme Soviet published on March 7th was merely an endorsement of a previous manoeuvre. The inner group that had directed the Council of Ministers since the time of the Nineteenth Congress was openly acknowledged. Under the leadership of Malenkov it now consisted of Beria, Molotov, Bulganin, and Kaganovich.

The second important decision concerned Malenkov's own fate. The other leaders apparently exerted their influence to make him give up one of his key positions in order to breathe life into the concept of collective leadership. If Malenkov had sufficient power to take an independent decision with regard to the initial make-up of the government, it is reasonable to presume that he could also choose which of his posts to relinquish. He gave up his stake in the party apparatus by resigning as secretary of the Central Committee.

This move left Khrushchev as the only top leader with a place in the

Secretariat, to which he was now appointed together with M. Suslov, P. Pospelov, N. Shatalin and S. D. Ignatiev. At first sight it seemed as though Malenkov and the other leaders ranged on the state side in the balance of power were bestowing too much influence on Khrushchev; Stalin had risen to supremacy through this position. But the decline of the party in relation to the state during the later years of Stalin's rule should be recalled to mind. Moreover Khrushchev now gave up his post as first secretary of the city of Moscow, where he was in complete control, to become one among five secretaries whose stature was insignificant beside that of the famous leaders heading the Council of Ministers. At the same time four of Khrushchev's future supporters were ousted from the Secretariat and Shatalin, a close associate of Malenkov, was brought in.

The short-lived rise of Beria and his arrest in 1953 may be treated at this point, since his fall and execution weakened the power position of Malenkov and also dealt a blow at some of the policies that were beginning to be associated with Malenkov's name. On March 6, 1953, the day after Stalin's death, security troops under Beria's command sealed off the city of Moscow, presumably at the time when he was arranging the government with Malenkov. Under the new dispensation Beria was put at the head of the Ministry of State Security and the MVD, which, as the chief instruments of the secret police, had been separated in 1946 but were now combined again. Together with Malenkov he was the chief proponent of a policy of relaxation. As we shall see, Malenkov identified himself with a promise of increased production of consumer goods and Beria on his part announced on April 3rd that the 'Doctors' Plot' had been a hoax. The harsh methods of the secret police were criticized and M. D. Riumin, deputy minister of the Ministry of State Security at the time of the plot, was arrested. There were also hints in 1953 and afterward that Beria at this time advocated a soft line with regard to the national minorities and to problems in agriculture.

Concessions within the Soviet Union led to similar demands in the satellites. The industrial strike at Pilsen in Czechoslovakia on June 1st and the general strike in Berlin and other towns in East Germany on June 16th were followed by the announcement on July 10th that Beria had been arrested. It seems likely that he was made the scapegoat for the crisis in Eastern Europe. Beria was accused of having attempted to seize power by using the security apparatus and of being a 'capitalist agent'. The first charge contained a good deal of truth, as we have noted, but the second was merely another fantasy in the long line of trumped-up accusations against fallen Soviet leaders. In December

1953 it was announced that Beria and six of his supporters had been executed without public trial.[1]

The fall of Beria heralded the gradual break-up of the secret police organization for which he had been responsible. This was the first part of the Stalinist system to be dismembered, and also one of the most typical. Its survival was vital if Stalin's method of rule was to be pursued after his death; but the new head of the security apparatus was not made a member of the Presidium, as Beria had been. The party began to regain the control of the security organs that Stalin had taken away from it, and several purges were carried out within the ranks of the Ministry of Internal Affairs and the Committee of State Security, both of which supervised state security after March 1954. The amnesties initiated immediately after Stalin's death in the attempts to relax the political tension also served to depopulate the labour camps; this entailed the transference of control over the economy from the Ministry of Internal Affairs to the economic authorities normally charged with such matters.

Beria's fate showed the link between the two fronts on which the battle among the surviving leaders was fought. Policies as well as power positions were now at stake. This was an innovation in Soviet political life. Since the rise of Stalin no doubt could be permitted as to the efficacy of any political line that the dictator chose to introduce. Both in domestic and foreign affairs his word had been law, and although occasional dissenting voices, such as that of Varga, could be heard, no objection on the part of any of Stalin's lieutenants ever came to light—though some of these lieutenants were occasionally taken to task for misinterpreting their master's orders, as was Khrushchev in the Ukraine in 1947 and Voznesensky in 1949.

Stalin's undisputed policies were executed on majestic, sweeping lines bearing the clear imprint of single rule. The grand design of Soviet foreign policy from 1947 to 1953 had the advantage of decisiveness of purpose, as well as the limitation of insensitive monolithic unity in the presence of a heterogeneous world. After 1953 the sureness of touch went out of the political scene, never to return with quite the same relentlessness that had characterized it under Stalin's rule. In the years 1953–7 especially, before Khrushchev acquired almost complete control of Stalin's legacy, Soviet politics were marked by a lack of direction and by contradictory movements that were chiefly the reflections of the acute power struggle going on among the leaders.

If we jump ahead in time for a moment with regard to the struggle

[1] It now seems almost certain that Beria was shot before his case could be heard.

for power at the summit of Soviet politics and look at the situation as it had evolved on the domestic front by 1955, it is clear that whereas Malenkov had lost the dominant position he had occupied in March 1953, Khrushchev was increasing his strength all the time. But it was not a primrose path to success. As we shall see, Khrushchev was submitted to severe criticism over the agricultural issue, and the relationship between the Soviet intellectuals and the government remained unsettled.

Behind the open discussion of political issues, however, the levers of power were being manipulated in Khrushchev's favour. Malenkov lost an influential colleague with the fall of Beria, while Khrushchev's following in the party apparatus gradually increased. Working through his position as *primus inter pares* on the Secretariat of the Central Committee, Khrushchev managed to replace ten first secretaries of regional committees between November 1953 and February 1954. All of those displaced had been appointed during Malenkov's tenure of control over party cadres. In September 1953, Khrushchev was nominated first secretary by the Central Committee, and in July 1955 he succeeded in enrolling three of his supporters to the Secretariat—A. V. Aristov, N. Beliaev and D. T. Shepilov. By flattering the Central Committee through using it rather than the normal administrative channels to carry out his agricultural reforms, and by packing it with his own men, Khrushchev obtained a firm hold over the body. This was to prove invaluable to him in June 1957 when his supremacy was disputed by other Soviet leaders.

By 1956 approximately 30 per cent of the total membership of the Central Committee was safely in Khrushchev's hands. Most of these men had been promoted through the Ukrainian and Moscow regional party machines, which had been run by Khrushchev in Stalin's time. Other supporters came from the Central Committee apparatus or else held senior agricultural posts under Khrushchev. Outside the Central Committee, the ex-boss of the Ukraine was not slow in finding key posts for old acquaintances. I. A. Serov, Khrushchev's police chief in the Ukraine from 1939 to 1941, became chairman of the new Committee of State Security; R. A. Rudenko, formerly procurator of the Ukraine, became procurator of the USSR as a whole.

So far in this chapter we have concentrated our attention on the struggle between Stalin's heirs to gain influence through *position* in the political hierarchy, that is, on the first front of the succession crisis. Now we must turn to their manipulation of *policies*, the second and scarcely less vital front on which they fought. If at this point in the narrative a general survey of developments between 1953 and 1956 in Soviet industry, agriculture, foreign policy, etc., were to be given without any explanation of how these developments were directed by the Soviet leadership—and more precisely by which members of the leading group and for what motives—the deeper significance of this period would be lost on the reader.

Until 1956 at least, each of the Presidium members was more concerned with his own political fate than with general governmental policies. This attitude resulted in a succession of muddled and often-changed policies that depended on the particular clique or man in control at any given time. The effects of the struggle for power through policies are discussed below. No field was left unscathed. Domestic arguments between 1953 and 1956 centred on the policies to be applied in industry, agriculture, and the arts, but dissension also flowed over into the sphere of foreign policy.[1] The debates on these matters are summarized below, except for the controversy in the literary field, which is described in Chapter VII.

Industry

Malenkov's 'new course' aimed at stepping up the production of consumer goods. Since he fell from power as early as 1955, it is difficult to tell whether his programme was intended to be permanent or whether it was a temporary manoeuvre to gain popularity. There are signs, however, that Malenkov's new line, initiated in the autumn of 1953, was only a makeshift effort undertaken for the sake of winning support, as was, indeed, the exaggerated propaganda campaign soon to be launched against it by Khrushchev and other leaders. Malenkov simply drew on various state reserves and expanded the proportion of imports made up of foods and consumer goods. These hesitant steps scarcely made any change in the ratio of increases in the consumer goods area to those in producer goods, although for the first time in many years light industry was given precedence in the increases made in 1953. After Malenkov's demotion in 1955 capital investment in light industry was only slightly reduced, and Khrushchev resumed concessions to consumers once his supremacy was established.

Malenkov's economic policy was not at first attacked openly, although some organs of the central press continued to stress the need for building up heavy industry. By December 1954, however,

[1] For a fuller account of the struggle for power after Stalin's death, see the author's study, *A Key to Soviet Politics—The Crisis of the Anti-Party Group* (London: Allen & Unwin, 1962; New York: Praeger, 1962).

the army was brought into the arena against Malenkov. Greater emphasis on light industry would entail a cut in heavy industry producing armaments, and the army was alerted to the danger of a war scare at this time—as was the general public—in a series of statements appearing in the Soviet press. That it was no more than a scare was apparent both from the general international situation and from the tactics of the opposition to Malenkov led by Khrushchev, Molotov, and Kaganovich: on February 8, 1955, the day of Malenkov's resignation from his post as chairman of the Council of Ministers, Molotov made a speech clearly showing that the war crisis had been artificially manufactured.

An article by D. T. Shepilov, the editor of *Pravda*, brought the quarrel to a head in January 1955. For the first time economists in favour of the Malenkov line were attacked by name, although as early as December 21, 1954, editorials with conflicting views had appeared on the same day in *Pravda*, the party organ, and *Izvestiia*, the government newspaper. An occurrence of this nature would have been unthinkable in Stalin's time, and gave an indication of the rifts appearing in the supposedly united policy of the 'collective leadership'. Khrushchev obviously played on the importance of the industrial issue, because by January 1955 his call for continued support for heavy industry was backed up by Bulganin, Mikoyan, Molotov, Kaganovich, and Voroshilov, who together formed a majority in the party Presidium. Bulganin had opposed Malenkov on this question since 1953, and he was to receive Malenkov's post as chairman of the Council of Ministers as his reward. In view of the fact that Khrushchev was opposed in the agricultural sphere by most of the leaders mentioned above, this particular triumph was very useful to him at the time.

Agriculture
On coming to power in 1953, Malenkov surveyed the fast growth of Soviet industry with satisfaction and considered allowing the country the luxury of diverting a small portion of its efforts in the field of heavy industry into that of light industry. In the agricultural sphere it was plain to all the Soviet leaders that there could be no cause for satisfaction.

Soviet agriculture, the Cinderella of the economy, recovered far more slowly than industry after the war. This was due to a variety of reasons. From the climatic point of view, the geographical position of the great bulk of Soviet land is such that the growing season is far shorter than in other countries. There are few agricultural areas in the

USSR where the average rainfall is as high as twenty inches. Natural disadvantages have been aggravated by the Soviet Union's economic policy, which since 1917 has been directed toward the increase of industrial production at the expense of agriculture.

The collectivization of agriculture under Stalin initially retarded expansion, and subsequent agricultural planning remained over-centralized, authoritarian, and stubborn in the face of opposition from the peasants. The collective farms were given orders from above as to what to produce and how to dispose of the product; they found that the more they produced the more their efficiency was penalized by the state demanding higher quotas for itself. Until 1953 at least, incentives of any kind were lacking in the public sector of farming. It was practically impossible for the peasants to foresee what economic benefits they were likely to receive in return for their labours.

Compulsory government procurement at very low prices virtually killed incentive, which was diverted into the private sector. In the years 1950–2 the peasants were able to sell meat from the private sector for twenty times as much as the price paid by the state. It was therefore understandable that even in 1950, after nearly twenty years of collectivization, two-thirds of the total meat production came from the private sector. In addition three-quarters of the milk supply and high proportions of the vegetable and fruit crops came from the peasants' private plots. The existence of two different methods of farming led to waste and confusion, labour was over-concentrated in the private sector and valuable animal products were not handed over to the public sector where they were badly needed.

The fifth Five-Year Plan (1951–5) envisaged a rise of some 50 per cent in agricultural output over the period, to be achieved mainly by increasing yields per hectare and productivity per animal. By the beginning of 1953 agricultural production as a whole had barely increased from the 1950 level and was no higher per head of the population than it had been in Tsarist times. The picture was very black in the first year of the post-Stalin era and called for drastic measures.

The agricultural question was soon caught up in the struggle for power among Stalin's heirs. It was connected with the consumer goods issue, since Malenkov's new line was intended to stimulate a rise in agricultural production by offering material incentives to the peasants. Conversely, the programme of increased consumer goods supply was based on the assumption that the output of agricultural goods would rise substantially as a result of the reforms in farming carried out at this time. In their major speeches on agriculture after

Stalin's death, Malenkov on August 8, 1953, and Khrushchev on September 13th, both admitted that output was being crippled by lack of incentives and by unsuitable planning for production. Thus they agreed on the two main shortcomings in Soviet agriculture and the need to eradicate them. It was only when the methods of solving the problems came up for discussion that they disagreed. As the chief Soviet authority on agriculture, Khrushchev had the whip hand in implementing the reforms.

The question of incentives was tackled in various ways. The prices paid by the state for obligatory deliveries were raised, and in some cases deliveries were reduced or abolished entirely. Particular encouragement was given to the weaker areas, including livestock products and vegetables. Finally the tax system for the private sector was simplified and rendered less oppressive.

Changes in production planning were introduced by a decree of March 1955. Initiative at the local level was greatly enhanced, since the reform permitted the individual collective farms in conjunction with the MTS (Machine Tractor Stations) to draft their own plans on the basis of a central procurement scheme. The plans were approved by district authorities, then consolidated regionally and only submitted to the central government agencies for final ratification.

The reduction of obligatory deliveries tended to diminish the control of *Gosplan* (the central State Planning Commission) as did the reforms in production planning. It was significant that the main planning changes were carried out just one month after Malenkov had lost his place as chairman of the Council of Ministers.[1] In his speech of August 1953, Malenkov was far less explicit than Khrushchev on the need for greater liberty in production planning. The reforms curtailed the powers of the economic élite exercised through *Gosplan*, which in turn had very close connections with the state apparatus.

Not only did the influence of the economic élite and the state, and therefore of Malenkov also, decline in this sphere, but the role of the party organs increased. Further reforms carried out in Khrushchev's name tightened up party supervision over the collective farms. This was done through the MTS, which exercised a monopoly over collective farm machinery. In September 1953 the first secretaries of district party organizations were placed at the head of groups of secretaries from the MTS zones. At the same time the MTS were given greater control over farm production. By 1955 Khrushchev was in a

---

[1] See the decree 'On the Reform in the Practice of Agricultural Planning', March 11, 1955.

position to declare: 'Now that the MTS decide the outcome of production of the main agricultural products, they are able also to take upon themselves responsibility for carrying out procurements on collective farms.'[1] In September 1953, at the time of his report on agriculture to the Central Committee, Khrushchev was elected first secretary. His confidence soon found expression in the decision of February 1954 to bring under the plough vast areas of virgin land in the Asian republics. The campaign was closely associated with Khrushchev's name. It involved reclaiming and farming 90,000,000 acres of virgin or waste land in Kazakhstan and south-west Siberia. In the first experimental year the Soviet Union claimed to have ploughed 17·6 million hectares and sown 3·6 million hectares, thus exceeding the planned targets of 13 million and 2·3 million hectares respectively.

This daring operation was carried out by approximately half a million *Komsomol* (Young Communist League) members and army units, as well as by the peasants themselves. 1954 proved to be a good year climatically, but the new areas were hit by drought in 1955 and a large part of the grain crop was ruined. Luckily, that same year the grain harvest in the Ukraine benefited from good weather conditions, thus proving the value of having alternate sources of supply. Despite this healthy measure of initial success, Khrushchev's virgin lands scheme met with much more serious opposition than had the agricultural reforms mentioned above.

In the first place Malenkov's policy in the past had been to increase crop yields per acre in areas already under cultivation rather than to sow new ground. Khrushchev's new scheme went completely counter to this system. It is probable that Malenkov was averse to the idea simply because it was put forward by the member of the collective leadership who was rapidly becoming his most serious rival in the power struggle; but he had other reasons as well. Since the new project entailed a reversal of the policy of increased yields per acre embodied in the fifth Five-Year Plan, the organizational work of the economic and state planners would be disrupted. More important still, tight party control was established in the new areas; local party men had greater influence than central state administrators in the large state-owned farms that were set up. The collective farm system was not applied, since it was easier to streamline party supervision over the state farms, where the farm workers were paid as government employees and did not share profits in kind and cash.

[1] *Pravda* (February 3, 1955).

Malenkov's personal attempt to thwart Khrushchev's plan in this respect has gone on record. A partisan of Khrushchev later reminded his boss:

> Malenkov and the other members of the anti-party group who were opposed to the appropriation of the virgin lands in the Altai were decisively beaten in their objections. You will remember, Nikita Sergeevich, that you were with us in the Altai in the summer of 1954 and saw how the wheat was growing in the state farms that had already been organized in the virgin lands. Malenkov, who was then chairman of the Council of Ministers, signed a decree at that time in which he blamed us for the organization of the virgin land state farms. We were forbidden to organize any more and so we were compelled to leave the organization of the next ten farms until 1955.[1]

In his opposition to the virgin lands scheme Malenkov was supported by the economic planners Pervukhin and Saburov, who no doubt also resented the curtailment of *Gosplan*'s activities in the other changes regarding incentives and production planning. After the event it became clear that Molotov and Kaganovich had also opposed Khrushchev. Both men had staked out their claim to power after Stalin's death chiefly in the state apparatus, as had Malenkov. Moreover they were politically conservative in temperament and probably distrusted a scheme that involved a considerable element of speculation. They remembered that once before, in his rather Utopian plan for agro-towns, Khrushchev had attempted without success to apply fanciful ideas to improve the agricultural situation. The virgin lands campaign was not Khrushchev's only brainchild. His drive to cultivate maize on a large scale, often regardless of soil and climatic conditions, earned him the nickname of *kukuruza* (the Russian word for Indian corn) at this time.

Thus the majority Khrushchev had won in the Presidium by advocating a conservative line in the controversy over heavy versus consumer goods production was lost to him over the agricultural debate. Luckily for Khrushchev, the reforms of 1953–4 paid off. Between 1953 and 1958 there was a 50 per cent increase in agricultural production; the prices fetched by produce sold to the state tripled during this period, and for the first time since collectivization prices really meant something in economic terms to the peasants.

But even by 1958 two separate worlds existed in the Soviet Union—

---

[1] K. G. Pysin: see the stenographic record of the Central Committee Plenum held from December 15 to 19, 1958, p. 408.

the urban communities clustered round the great industrial centres that had been plunged into twentieth-century methods by Stalin's Five-Year Plans, and rural Russia, remote and lethargic, lagging far behind both economically and psychologically.

By early 1955 Khrushchev had accumulated enough influence, through his stronger position in the party and his victories over Malenkov and others on domestic policy issues, to bring about Malenkov's dismissal from the Council of Ministers. In the section devoted to foreign policy during the interregnum we shall observe how Khrushchev scored a similar triumph over Molotov, his other chief opponent, at almost the same time.

The culmination of this early period of post-Stalin politics was marked by the demotion of Malenkov in February 1955, and by harsh criticism of Molotov in July of the same year. The published speeches of the Central Committee meeting at which Malenkov offered his resignation as chairman of the Council of Ministers alluded to his 'failures' in agricultural and economic matters alone, but in themselves these 'failures' would hardly have been sufficient to deprive him of his post. Khrushchev rather than Malenkov had been responsible for agriculture since the war, and the former had greatly magnified the potential danger of Malenkov's industrial policy.

Other reasons lay behind the façade that was presented to the Soviet public and the world at large. In the same way that Khrushchev undermined Malenkov's influence after Stalin's death by fighting him on the double front of political issues and manoeuvring for a position of strength within the 'collective leadership', so he now attacked Malenkov not only for his mistakes in economic policy, but also for unusually foul play in the race for position.

Malenkov was secretly charged with two serious errors. 'The Soviet Presidium accused Malenkov of a conciliatory attitude toward Beria, and of co-responsibility for the "Leningrad trials".'[1] The first charge referred to Malenkov's and Beria's joint manipulation of the ruling bodies immediately after Stalin's death. 'In effect the Central Committee was confronted with a *fait accompli*. In view of the serious position at that moment [*in March 1953*], no one raised any ob-

[1] S. Bialer: *Hearings Before the Subcommittee on the Judiciary, US Senate, 84th Congress, Second Session, on the Scope of Soviet Activity in the United States.* Part 29, p. 1560. Bialer was a party activist of the Central Committee of the Polish Communist party who saw a circular letter from the Presidium of the Soviet Central Committee shortly after Malenkov's resignation. This letter was addressed primarily to the Soviet party *aktiv* and concerned the reasons for Malenkov's dismissal.

jections: but it was not easy to forget such an odd procedure.'[1]

The second accusation was even more threatening, since Malenkov was declared guilty of criminal activities in connection with the purge of Zhdanov's supporters from the Leningrad party machine after the latter's death in 1948. (It is even possible that Malenkov's part in the 'Leningrad Affair' had already been discussed behind closed doors in the Central Committee meeting of September 1953 that endorsed Khrushchev's agricultural policy.)[2] Edge was added to the accusation by the execution of Abakumov, which had occurred two months earlier, in December 1954, for his part in the 'Leningrad Affair'. There is little doubt that this association of Malenkov with past crimes committed by Beria and Stalin had considerable impact on the minds of the Central Committee members who were already turning against this aspect of the Stalinist past. In July 1957 this accusation was made public by Khrushchev and used as a trump card in denigrating his opponent's reputation in the eyes of the Soviet population. By the time the Twentieth Congress was convened in 1956, Khrushchev had already antagonized Malenkov, Molotov, and Kaganovich, who were to form the core of the 'anti-party group' of June 1957. Why did these three formidable men not pool forces in 1955–6 and strike back at Khrushchev?

By the end of 1955 their combined influence was much less than it was to be in the first half of 1957. In particular Malenkov's personal stock was very low because of the revelation to some party members of his role in the 'Leningrad Affair'. Also, in January 1955, his consumer goods policy was opposed by Khrushchev, Bulganin, Mikoyan, Molotov, Kaganovich, and Voroshilov, who formed a majority in the Presidium. Although Malenkov remained a deputy chairman of the Council of Ministers and a member of the Presidium, he was now deprived of followers like Shatalin in the Secretariat and Alexandrov in the Council of Ministers. Molotov's extremist position on foreign policy, referred to below, alienated at least four Presidium members.[3]

FOREIGN POLICY

In the period covered by this chapter Soviet foreign policy departed further from Stalinist traditions than did domestic policy, although

---

[1] G. Boffa, *La Grande Svolta* (Rome, 1959), pp. 29–30.
[2] See R. Conquest, *Power and Policy in the USSR* (London: Macmillan, 1961), pp. 229–30, 232.
[3] Pervukhin, Suslov, Bulganin and Shepilov, who were either back on the side of the 'anti-party group' or at least neutral (in Suslov's case) in June 1957.

the same hesitancy and experimental approach were in evidence. At the Twentieth Congress even Molotov, the most conservative spokesman on foreign affairs, was to say, 'We not infrequently still remain prisoners of habits and patterns formed in the past. . . . We not infrequently still suffer from an underestimation of the new possibilities opened before us in the postwar period.'

What were the 'new possibilities' in the year of Stalin's death? In the first place, the Soviet Union could now further its interests abroad from a home base that was immeasurably more secure, economically and politically, than it had been in 1945. Time appeared to be on the Communist side in the bipolar struggle for the world that had arisen since the reaffirmation of the Cold War. Malenkov's announcement to the Supreme Soviet in August 1953 that Russia as well as the United States possessed the hydrogen bomb reinforced this view.

The Communist homeland, which had survived alone until 1945, was now surrounded by a ring of friendly satellites, none of which could as yet remotely contest Russia for the leadership of the Communist bloc. Also, the carefully built up group of states in Eastern Europe had been unexpectedly joined in 1949 by Communist China.

In March 1953 the only cloud of any dimension on the Soviet horizon was Yugoslavia. Soviet-Yugoslav relations were an omen of much future dissension within the Soviet bloc. The course of future history may show that by the time of Stalin's death the world Communist movement had reached an all-time peak in terms of solidarity and cohesion, if not of geographical expansion.

No longer hindered by the whims of a ruler whose weakness lay in a rigid theory-bound view of Soviet foreign policy, the new leaders slowly adapted themselves to the realities of the world situation. The doctrine of peaceful coexistence announced at the Twentieth Party Congress in 1956 was merely the intellectual crystallization in thought of the pragmatic moves made after Stalin's death. These moves were based on the hypothesis that the Cold War in Europe had reached a stalemate: for the time being there seemed to be little chance of Soviet advances further west. Consolidation in Eastern Europe was therefore the chief aim, and this included a settlement of the German and Austrian questions that would be favourable to Russia.

Subsequently more attention would be paid to Asia and other parts of the world where there were many opportunities for Communist subversion. The massive retaliation evoked by the Korean episode and the abortive attempts at violent Communist revolution in Asia pointed to the failure of Stalin's hard line. The Soviet leaders' most important innovation in the years from 1953 to 1956 was the early recognition of the 'third camp' of uncommitted nations in Asia, which were coming to political maturity under the leadership of India. From now on they were wooed with Soviet aid and peaceful overtures instead of being subjected to the constant threat of Communist revolution. With the abandonment of Stalin's rigidly dichotomic view of the world '... the tasks of Soviet foreign policy have become immeasurably greater and more complex. They include not only the Soviet Union's relations with the capitalist countries, but also the wide field of relations with the friendly and fraternal countries of the camp of peace, democracy and socialism which have come to be of great importance in our country's foreign policy.'[1]

Eastern Europe
In Eastern Europe the aim of consolidating Stalin's empire was not realized during this period, and it became an even wilder dream after the Polish and Hungarian uprisings of 1956. The Soviet Union's own policy prevented its implementation as much as did recalcitrance on the part of the countries under Soviet influence. At the time of Stalin's death men like Mátyás Rákosi in Hungary, Boleslau Bierut in Poland, and Walter Ulbricht in East Germany were willing to submit to consolidating trends in Soviet policy, as they had been in the past. But being loyal Stalinists they were ill-equipped to understand and imitate the subtle gyrations of the new 'soft' line in Soviet policy carried out by a somewhat undecided collective leadership. Furthermore they did not agree with the wing of the collective leadership headed by Malenkov, since increased attention to consumer goods production entailing a slower pace in heavy industrial growth was anathema for East European Stalinists.

There were, it is true, influential Communists near the top of the East European parties who wholeheartedly agreed with Malenkov's New Course. But their views on other subjects veered even further away from the Stalinist line and did not coincide with those of any member of the Soviet collective leadership; they were eager to acquire some measure of independence from Moscow in matters of economic planning and the conduct of their foreign relations.

Thus within the Soviet-controlled countries of Eastern Europe the collective leadership had to choose between two unpalatable alterna-

[1] K. Ivanov, 'Soviet Foreign Policy and the Present International Situation', *International Affairs* (Moscow; November 1955), p. 19.

tives—on the one hand the subservient Stalinist bosses in power, who knew only too well how to align themselves with Moscow and carry out a policy of consolidation, but who looked askance at the new elements of Soviet domestic and foreign policy; on the other hand slightly less prominent leaders who could be relied upon to fulfil the new line, but who were likely to press for more independence. Indeed their views contained more than a whiff of Titoism.

The years between the death of Stalin and the final settlement of the problems raised by the Hungarian revolution in 1956 witnessed the evolution of a makeshift compromise between the Stalinist and Titoist extremes. The Soviet attempt to impose the frequently conflicting policies of consolidation *and* relaxation met with numerous setbacks and opened up wide rifts in the governments of some of the East European countries. The uncertain course of Russian policy due to the changing fortunes of the members of the rapidly disintegrating Soviet collective leadership only served to enhance the general instability. Until the final emergence of Khrushchev as Stalin's successor in the summer of 1957 Soviet foreign policy in Eastern Europe operated in a curiously haphazard fashion and the various countries reacted to it in widely differing ways.

The immediate reaction to Stalin's death both in government circles and among the masses in Eastern Europe was almost the opposite of that in Russia. At first there was no change in Stalinist policies at the top, but considerable ferment occurred at lower levels. As might be expected, Czechoslovakia and Bulgaria, both heavily committed to Stalinism, continued to apply the old hard line. In June 1953 the Czech government enforced a severe currency reform in an effort to make the labour force work harder; as late as September 1954 trials reminiscent of the later Stalinist period were staged in Bulgaria. There was also no immediate change of policy in Poland, where it was announced that Wladyslaw Gomulka, who had been removed from power in the purges of 1948, was about to be tried.

On the other hand the summer of 1953 was marked by the first wave of serious popular outbreaks in Eastern Europe (the second wave, far more significant in its implications, was kept back until the summer and autumn of 1956). In June a strike occurred at the former Skoda works in Pilsen, Czechoslovakia, and in the same month a general strike and disturbances on a much larger scale took place in East Germany. The local police were unable to quell the disorder in East Germany and Soviet troops intervened.

After the initial upheavals in Eastern Europe the Soviet Union attempted to impose a system that appeared to come closest to

Malenkov's domestic line of economic relaxation, while conserving Stalin's political ideas. Following on Malenkov's announcement of the New Course on August 8, 1953, planning commissions in Eastern Europe adapted their programmes to the Soviet model: a brake was put on the development of heavy industry and greater attention was paid to the output and exchange of consumer goods.

The spring of 1954 saw the resuscitation of the Council for Mutual Economic Aid, which had been formed by Stalin in January 1949 to weld together Soviet-controlled economies in Europe but which had remained a dead letter. It was now admitted, at least tacitly, that Stalin's effort to mould each East European country on Soviet lines had resulted in the uneconomic duplication of heavy industrial plants within national boundaries, thus making for over-investment in primary production and for economic autarchy.

At the same time the transfer of scarce labour, materials, and foreign exchange from half-finished investment projects to consumer goods production was considered ruinous by economists in Eastern Europe, where heavy industry was far less advanced than in the Soviet Union.[1] We have already seen that Malenkov's makeshift economic policy met with considerable opposition inside Russia and was soon reversed to some extent. Similarly the aim of the East European Five-Year Plans for the years 1956–60 was in the event more in line with Khrushchev's than Malenkov's ideas; the priority of heavy industry was maintained both in Russia and in Eastern Europe, but over-investment in this sphere was reduced.

On other economic questions the same half-hearted approach was in evidence. Thus while many joint stock companies,[2] those overt signs of Stalinist economic dominance in Eastern Europe, were now dismantled, the outworn price systems were allowed to continue.

The pattern of East European agriculture in the years from 1953 to 1956 reveal the same muddled outline. Toward the end of 1953 substantial concessions were made to the peasants in Poland, Czechoslovakia and Hungary. In some cases they were even allowed to revert to private farming after having been members of collectives. By 1954 a partial reaction to this policy set in.

Inevitably, economic relaxation in several areas brought in its wake hopes for some measure of political détente. The spark that set off the strike of the Czech workers at Pilsen was the currency reform that

---

[1] See an article by F. Schenk in the *Observer* (November 1958).
[2] Bilateral agreements signed between the Soviet Union and individual East European countries after the war for the purpose of exploiting East European economic resources almost entirely in Russia's interest.

slashed their wages, but the memory of the short period of American occupation at the end of the war and the deeper remembrance of the more liberal past spurred them on to protest against the political regime as well. Symbolic gestures were made by East European governments in response to this and other outcries from below. In 1954 elections were held in some countries and National Fronts were temporarily revived in an effort to woo sectors of public opinion that appeared to be deviating from the party line. A more permanent liberal trend was imported from the Soviet Union: the execution of Beria and the considerable diminution of the powers of the secret police had direct repercussions in Eastern Europe, where to a great extent Soviet domination of the police was abandoned. The national police systems released their grip on the parties and the population.

In the period under review Hungary may be taken as an interesting though untypical illustration of the impact of Soviet influence on the East European countries. More violently than any other country in the area, Hungary reflected the vacillations in the Soviet attitude, and showed how economic changes led in turn to political innovations.

The wildly fluctuating reactions to Russian events and pressure, culminating in armed revolt in 1956, were partly due to the internal situation in Hungary and partly to Soviet changes of mind. At the time of Stalin's death the Hungarian population was engaged in an industrial programme that was more arduous than that existing in any other country of Eastern Europe and which had been hastily imposed on a backward economy. The political purges in Hungary had also been exceptionally harsh.

At one blow this legacy from the Stalinist era was removed in June 1953 by the replacement of the Premier, Mátyás Rákosi, by Imre Nagy. Rákosi had been personally responsible for the policies applied prior to 1953, whereas Nagy was known to be a supporter of Malenkov's New Course. In fact the change in the government was arranged by the Soviet collective leadership at a meeting with Rákosi and Nagy in Moscow in May–June 1953. The Soviet leaders apparently decided to apply their concept of a balance of power to the Hungarian political scene: Nagy was given the equivalent of Malenkov's post as chairman of the Council of Ministers, while Rákosi was maintained as first secretary of the party, the equivalent of the post that was to fall to Khrushchev in September of the same year.

However, Rákosi's views were much more Stalinist than Khrushchev's, and Nagy's new economic programme immediately led to demands for greater political freedom, which did not happen in the Soviet Union. The strain imposed on Hungary by a 'collective leadership' made up of leaders with diametrically opposed views eventually proved too great. The collective leaderships broke up in both Russia and Hungary, with consequences that were far more violent in the latter country.

After his appointment Nagy made various price reductions and wage increases, slowed down heavy industrial production, and abolished some compulsory agricultural deliveries to the state. Peasants were allowed to leave the collective farms in large numbers. The contrast with the pre-1953 period was very great. Political changes took place in the wake of economic reform. A serious effort was made to resuscitate the Independent People's Front, which was now joined by 'Titoists' newly released from prison.

In Hungary the tight political spring that had been wound by Moscow-inspired Communists over the years since the end of the war was suddenly uncoiling with serious effects on the Stalinist state machine.

The mere fact that Hungary was now acting differently toward other East European countries showed that the rigid conformity to Russian practice of the period from 1948 to 1953 was rapidly becoming a thing of the past. It gradually became apparent to the more liberal Soviet leaders that within the looser system of Communist states, as it was now evolving, a niche could even be found for outlawed Yugoslavia. Yugoslavia's re-entry into the Communist bloc would be a big step toward consolidation in Eastern Europe. The slow rapprochement between Russia and Yugoslavia that took place from 1953 to 1955 was conducted entirely from the Soviet side—to the surprise and for the instruction of the rest of the Communist bloc.

The Soviet approach was insistent. As early as April 29, 1953, the Yugoslav chargé d'affaires in Moscow was sounded out on the subject of re-establishing normal diplomatic ties. By the end of the year, no doubt with Russian encouragement, Bulgaria, Hungary and Albania had entered into negotiations with Yugoslavia with the intent of reducing tension between themselves and that country. Once again economic changes preceded political openings; a barter agreement between Russia and Yugoslavia was concluded in September 1954, and in May 1955 an announcement that a delegation of Soviet leaders was going to Belgrade with the aim of achieving 'a further improvement of relations' heralded the decisive Russian move. It proved to be a twentieth-century Canossa.

The Soviet delegation included Khrushchev, Bulganin and Mikoyan, but the Stalinist Molotov was ostentatiously omitted. After making an abject apology in public for the way in which Yugoslavia had been treated since 1948, the Russians proceeded to negotiate for an agreement. Russia's aim was to re-establish full party relations. Tito not unnaturally wavered, because in their apology the Soviet leaders frequently rejected the Cominform resolution of November 1949, accusing the Yugoslavs of many crimes, but little apology was made for the 1948 declaration, which had explicitly accused the Yugoslavs of ideological errors. The joint statement issued at the end of the Soviet visit merely stressed the inter-state, as opposed to the inter-party, relations between the two countries, which were now to be renewed. Economic and cultural exchanges figured most prominently in the agreement, although lip service was paid to the desirability of ideological rapprochement.

This major diplomatic move on the part of the Soviet Union could not help but have far-reaching consequences, especially in the context of the other measures of relaxation that had been taken by Russia since the death of Stalin. Until May 1955 Eastern Europe could presume that its economic grievances would be heard to some extent; at that time it became clear that even outright political opposition to the Soviet Union was not always followed by annihilation. Khrushchev's revelations on Stalin at the Twentieth Congress were the final stimulus responsible for the second and much larger wave of uprisings in Eastern Europe in 1956. From 1953 onward the mounting crisis in the area was continually fanned by the more liberal breeze coming from the Soviet Union.

Among the Russian leaders only Molotov appeared to foresee the dangers inherent in Soviet foreign policy. At a Presidium meeting in March 1955 he opposed the plan for a rapprochement with Yugoslavia and did not join the delegation to Belgrade two months later. At a plenary meeting of the Soviet Central Committee in July he was strongly criticized for his opinion, though he was retained as Foreign Minister for almost a year afterwards.

Molotov also wished to continue the Stalinist line on a number of other foreign policy issues. For instance he did not agree to the proposed signing of peace treaties with Austria and Japan, nor to Khrushchev's and Bulganin's goodwill visits to Asia during this period. His obstinacy must have caused considerable embarrassment to Malenkov and Khrushchev, who both wanted changes in Soviet policy, although they did not agree on the extent of these changes. Stalin had delegated so little authority to his lieutenants that on his death no single Soviet statesman had an overall view of the political problems involved in running the country's affairs. The only man who had long experience of foreign policy was Molotov, who was thus in a position to influence and possibly to thwart his colleagues' intentions in this field. He was probably able to defend and in part execute his own ideas on foreign policy in the early days of collective leadership. However, in July 1955 he was attacked for having allowed his nominees to ambassadorial posts in Eastern Europe to issue orders to local party leaders.

The struggle for power inside the Soviet Union had great influence on the conduct of foreign policy until Khrushchev's final victory. The connection between the policies of Nagy in Hungary and Malenkov in Russia has been mentioned above. With regard to the New Course, we know from the former secretary to the chairman of the East German Planning Commission that all correspondence on the subject between East Germany and the Soviet Union was conducted between the Soviet *state* administration and the East German Government. Party channels were excluded. But in August 1954 correspondence on economic matters was suddenly taken over by the respective *party* Secretariats; at the same time Khrushchev began to replace Soviet economic advisers with his own nominees from *Gosplan*.[1] With the decline of Malenkov the state machine crumbled under the revived influence of the party organs.

Towards 'Summit Diplomacy'

As a result of Stalin's isolationist policy toward all non-Communist countries, by 1953 it had become very difficult for Soviet foreign policy to intervene with positive effect in international affairs beyond the bounds of the Soviet bloc. The attempts of the new leadership to restore contacts abroad and to reduce tension while the succession crisis was weathered at home were the first signs of political change in the USSR to make an impression on the West. A whole series of minor diplomatic moves on the part of the Soviet Union indicated that she was seeking some form of accommodation with her ideological enemies; substantial progress in the Korean War armistice talks in 1953 helped to reduce one of the main issues of tension between capitalism and Communism.

The member countries of NATO were heartened by the Soviet moves. At Churchill's instigation they proposed in July 1953 that the heads of government of the four great powers, Britain, France, the United States and the Soviet Union, should meet to settle outstanding problems. At first the Soviet Union turned this suggestion down, and in August 1953 Malenkov made a positively anti-American speech to

[1] See the article by F. Schenk in the *Observer* (November 1958).

the Supreme Soviet; but the government gradually took to the idea. An international meeting at the highest level was the only method of achieving the Soviet aim of consolidation in Eastern and Central Europe; the signing of German and Austrian peace treaties concerned all the great powers.

Following top-level negotiations over the German, Austrian and Indochinese questions, which are considered below, the West again suggested a 'summit' meeting. This time the Soviet Union was more amenable, and in July 1955 President Dwight Eisenhower, Sir Anthony Eden, Guy Mollet and Nikolai Bulganin met at Geneva. Bulganin went to Switzerland in his position as head of the Soviet Government. His visits to England and India shortly afterwards in the same capacity led the West to believe that he was as influential as Khrushchev, who accompanied him on all three occasions; we now know that he acted mainly as a figurehead. By 1955 Khrushchev and the party apparatus at his back were already in the ascendant over the government interest group.

The Geneva agenda covered four main items. The unsolved German problem is treated below. Linked to it was the pressing need for European security. The heads of government decided to refer the matter to a meeting of their foreign ministers, who were instructed to draw up a security treaty including the renunciation of force and provision for the international inspection of armed units. General disarmament was the third item discussed. The United States Government offered to provide the Soviet Union with information about its military establishments in return for similar details from that country. The question was handed to a sub committee of the United Nations disarmament commission for further consideration. Finally, preparations were made to improve East-West contacts at every level.

The 'Geneva spirit' of optimism was perhaps justified up to and during the negotiations of July 1955, but later it was to prove almost as ephemeral as the spirit of wartime co-operation between Russia and the West. At the time, the chief omens of continued Soviet intransigence were visible in the Soviet refusal to discuss Eastern Europe or the problem of international Communism. Very soon, at the meeting of the foreign ministers in November 1955, the Soviet Union's reluctance to translate its new willingness to negotiate into concrete actions became apparent. The 'Geneva spirit', like the Soviet-inspired theory of peaceful coexistence that was to follow it in 1956, was welcomed a little too sanguinely by some quarters in the West.

Central Europe
During this period consolidation appeared to be the keynote of Soviet policy toward the buffer states bordering on Soviet-controlled areas in Europe. There was certainly a need to tidy up the international situation with regard to Germany and Austria. In view of her potential strength, geographical position and history, Germany remained the greatest unsolved problem in postwar politics. Neither side in the Cold War was willing to let Germany fall into the camp of the other, yet the unstable, temporary arrangement that had been reached at Potsdam, especially with regard to Berlin, continually threatened to explode—as had the Danzig question before the Second World War.

The efforts of the ex-Allies at the Berlin Conference of January–February 1954, the Geneva Summit Conference of July 1955 and the meeting of foreign ministers at Geneva in October–November 1955 had no tangible results. It was clear that the Berlin meeting was doomed to failure even before it had begun. Molotov's conservative policy scarcely differed from the Soviet position of 1952. Germany was first to be reunited under a coalition government; only afterwards would general elections be held. This policy was mistrusted by the Western powers. They foresaw another Communist take-over of the type that had been begun in Eastern Europe in 1945. Molotov's sole innovation was his suggestion that two separate German states be created for a period after the signing of a peace treaty. The Soviet aim was to obtain Western recognition of East Germany as a sovereign state and to sever ties between Adenauer's government and the Western camp. The idea was rejected, but Russia proceeded to recognize the sovereignty of Eastern Germany on March 26, 1954. Diplomatic relations with West Germany were established in September 1955.

At the Geneva Summit Meeting of July 1955 the question of a European security system came to the fore. In 1954 Molotov had suggested that all the European countries including Russia and the two Germanies, but excluding America, should form an alliance—a plan that could have led to Soviet hegemony over the whole continent. At Geneva the West insisted that the German question could only be settled by establishing a different kind of security system. In the autumn of 1955 the foreign ministers of Russia, the United States, Britain and France made another attempt to settle the German problem. Eden, the British Prime Minister, put forward the idea of a neutral zone on either side of Germany, but Molotov insisted that it would be wiser to set up a neutral and reunited Germany in the centre of Europe. It seemed impossible to castrate such a great power politically. The USSR probably counted on Communist subversion to swing Germany over to the Communist camp at a later stage.

Soviet arguments in 1954–5 took on an urgent note because of West German admission into NATO in October 1954. With the passing of time, it became more apparent that Germany would remain divided for years to come, with Russian control extending over the smaller slice of the cake. After their exertions of 1954–5 to bring all Germany under Soviet control, or at least to neutralize the country, the Russian leaders resigned themselves gradually to tightening their hold on East Germany alone and, above all, to removing Western influence from Berlin.

At the Berlin Conference of 1954 Molotov stressed that a peace treaty for Austria could only be signed at the same time as one with Germany, but in February 1955 Russia agreed to sign a separate peace. From the international angle, Austria's problems were not as acute as those of Germany. Only one government ruled from Vienna, and it ruled over a population of 8,000,000 as compared with 65,000,000 for Germany as a whole. Neither Austria's geographical situation nor her position as a European power was as strategic as that of Germany.

The change of Soviet opinion was due to a variety of reasons. In the first place it was recognized that the solution of the German problem was as remote as ever; there was no point in delaying an Austrian agreement that would help to normalize the situation in Eastern Europe and also serve as propaganda in the Soviet campaign to woo the uncommitted countries. In the words of a Soviet textbook:

> Austria's acceptance of neutrality serves as an example for many other countries and shows that in the present international conditions even a small capitalist country which relies on the support of peace-loving powers can conduct an independent policy and abstain from participating in the blocs of imperialistic powers.[1]

Russia was obviously addressing her Asian public. No doubt she was also interested in softening Austria's neighbour, Yugoslavia, by this instance of goodwill to a non-aligned state. The Austrian Peace Treaty was signed on May 15, 1955, the day after the announcement of the Soviet pilgrimage to Belgrade. By the spring of 1955 Molotov's influence in the Presidium had waned considerably and his opposition to the signing of an Austrian treaty could be overridden. Finally, the

[1] *Mezhdunarodnye Otnosheniia i Vneshniaia Politika Sovetskogo Soiuza 1950–59* (Moscow, 1960), Vol. II, pp. 17–18.

USSR probably reckoned with the fact that a neutral Austria would create a strategic barrier between Italy and Germany, now both members of NATO.

In a similar spirit Russia announced in September 1955 that the naval base of Porkkala would be returned to Finland and Soviet troops withdrawn. The example of postwar Finland proved what a small country could do to evade Soviet domination, despite a precarious geographical and political position (the postwar elections of 1945 in Finland had seen the return of as many as forty-nine members of the Communist-led bloc of 'Popular Democrats' to Parliament). The ingredients of Finland's success included the absence of Soviet troops on her territory apart from the small Porkkala enclave; genuine Western sympathy after the Russian attack on Finland in November 1939; and finally, Finnish determination to fight, alone if necessary, against Russian domination. The torch of Finnish independence remains alight to this day as an inspiration to the 'People's Democracies' of Eastern Europe.

In September 1955 the eight-year treaty of mutual assistance between Russia and Finland was renewed for twenty years without change, although NATO's extension into Scandinavia since the original signing of the pact gave added significance to its prolongation. In 1956 Finland was encouraged by Russia to take part in the deliberations of the Nordic Council in Copenhagen, and in the same period the prime ministers of Norway and Denmark paid official visits to the Soviet Union. As in Asia, Russia's new policy of goodwill seemed to be bearing fruit, at least on a short-term basis.

Before turning to Soviet policy in Asia, the signing of the Warsaw Pact on May 14, 1955, by the European Communist states and the USSR should be noted. Essentially a military agreement, it legalized the stationing of Soviet troops in Eastern Europe and established a political advisory commission on foreign affairs for the whole bloc. It was intended as a riposte to the entry of West Germany into NATO and also as a confirmation of basic Soviet military control over East European regimes that were becoming increasingly heterogeneous.

Asia

Soviet policy in Europe from the death of Stalin until the Twentieth Congress was of a patchwork nature. In Asia and the Middle East changes were much clearer and far more sweeping. In comparison with Eastern Europe these areas had scarcely been touched by Stalinist influence and therefore represented a clean slate on which the dictator's heirs could inscribe their new policies, unencumbered by the necessity to erase much of the past. It was easier for the so-called 'collective leadership' to agree on policies for the less-developed countries than for the more complex situation in Europe. The Malenkov-Khrushchev quarrel on the merits of heavy versus light industry lacked all relevance to the Asian scene. Both men appeared to favour a 'soft' approach to the emergent uncommitted nations. As early as 1952 Malenkov took an interest in Asian developments, and after his fall in 1955 Khrushchev took over his role, undertaking official journeys in the area. Since the two men's views were not so disparate, it seems likely that together they were able to ignore the 'hard' line of Molotov, whose claim to authority on the basis of long experience held little water beyond the European stage.

The new Soviet policy in Asia was dynamic because it found an echo in the needs of the countries concerned. It did not take long to establish a working relationship.

Asian political leaders were eager to bring technological and economic progress to their countries in the shortest possible time. By 1953 the Soviet economy was in a position to supply at least some of the aid required in the form of equipment and expertise. For countries in a hurry, Russia's fast industrial development and her planned economy seemed in some ways a better model to follow than the capitalist system of Western Europe and North America. Many of the ex-colonial Asian countries came to maturity in the period 1953–6, working out for themselves a position in the world apart from the two main power blocs thrown up by the Cold War. The Soviet Union wasted no time in declaring its sympathy for the aims of the uncommitted nations. The Russian leaders subscribed to the Five Principles of peaceful international conduct laid down by China and India *before* the Western bloc formed SEATO to ward off the effects of Soviet aggression, which was less probable than formerly in Asia. Having failed by a wide time-margin to take advantage of the anti-colonial revolutions of the immediate postwar period, the Soviet Union was now determined to outstrip the capitalist powers on the next leg of Asian political development. It was afforded a good start by the prejudices of Asia, where the memory of Western domination was still fresh and any experience of Communist rule virtually non-existent.

The Soviet Union had first to obliterate the evidence of past policies. In the spring of 1953 the Communist side in the Korean armistice negotiations began to express a genuine interest in achieving results, and an armistice was signed on July 27th. The civil war in

Indochina, epitomizing the earlier Communist method of taking over areas in Asia by subversive revolution, was brought to an end in July 1954 at the Geneva Conference. A provisional demarcation line was established at the seventeenth parallel in Vietnam. Laos and Cambodia were neutralized. Thus at one blow the Communists procured a considerable extension of their influence in south-east Asia and the prospect of gaining more goodwill from the uncommitted countries in the region.

While the guns were being silenced throughout Asia, political leaders from the area met at Colombo in April, 1954, in an attempt to promote the growing solidarity of the newly-independent countries. India, Pakistan, Burma, Indonesia and Ceylon were represented, though Pakistan soon went over to the Western camp when she joined SEATO on its formation in February 1955. The positive aims of the Colombo powers were ill-defined, but it became clear that they wished to avoid modelling their future development on either Soviet or capitalist lines.

This nucleus was joined by twenty-six other Asian and African delegations at a meeting of the independent countries of the two continents held at Bandung in April 1955. Russia was not represented, although President Voroshilov sent greetings, as did also the Central Asian republics of Uzbekistan, Turkmenia, and Kazakhstan, thus showing the Soviet Union's ethnic stake in the conference. Communist leaders were ably represented by the Chinese Premier Chou En-lai. He offered to extend his country's agreement of April 1954 with India—the Five Principles—to all Asian and African peoples. The principles were significant in that they foreshadowed the revised theory of Soviet foreign policy as expounded at the Twentieth Congress in February 1956. They were as follows:

1. Mutual respect for each other's territorial integrity and sovereignty.
2. Non-aggression.
3. Non-interference in each other's internal affairs.
4. Equality and mutual advantage.
5. Peaceful coexistence and economic co-operation.

The Bandung Conference was a triumph for Chinese diplomacy and hinted at a future in which Chinese rather than Soviet Communism would hold the greater sway over Asia. By 1955 China was already winning a wide audience for her political theories with regard to the newly-independent countries of Asia, but she was in no position to hold out offers of practical aid. In this field Soviet superiority carried great weight. By virtue of her enhanced stature in world affairs and her growing industrial might, Russia could use her influence in support of the uncommitted countries. This she did in 1953–6 and afterwards. Her actions were prompted by a clearly-conceived policy that was in sharp contrast to the vagueness and neglect typical of Stalin's line in Asia. It was all the more effective for concentrating on deeds rather than words. Although the full-fledged theory of peaceful coexistence was not made public until 1956, Russia was making her aims clear not long after Stalin's death by means of political and economic aid to Asia.

Political interest in the period under review centred on Khrushchev's and Bulganin's visit to India, Burma and Afghanistan in November–December 1955. The Soviet choice of countries for this initial visit was significant. On account of her size, potential and comparative political maturity, India was the obvious cornerstone on which to build future relations with the neutral states of Asia. Burma was also near the hub of the emergent bloc. Geographically she had the longest frontier bordering on China after Russia and India. In 1955 she urgently desired to export her large rice surplus in return for industrial equipment. U Nu, the head of state, had made a visit to Moscow immediately before the Soviet leaders' journey. Afghanistan was a special case. Because of her political and economic weakness and her proximity to the USSR, it was not inconceivable that the Soviet Union hoped that she would eventually fall into the category of a country like Outer Mongolia and become another Soviet satellite.

During their visit to India, Khrushchev and Bulganin took care to present Soviet policies in a favourable light and to contrast them on every possible occasion with Anglo-American machinations. India's claims to Kashmir and Goa were wholeheartedly supported—while the Soviet leaders were in India, John Foster Dulles confirmed American approval of Portuguese policy with regard to Goa—and Pakistan was branded as a traitor to the Asian cause for participating in the Baghdad Pact sponsored by the West. Projecting their propaganda into the past, the Soviet leaders stressed that their own revolution would have been bloodless, conforming to Gandhi's tenets, if it had not been for capitalist intervention. The Western Allies were accused of having provoked Hitler's Germany into attacking Russia in 1941.

The Soviet visit to Asia was accompanied by substantial trade agreements, providing concrete evidence of Russian goodwill. In the years from 1945 to 1952 Stalin's policy and Russia's weak economic position had barred the prospect of trade with the less-developed countries of the world. At a time when the Soviet Union was stripping Eastern Europe and Manchuria of industrial plants, it was in no mood to barter machinery against Asian raw materials. But by 1952, when an international trade conference was held in Moscow, Russia demonstrated an evident interest in trading her heavy industrial equipment for primary goods. It only needed Stalin's death to let loose a growing flow of Soviet trade and aid to the newly-independent countries.

Khrushchev frankly told United States congressmen in 1955: 'We value trade least for economic reasons and most for political purposes.' In actual fact both motives were apparent in Soviet expansion in Asia and the Middle East after 1953, though it is true that political consideration took pride of place. Credit extended to the new countries was inevitably accompanied by a fanfare of political propaganda and was expended on showy projects in order to catch the popular imagination. Heavy industrial projects were the most favoured by the Soviet Union because they were seedbeds for the rising proletariat. Particular attention was paid to Russia's weak neighbours—like Afghanistan—which could be more easily submitted to maximum political pressure at minimum economic expense.

From the economic point of view the USSR found it profitable to exchange machinery for cheap raw materials and tropical foods, particularly in the case of Soviet border republics in close touch with foreign under-developed areas. Although economic autarchy continued to flourish to a great extent inside Russia after 1953, foreign markets were used for taking Soviet plan surpluses, and also as suppliers of scarce products in order to stave off domestic inflation.

Much has been said on the subject of Soviet economic aid, but virtually the only element of aid in Soviet economic agreements with the submerged two-thirds of the world consists of a low interest rate. Until 1958 Russia only made thirteen outright grants of little value, as compared with the 1·8 billion[1] dollars handed out by the United States up to the end of 1957. The great bulk of Soviet 'aid' went into long-term credits, to the tune of 1·5 billion dollars contracted for but not fully paid out by the end of 1957. Technical assistance figured prominently in both Soviet and American programmes. Despite frequent delays and occasional fiascos, there is no doubt that the Soviet Union's economic interest in the countries of Asia, Africa and the Middle East paid off quite handsomely in political dividends.

[1] Here, and elsewhere, the US billion, i.e. 1,000,000,000, is referred to.

Communist China

The period 1953–6 witnessed the fast growth of Chinese political power, although it was obscured to some extent by China's continued economic dependence on the Soviet Union and the almost unchanged nature of the Sino-Soviet relationship during these years. China's enhanced position in the Communist bloc began to have its effect soon after the Soviet Twentieth Party Congress. The trade agreement between the two countries arranged in March 1953 did not differ from earlier pacts: Soviet aid was again directed mainly to Manchuria and northern China, areas that had been Stalin's chief interest. In the theoretical sphere, Chinese Communist experience provided Russia with a valuable link through which the under-developed countries of Asia could be influenced politically. Although China's version of Marxism-Leninism as applied to her domestic problems was unorthodox by Soviet standards, it did not as yet affect Soviet ideological primacy within the Communist bloc.

Chinese prestige grew in connection with the Cold War in Asia and later with the cultivation of the new 'soft' line. The Korean War, in which China played a leading role, was portrayed as a great Communist victory and proved to the Chinese, as the Japanese had proved to the rest of Asia during the Second World War, that North American and European armies were not necessarily invincible. During the transition to peaceful coexistence Communist China acted for the first time as a great international power in the settlement of the Indochinese problem, which could not be solved without her help. The Chinese leaders took advantage of the occasion to display themselves with pomp at Geneva in 1954. By 1955 Chou En-lai was scoring quieter, though no less impressive, gains for Chinese influence by attempting to minimize the differences of outlook between his country and the uncommitted nations at Bandung.

The celebration of the fifth anniversary of the Communist Chinese regime in October 1954 was marked by the visit of a Soviet delegation headed by Khrushchev. Neither Malenkov nor Molotov took part in this goodwill tour, which resulted in Soviet concessions to China that implied some readjustment in the balance of power between the two states. The last Soviet forces in China left Port Arthur in 1955. The joint stock Sino-Soviet companies formed in the Stalinist era and characteristic of its dominating ethos were liquidated by January of the same year. Also in 1955 Chinese influence made inroads into Outer Mongolia by means of greater economic aid and technical assistance. Sinkiang, another crucially-located area near

Soviet Asia, received increasing numbers of Chinese, who ran the Communist machine there.

During this period China made substantial grants to North Korea and North Vietnam, and also provided assistance for Outer Mongolia. These measures were extraordinary at a time when China was still obtaining vast loans from the Soviet Union, but they were indicative of her attitude. For reasons of prestige China wished to maintain her hold over the first two areas, which owed as much to her as to Russia in the recent past. The Chinese Communist leaders and the Chinese population as a whole were beginning to shed a national inferiority complex brought on by past humiliations. The Chinese Nationalist Government still lay like a thorn in her side on the island of Formosa. An overwhelming majority of nations still refused to give diplomatic recognition to the Communist regime. Soviet Russia remained China's chief support in a hostile world.

The Middle East
Soviet policy in the Middle East in the period between the death of Stalin and the convocation of the Twentieth Congress casts further light on the new line in under-developed countries.

The state of flux in Soviet foreign policy towards under-developed countries immediately after March 1953 was clearly illustrated by Moscow's equivocal attitude to the national bourgeois revolt under Premier Mohammed Mossadegh in Iran. This came to a climax in July 1953 when the Shah attempted to dismiss Mossadegh. Soviet policy had not yet had time to evolve sufficiently to a point where it was possible to give unabashed support to a bourgeois nationalist government like Mossadegh's, even though its political cast was violently anti-Western. It is conceivable that if Stalin had still been alive, Russian troops would have been sent into Iran to put the pro-Communist Tudeh party into power. As it was, the new Russian government had already, on May 30, 1953, sent a conciliatory note to Iran's nationalist neighbour, Turkey, and was in the process of making similar gestures all over the world. Consequently the Soviet Union fell between two stools in the summer of 1953. Both the Tudeh party and Mossadegh fell, for lack of sufficient outside help, before the forces of the pro-Western Shah.

The evolution of Soviet relations with the Middle East and in particular with the Arab world showed to a greater extent than in Asia how at first the initiative came as much from the countries themselves as from Russia. It should not be thought that any clear-cut theoretical policy was worked out in the Kremlin soon after Stalin's death. On the practical level a plan of action was gradually elaborated as a result of the quarrels in the collective leadership and the turn of events in the countries concerned. An expert on the Middle East has written of this period:

> The Soviet reorientation in the Middle East in 1954-5 did not come as the result of any startling new discovery made by Soviet Middle Eastern experts, nor did a new Marxist-Leninist analysis *precede* the change. The Middle East experts modified their approach after, not before, the politicians did.... If there had been a Leninist reappraisal of the Middle Eastern situation, it was carried out by the diplomats and the Presidium rather than by the experts—who followed a lead given from above.[1]

On Asian questions Russian experts (and politicians) could mould their new outlook on the theory expressed in 1954 by China and India through the Five Principles, but in the Middle East Soviet moves were not guided by a friendly Communist power like China with an intimate knowledge of the area. Besides, the original idea of a bloc of uncommitted nations arose in Asia, and not in the Middle East.

The Turkish-Pakistani pact of 1954, and later agreements culminating in the pro-Western Baghdad Pact of February 1955 aroused the anger of several Arab countries, and also of the Soviet Union, against which the defensive military coalition was directed. Like SEATO, the pact was formed too late to counter an aggressive Soviet line that had already disappeared. No longer, as in the postwar years, was Stalin's land empire an expansionist force in terms of military might. Turkey and Iran, countries with long borders on the Soviet Union, joined together with Britain, Iraq, and Pakistan to ward off the threat of Communist invasion—a threat that had gradually waned since the early postwar days when the Russians occupied Iran and sent belligerent notes to Turkey on the Dardanelles question.

The imposition of a defensive cordon along Soviet Middle Eastern frontiers spurred Russia to take a step that was completely alien to Stalin's way of thinking and which represented a break-through out of the impasse to which his policy had led. Instead of putting crude military and political pressure on geographical neighbours, the Soviet Union now discarded the vision of a monolithic Communist land bloc, jumped over the hostile barrier set up by the Baghdad Pact, and started to woo a compliant Egypt with offers of trade and

[1] W. Z. Laqueur, *The Soviet Union and the Middle East* (London: Routledge & Kegan Paul, 1959), p. 156.

military aid. The new line was a success, thanks to the growth of Russian political and economic prestige and the fact that it was addressed to a sympathetic and not too sophisticated political audience. Russia's initial gains eventually encouraged her to turn to areas as far afield as Africa, South America and Cuba.

Soviet policy in the Middle East reached a major turning point with the arms deal with Egypt in September 1955. As early as the winter of 1953-4 Soviet-Egyptian relations had improved during a period of tension between Britain and Egypt over the Suez Canal, but they were damped by the Anglo-Egyptian agreement of July 1954. By February 1955, however, Soviet officials in the Middle East were making offers of Soviet economic assistance, and in March the Soviet ambassador to Egypt approached Nasser in confidence and proposed the sale of Russian arms. The timing was significant, because the suggestion came near the time of Stalinist Molotov's downfall.

The arms deal was conducted with discretion, since it coincided with the Geneva Summit Conference and in view of its military overtones was hardly apt propaganda for the new 'soft' Russian line. Some Egyptian Communist groups, like the Soviet foreign policy experts alluded to above, found it hard to adapt themselves to the dramatic change of climate and continued to oppose Nasser and his bourgeois nationalist government as they had been taught to do by Moscow in the recent Stalinist past. Both in Russia and abroad it took some time for the new flexibility in policy to seep down through the Communist ranks.

If Soviet achievements in foreign policy during the interregnum are compared with the rather muddled attempts at reform in domestic affairs, it is clear that the greatest gains were made abroad, especially in Asia and the Middle East. Internal Soviet issues were too often used and misused as pegs on which to hang individual hopes of becoming the master of the state; it was not as easy or as profitable to manipulate foreign policy in the same way. Furthermore the two main rivals, Khrushchev and Malenkov, were nearly of the same mind on numerous international problems. Molotov's fierce opposition could be discounted, particularly as his views on domestic affairs coincided on some occasions with those of Khrushchev, but on others with Malenkov's. In this way his influence was dissipated in the struggle for power.

Molotov's ideas on foreign policy and domestic matters were Stalinist in type and by 1956 came to be almost completely disowned by his colleagues. Their disassociation from Stalin's precepts in foreign policy reaped immediate success in the world because it came so quickly. The Soviet leaders found it relatively easy to captivate the less-developed countries with their new line, and even hardened capitalist opinion in the NATO group awoke to the new Soviet charm. But the element of quick change brought trouble as well as success. Molotov sensed that the sudden thaw in East Europe might become an avalanche, and he was to be proved right after the Twentieth Congress in 1956.

Moreover there was the danger for the future that disillusionment would set in among foreign observers of Russia's new flexibility. The Soviet government had certainly revised Stalin's methods of conducting foreign policy, but it was not yet certain that it had abandoned his aims—and those of international Communism since its birth. The note of continuity in the Soviet approach to the German problem should have forewarned the world in this period that these aims had in fact been largely preserved.

CHAPTER V

THE KHRUSHCHEV ERA: DOMESTIC POLICY

In the previous chapter we recorded the critical struggle for power that ensued in Russia after Stalin's death. It involved much more than the personal fates of the contestants for Stalin's mantle. Fundamental issues concerning the management of the state, the direction of the economy, and the course of foreign policy were bound up in the gigantic upheaval caused by the removal of a dictator whose word alone had decided all Soviet policies for a period of twenty-five years.

Khrushchev was the victor in the fight, which eventually produced another single dictator after a short experiment in collective leadership. But by the time of the Twentieth Congress in February 1956 a fresh breeze had blown into many areas of political thought and action, spreading out from the central whirlwind generated by the rivalry in the Presidium. Makeshift changes had occurred in the direction of industry and agriculture; Stalinist foreign policy had been questioned and on some points rejected; and the party apparatus had been stimulated from its previous torpor in order to serve Khrushchev on his way to the top of the political ladder. The Stalinist inheritance was slowly being rejected.

Until the years 1956–7 the traditional political climate was allowed to crumble slowly without any attempt being made to replace it with positive, long-term aims. The leaders in the Presidium could not agree with each other on policy, and no one man was powerful enough to forge a new vision for the Soviet state. Between 1953 and 1956 it was a case of every man for himself—there was no time or opportunity for a systematic revision of Stalin's Russia.

The first sign of a more thoughtful, rational approach to the huge problem of releasing the Soviet Union from the weight of Stalin's influence was apparent at the Twentieth Congress. The only man in a strong enough position to take such an initiative at that time was Khrushchev. His famous secret speech to the awestruck congress on Stalin's crimes and errors was a turning point in the progress of the Soviet state. His enunciation of the theory of peaceful coexistence at this time had a similar effect in the sphere of foreign policy, clarifying and appraising the uncertain moves that had been made since Stalin's death and setting out a blueprint for future action.

Khrushchev's temerity at the Twentieth Congress nearly led to his downfall and the loss of all the influence he had acquired since 1953, for his opponents in the Presidium capitalized on the unfortunate effects of the secret speech in domestic and especially in foreign affairs. But we shall see that by the summer of 1957 Khrushchev had regained the whip hand and was holding his power with an even firmer grasp.

The present chapter opens with a discussion of the Twentieth Congress as it affected domestic policy, continues with the history of Khrushchev's brief reversal toward the end of 1956 and his swift recovery in the first half of 1957, and concludes with an account of some of the long-term changes introduced during the Khrushchev regime. Stability of government after June 1957 was reflected in more solid, more confidently-planned policies that contrasted sharply with the piecemeal schemes thrown up during the succession crisis.

Yet in some areas, such as the increasing power of the party apparatus and the reform of the economy, post-1957 policies merely enlarged on trends that had begun almost immediately after Stalin's death. The examination of how the party apparatus reasserted its hold over the other main interest groups in the state will be pursued in this chapter and extended to include new spheres of Soviet life penetrated by its octopus-like influence. After 1957 greater confidence in its own power and that of Khrushchev, its master, encouraged it to carry out a certain amount of decentralization and delegation at the lower levels of political control. The same confidence led to a recasting of major elements of economic theory in an attempt to sweep away Stalinist rigidity and lay the base for a streamlined economy that would be capable of producing the material abundance envisaged by Khrushchev at the Twenty-first and Twenty-second Congresses. Remnants from the past still littered the stage at the end of the period covered in this book: agricultural theory and practice in particular remained backward in an optimistic community. But by the winter of 1961 Khrushchev had already left an indelible impression of his political will on the country he ruled. Not only were the results of his government different from Stalin's but his style was unique too. In the years covered by this chapter, the great changes that were still inchoate during the unsettled three years after Stalin's death were submitted to inspection, put in order and launched as long-term policies.

THE FINAL STRUGGLE FOR POWER

By the end of 1955 only a drastic change inside Russia could have resuscitated the prestige of Malenkov and Molotov, who appeared to be almost annihilated politically. Ironically Khrushchev himself threw his opponents the vital political lifebelt by his denunciation of Stalin in his secret speech to the Twentieth Congress in February 1956; this speech led to unrest in Eastern Europe that could be blamed directly on the First Secretary of the Soviet party.

Surprising though it may seem after the event, Khrushchev grossly underestimated the effect his speech would have on the People's Democracies. This apparent misjudgment may be explained in part by the fact that he intended his speech primarily for domestic consumption. Khrushchev wished to make an appeal to his audience at the congress, which chiefly consisted of the higher élite of the party and the state—the class that had suffered most from the Great Purge of the 1930s and wanted a guarantee against any repetition of Stalinist error.

The speech itself was very strong meat. Although Khrushchev insisted that Stalin had played a positive role in defeating Trotsky, Zinoviev, and Bukharin and in carrying out his own industrialization and collectivization policies in the late 1920s and early 1930s, the dead leader was accused of introducing the 'cult of personality' and ruling despotically after 1934. According to Khrushchev, Stalin had distorted Lenin's teaching by proclaiming that the class struggle became stronger as socialism drew nearer, and had used his thesis as an excuse to conduct terrorism on a vast scale. Khrushchev's language was inflammatory: 'Men came to fear their own shadows,' he exclaimed; they were haunted by 'mass repressions and brutal acts of violation of socialist legality'.[1]

Although the speech came as a revelation to the outside world, it was marked by a sensitive reticence on some points, since even Khrushchev must have realized that it was impossible to inculpate Stalin without incurring some of the blame himself for having cultivated his late master. However, he had an edge on his main opponents in the Presidium, Malenkov, Molotov, and Kaganovich, who had been more closely connected with Stalin than he himself had been. The secret speech was carefully slanted in order to bring out this connection. For instance, Khrushchev went into the 'Leningrad Affair' of 1948–9 in great detail, knowing the effect this would have on Central Committee members who already knew of Malenkov's guilt. Molotov was directly attacked for his connivance in Stalin's attack on Yugoslavia in 1948; and both Molotov and

[1] See the text of Khrushchev's secret speech, together with a commentary, in Bertram Wolfe, *Khrushchev and Stalin's Ghost* (New York: Frederick A. Praeger, Inc., 1956).

Kaganovich were mentioned as the two men who were first informed of Stalin's decision to make Ezhov People's Commissar for Internal Affairs, a move that heralded the dreaded Great Purge. In their subsequent speeches to the congress Kaganovich and Molotov hinted that they did not approve of Khrushchev's secret speech.

Khrushchev's bold attack on the originator of all past policies struck at the heart of the problem created by the Stalinist legacy. Once the apex of the Stalinist pyramid was assailed, the whole edifice tottered. We shall have occasion to note the widespread effects of the secret speech within the Communist bloc in the next chapter. Inside the Soviet Union it soon led to the final struggle among the rivals for Stalin's position. Also, after the Twentieth Congress profound changes were made in the economy, resulting in the elimination of the pre-1953 structure and going far beyond the modifications introduced between 1953 and 1956. The secret speech thus not only lent added momentum to a process initiated beforehand, but also launched de-Stalinization on a path of no return.

It was evident from the changes in the top party organs that followed immediately after the Twentieth Congress that Khrushchev had won a moderate personal victory on the home front. Five new candidate members were elected to the Presidium; all of them were Khrushchev's supporters at the time. One of them, Shepilov, replaced Molotov as Minister of Foreign Affairs in June 1956. However, all the full members of the Presidium remained in their places. The secret speech probably delayed Khrushchev's further progress toward sole leadership in so far as it was a polemic against one-man rule.

A far more serious obstacle to Khrushchev's further rise lay in the revolts that followed in Eastern Europe. The Soviet decisions on how to deal with the precarious situation were taken with the full participation of Khrushchev's opponents. Molotov, who had not accompanied Khrushchev on his earlier visits to Peking and Belgrade, went to Warsaw on October 19, 1956, to treat with the angry Poles, and Malenkov joined Khrushchev on a trip to a five-power meeting with the People's Democracies in Budapest in January 1957. An effort was even made to reverse the dicta of the Twentieth Congress through articles in Soviet journals questioning the theory of peaceful coexistence and attempting to rehabilitate Stalin.

The nadir of Khrushchev's prestige was reached at the Central Committee meeting of December 1956. The meeting was called late. Khrushchev was obviously trying to gain time in order to improve his position. Two groups of problems were discussed; their economic

THE KHRUSHCHEV ERA: DOMESTIC POLICY 161

implications will be dealt with in the appropriate place, but at this point their political significance should be observed.

First, the economic planner Saburov gave a report on the sixth Five-Year Plan in which he criticized investment policy and low labour productivity. He was joined by Pervukhin in a plea for a revision of the Soviet bloc economic integration programme established at Budapest in 1955. As economists both men must also have viewed the drain on Soviet resources, resulting from the effort to appease Eastern Europe, as a sorry consequence of Khrushchev's ill-timed Stalin speech.

The expert criticism of these two men, who had already come out against other economic policies introduced by Khrushchev between 1953 and 1956, put wind into the sails of his opponents, who now felt strong enough to confront him over the other main problem that arose at the meeting—the issue of economic decentralization within the Soviet Union. In addition to purely economic reasons, Khrushchev was also anxious to put the Soviet economy on a more regional basis for his own political ends: decentralization would break up the Moscow empires of the government and economic interest groups represented by Malenkov, Saburov, and Pervukhin in the Presidium, and would allow more intervention by the party apparatus at local levels under Khrushchev's control.

Khrushchev's aims were thwarted in December by the reinforcement of the traditional centralized approach to Soviet economic organization. Pervukhin was made chairman of the State Economic Commission. The closer ties between the state and economic groups were underlined by the transference of nearly all the first deputy chairmen and deputy chairmen of the Council of Ministers to the commission. The stage was set for the final battle between Khrushchev and the party apparatus in the Central Committee Secretariat on the one hand, and Malenkov, Molotov, Kaganovich, together with Saburov and Pervukhin in the state and economic caucus on the other. The State Economic Commission, still maintaining a firm grasp over the galaxy of Moscow ministries, arrayed its forces in combination with the state bureaucracy. Significantly, the reduced Council of Ministers now consisted of the entire 'anti-party group' that was to attack Khrushchev in June 1957 (Bulganin, Molotov, Kaganovich, Pervukhin, Saburov, Malenkov) plus Mikoyan, but excluding Shepilov.

The opposition to Khrushchev looked formidable enough in the spring of 1957, but some qualifications should be made. Before this time his adversaries had consisted of a mere array of malcontents, each of whom resented Khrushchev's increasing prominence, but who often disagreed among themselves on the major political issues at stake and who only combined when it was too late to smash Khrushchev's accumulated power in the Central Committee—even though they represented a majority in the Presidium. Pervukhin and Saburov only came down on the side of the 'anti-party group' in December 1956 while Bulganin and Shepilov moved away from Khrushchev at an even later stage, as we shall see in a moment. Finally, it should not be forgotten that Molotov and Malenkov, the ringleaders of the 'group', had already suffered crushing blows to their reputations in 1955.

Khrushchev struck back at his enemies through a Central Committee resolution of February 17, 1957, proclaiming the need to rearrange the work of the State Economic Commission, i.e. to decentralize the economy. Six weeks afterward Khrushchev published his 'theses' calling for a major reorganization of industry. At the May session of the Supreme Soviet, which dealt with the 'theses', Khrushchev managed to have ten national ministries and fifteen union republic ministries abolished, although he had originally proposed far more sweeping plans. At this meeting none of the economic planners or factory directors made statements; they objected in silence. Of the Presidium members, only Kirichenko spoke out in favour of Khrushchev.

Khrushchev's partial victory won him the temporary support of Marshal Georgi Zhukov, who realized that the economic changes benefited military security in the USSR by pushing vital services out of the big cities, which would be the primary targets in the event of atomic war. Moreover six of the remaining eight central industrial ministries became part of the defence establishment.

In the same period Khrushchev's boasting loquaciousness lost him a supporter in the person of Marshal Nikolai Bulganin, who objected to his consumer goods plan to overtake the United States in four years in the production of meat, butter, and milk *per capita* of the population.[1] Bulganin had been Khrushchev's keenest aide in the dispute with Malenkov over the question of heavy industry versus consumer goods in 1953–5. The new programme appeared to him to be a reversal of Khrushchev's previous position in support of heavy industry.

Embittered by Khrushchev's reversal of their economic arrange-

---

[1] See R. W. Pethybridge, *A Key to Soviet Politics—The Crisis of the Anti-Party Group* (London: Allen & Unwin, 1962; New York: Frederick A. Praeger, Inc., 1962), p. 80.

ments of December 1956, the opposition gathered their forces once again and staged a showdown at a Presidium meeting that opened on June 18, 1957. In the first phase of the battle from June 18th to June 22nd, Khrushchev's opponents were on the offensive; they took the initial move on what was for them safe ground in the Presidium, where they had a majority. On June 22nd Khrushchev managed to shift the fight to the Central Committee, which condemned his attackers. The third phase followed on July 4th, as late as seventeen days after the start of the crisis, with the public announcement and discussion of the quarrel.

Malenkov and Molotov organized the Presidium meeting and the assault on Khrushchev that took place there. Their pretext for calling a meeting was the need to discuss the content of speeches to be made at Leningrad on the occasion of the 250th anniversary of the city. The alignment of the Presidium members was as follows:

The Opposition	Neutral	Khrushchev Group
Malenkov	Suslov	Khrushchev
Molotov		Mikoyan
Kaganovich		Kirichenko
Bulganin		
Pervukhin		
Saburov		
Voroshilov		

According to Saburov, the charges levelled against Khrushchev dealt mainly with topical economic questions like the threat of agricultural ruin and Khrushchev's programme to overtake the United States in the production of dairy products; but many other complaints that had been mounting up since 1953 must have come to the surface in this all-out attack.

Khrushchev's opponents felt confident enough to propose changes in the government. Khrushchev and some Central Committee secretaries would be required to withdraw. Molotov was to become first secretary, while Malenkov would head the government for a time before replacing Molotov as first secretary. At this desperate moment, Khrushchev appealed from the majority against him in the Presidium to the Central Committee, but his enemies affirmed that the Presidium had to take a formal vote on the matter before consulting the Central Committee.

Khrushchev had his way, thanks to the insistence of several Central Committee members resident in Moscow who heard of the dispute and came to the doors of the Presidium conference room demanding to be admitted. Meanwhile Zhukov did Khrushchev a good turn by putting military planes at the disposal of Central Committee members living in the provinces who wished to support Khrushchev. When the Central Committee met formally on June 22nd, it passed a resolution condemning the opposition to Khrushchev. Three hundred and eight of the 309 persons at the meeting voted in favour of the resolution, with one abstention by Molotov. Although the crushing majority was possibly exaggerated for political reasons after the event, it was true that since 1953 Khrushchev had built up a solid personal backing in the Central Committee that could be relied upon to side with him in a crisis.[1]

Molotov, Malenkov, Kaganovich and Saburov were removed from both the Presidium and the Central Committee. Pervukhin was merely demoted to candidate membership of the Presidium. Bulganin and Voroshilov retained their posts for the time being, either because they represented less of a threat to Khrushchev than the other men, or because by leaving them in power Khrushchev managed to cover up the fact that he had been in a minority in the Presidium quarrel. Molotov became the Soviet ambassador to Mongolia before moving on in October 1960 to the Soviet mission to the International Atomic Energy Agency in Vienna. Malenkov was made head of a hydroelectric power station in east Kazakhstan, while Kaganovich was sent to the Urals to become the director of a cement factory.

In the course of the public attack on these men a vigorous attempt was made to bundle the uneasy fellows of the 'anti-party group' into the same political bed. Khrushchev distorted the outline of recent events in order to portray himself as representing the liberal wing of the party, while it was made to appear as if Molotov's and Malenkov's political views coincided in their conservative leanings. This effort on the part of Khrushchev to gain popularity for his cause was not supported by the facts. It was Malenkov and not Khrushchev who first introduced a policy of providing the people with more consumer goods; it was also Malenkov who first realized that the advent of the hydrogen bomb entailed some revision of Lenin's maxim that war between capitalism and Communism was inevitable. Finally Malenkov's fall from power coincided with the political onslaught against Soviet writers after the intellectual thaw.

As we have seen, the 'anti-party group' was not a group at all, but a sundry collection of politicians of varying hue who had happened to join together at one particular moment to oppose Khrushchev. However, Khrushchev now instructed the Soviet propaganda

[1] See Chapter IV.

machine to stress that these men had been united in their opposition since Stalin's death.

Although the distortion of his opponents' views put Khrushchev on a par with Stalin, he did not copy his old master by exterminating his enemies physically, nor did he extort confessions from them under duress. To this day Malenkov, Molotov, and Kaganovich have never recanted. But Khrushchev hung a sword of Damocles over Malenkov's head by making his complicity in the 'Leningrad Affair' general knowledge in July 1957. Nor could he allow any potential rivals to stay in office once the crisis of June 1957 had passed over.

The largest political upheaval in the Soviet Union since Stalin's death had direct repercussions both inside and outside the country.

The Presidium as it was set up after Stalin's death contained only one man whose whole career and chief interest lay in the party apparatus, Khrushchev himself. After the Twentieth Congress the scales were about to tip in Khrushchev's favour, since government and party interest groups were nearly equally represented. By July 1957 the reformed Presidium consisted of fifteen full members, of whom eleven were party apparatus men. After a period of decline, which was short in terms of the full length of Soviet history, the party apparatus recovered from the setbacks of Stalin's last years and under Khrushchev's guidance achieved a dominating position once again.

The East European countries in the Soviet sphere were greatly interested in the crisis, since its outcome was bound to affect them deeply. Subsequent comment in the People's Democracies fell into two well-defined camps, according to whether the country concerned was Stalinist or liberally inclined. The more liberal Poles, Hungarians, and Rumanians stressed a supposed victory of the Soviet revisionist wing and claimed that the 'group' that had opposed the freer trends inaugurated at the Twentieth Congress had finally been cast out. The more conservative countries of Czechoslovakia, East Germany, Bulgaria and Albania restricted themselves in the main to an indictment of the 'anti-party group' for its attempt to overthrow the existing government and to destroy the political equilibrium at such a crucial stage in developments within the Soviet bloc. The Yugoslav view of the crisis was coloured by the hope that the changes would usher in an era of better relations with the Soviet Union.

In October 1957 Khrushchev deprived Marshal Zhukov of his Presidium post. This unexpected move underlined the subordination of the army to the party apparatus, which had already triumphed over the state bureaucracy and the economic experts in June. Khrushchev's action against the 'anti-party group' was a counter-attack, but his deposition of Zhukov was essentially a prophylactic measure against a potential Bonaparte—who, despite his great popularity, had never attempted to cast himself in this role as far as is known. But prior to October 1957 he disagreed with Khrushchev on three matters concerning the military: he pressed for the rehabilitation of the army leaders who had been victims of the Great Purge and for a fairer view of the military versus the party role in the Second World War; he differed from Khrushchev in his view of the effects of an atomic war on the Soviet Union; and finally, there is some evidence that he collaborated with Bulganin in the summer of 1957 in an effort to reinstate the latter. It seems that Bulganin was silently dropped from the Presidium at the time of Zhukov's fall.[1]

Like Stalin before him, Zhukov was charged with an attempt to build up a personality cult. He was also accused by Marshal I. S. Konev, an ally of the party in the ranks of the military, of trying to curtail party surveillance in the armed forces. Zhukov was replaced as Minister of Defence by Marshal R. Ia. Malinovsky.

Bulganin's public demotion was carried out in several stages. Following a carefully-planned drive against his reputation begun in December 1957, he was removed from his post as chairman of the Council of Ministers in March 1958, condemned as a member of the 'anti-party group' in November, and called upon to confess his guilt at a Central Committee plenary session in December 1958. In the course of his statement at that time Bulganin admitted: 'In my position at that time as chairman of the Council of Ministers, I was not only an adherent of their group, but their nominal leader as well. The anti-party group used to meet in my office. . . .'[2] It has been noted that the Council of Ministers did in fact serve as a nest of conspiracy against Khrushchev, though it is doubtful whether Bulganin's leadership was anything but a formality. Bulganin did not list his errors in sufficient detail to please Khrushchev's more ardent supporters, and he further annoyed them by differentiating between what was for him the greater guilt of Molotov and Kaganovich and the lesser faults of Malenkov.

At the Twenty-first Congress in January 1959, Khrushchev's men, led by members of the Leningrad party organization who had special cause to hate Malenkov, tried to whip up antagonism to the

---

[1] Bulganin's name is omitted from the list of Presidium members re-elected at this time in the *History of the Communist Party of the Soviet Union* (Moscow, 1959), p. 658.

[2] *Plenum tsentral'nogo komiteta kommunisticheskoi partii, stenograficheskii otchet* (Moscow: December 1958), p. 338.

'anti-party group' so as to make its members confess; but they only succeeded in persuading Pervukhin and Saburov, the smaller fry, to admit that they had been wrong in opposing Khrushchev's economic policies.

Although it falls outside the period covered in this chapter, a subsequent attack on the 'anti-party group' may be included here. At the Twenty-second Congress in the autumn of 1961 the 'group' was involved in the responsibility both for the purges of the 1930s and for the later ones. Its members, and Molotov in particular, were accused of putting up further resistance to the Soviet leadership after 1957. Molotov was supposed to have sent a letter to the Central Committee in which he declared that the draft party programme submitted to the congress was 'anti-revolutionary in spirit' and 'contained pacifism and revisionism'.[1] For the first time Voroshilov's complicity in the 1957 crisis was made public by Khrushchev, but all the same the latter pleaded for the harmless veteran who had been relieved of his duties as chairman of the Presidium of the Supreme Soviet in 1960 for health reasons.

Khrushchev's stage-by-stage assault on the power of the 'anti-party group' members after 1957 was very reminiscent of Stalin's treatment of the opposition in his time, as was Khrushchev's use of the 'group' as a scapegoat. Stalin's butts were Trotsky, Zinoviev and Bukharin, but their images paled for later generations to whom they were mere names. They have their living replacements now.

Having recovered from the initial shock of the June crisis of 1957, Khrushchev appeared to realize that his massed support in the Secretariat and the Presidium represented an over-display of power. The Secretariat, the hub of the party apparatus, was now twice as large as it had been in Stalin's time and afterwards up to 1957. All but one of its members were full members of the Presidium as well. Therefore, like Stalin before him, Khrushchev in May 1960 moved key party officials over into important posts outside the party machine in an attempt to consolidate his control over the state bureaucracy, which had harboured his chief opponents until 1957 and no doubt still employed some of the latter's erstwhile supporters. The party Secretariat was reduced from eleven members in 1957 to five in 1960 but it remained Khrushchev's main lever of influence.

At this stage some general remarks may be made concerning the long-term effect of the post-Stalin struggle for power and its aftermath on the position of Khrushchev.

During 1958 and 1959, when Khrushchev was ridding himself of

[1] *Izvestiia* (October 27, 1961).

the remnants of real and potential opposition, a number of non-Communist observers of the Soviet scene compared his new position to that of the all-powerful Stalin after the purges of the 1930s. Their opinion appeared to gain considerable weight when in February 1958 Khrushchev copied Stalin's move of 1941 by becoming chairman of the Council of Ministers, while retaining his post as first secretary of the party. As chairman he could speak for his country on an official basis at meetings with foreign heads of state and also have formal control over his major economic projects for industrial reorganization and agriculture. In practice he already had what appeared to be a pretty free hand in all three fields; but there was always the possibility that officials in the government bureaucracy who regarded his policies unfavourably could take steps to hamper them.

Khrushchev's manoeuvres on his way to the party summit bore a considerable resemblance to Stalin's tactics. Both men pinned their faith on the strength of the party apparatus and built up a following inside it. After the death of an unchallenged leader both of them had to assert their primacy among their equals or superiors. Khrushchev manipulated the political issues at stake after 1953 in a way that was reminiscent of Stalin's methods: Stalin had jockeyed himself into what appeared to be a central position between Bukharin and Rykov on the right wing and Trotsky on the left. He then dealt with each wing in turn, meanwhile appealing constantly for unity in the party ranks.

In 1957 Khrushchev also occupied a central position politically between the more reactionary Molotov and the more progressive Malenkov—though this was deliberately obscured by the Soviet press, which represented Khrushchev as the only progressive element in the struggle. Khrushchev also dealt with his rivals piecemeal. Molotov, Malenkov, Kaganovich, and Shepilov were demoted immediately after the crisis of June 1957, but Bulganin's fall was held over until the autumn of 1958, and though Pervukhin and Saburov had been silently demoted in June 1957, they were not submitted to public disgrace until the meeting of the Twenty-first Congress in 1959. After 1957 Khrushchev called continually for unity, which had been Stalin's cry also. Like Trotsky and Zinoviev, Malenkov and Molotov joined forces when their powers had already been sapped, and therefore they failed just as had their predecessors.

Although any reference to 'collective leadership' had disappeared from the Soviet press by 1959, Khrushchev's victory over all his rivals did not lead to the kind of unqualified dictatorship that had prevailed in the past. What is most instructive about the events of

THE KHRUSHCHEV ERA: DOMESTIC POLICY

June 1957 is not that Khrushchev won, but that he came so near to defeat. After that time, he was not able to extort confessions from the hard core of the 'anti-party group'.

At the highest political level inside Russia, the group of men who surrounded Khrushchev after 1957 were much less closely knit and irrevocably bound to his policies than Stalin's henchmen had been to his. To give one example, it looked at the Twenty-first Congress as though Kirichenko was being groomed as Khrushchev's right-hand man and even as his successor. A year later, in January 1960, he was suddenly demoted and accused of inefficiency, although he was a Ukrainian who had been close to Khrushchev for many years.

Outside the Soviet Union, the conduct of foreign policy in the Communist bloc was a far more delicate matter than it had been prior to 1953 and it did not allow Khrushchev to manoeuvre as independently or powerfully as Stalin had done. China had a large say in Communist affairs; Yugoslavia remained as adamantly independent as ever; and the People's Democracies required more careful handling than before. Khrushchev's position grew stronger after 1957, but this did not necessarily mean that he was attaining a position above the party and the state comparable to that of Stalin after the 1930s. In fact Khrushchev was never so securely placed at the summit of Soviet politics as Stalin had been. The difference has been clearly put in this way: 'Stalin's successor at the head of the party, unlike Stalin, governed through and with the party, and not as Stalin before him, over its head. His power derived from the fact that within the party, which was itself supreme, he was hierarchically in the position of the highest command, but it derived nonetheless from the party.'[1] This sober judgement was to be confirmed by the fall from power of Khrushchev in 1964, a major turning point in Soviet politics that lies outside the scope of this book.

POLITICS AT THE LOWER LEVELS

What repercussions did these events have on the lower reaches of political power? Below the figures of the Soviet leaders caught up in the post-Stalin struggle were ranged the interest groups and the personal followings that the leaders represented at the summit.

If we take the major interest groups to be the party apparatus, the state bureaucracy, and the economic managers, the ascendancy of the former over the other two groups was a cardinal feature of the post-

[1] L. Schapiro, *The Communist Party of the Soviet Union* (London: Eyre & Spottiswoode, 1960), pp. 588–9.

Stalin period of Soviet history. In the years before 1957 we noted the party's reaffirmation of power, which went hand in hand with the rise of Khrushchev. The party apparatus emerged triumphant from the struggle of June 1957. The state bureaucracy on the other hand was paralysed. Its very core, the deputy chairmen in the Council of Ministers, were decimated, leaving a temporary power vacuum: the five leading deputy chairmen, Malenkov, Molotov, Kaganovich, Pervukhin, and Saburov, were demoted in June, and some of the older deputy chairmen became sectional heads of the reorganized *Gosplan*. Only Mikoyan and Kuzmin, the new head of *Gosplan*, were left with the title of deputy chairman. Thus Khrushchev could afford to leave Bulganin in his position as chairman of the Council of Ministers even after his defection, because he knew that he was merely a figurehead without influence in the government as a whole.

Two minor interest groups, the army and the intelligentsia, emerged from the political shadows in June 1957, and played a subsidiary role in the crisis. They were brought to the fore and marshalled for battle at a time of great stress. Neither group was directly represented in the party Presidium, as were the major groups, but Zhukov's intervention and the reaction of the literary press did have a little influence on the outcome of the struggle.

Once Khrushchev was firmly in the saddle, he saw to it that the party infiltrated even further into the domains of the other interest groups. Some consequences of the economic reorganization of May 1957 began to tell against the state bureaucracy and the economic managers, and in favour of the party. Although some former heads of disbanded central ministries were transferred to the new regional economic councils, in many cases they were sent to distant provinces. Friction later arose between them and local administrators, who were either too narrow-minded or too ambitious for their new masters. When this happened the party took the opportunity to intervene. Regional economic council officials, including those chairmen who retained the rank of minister, had a lower position in the hierarchy than the secretaries of the local party committees. At the central level, the directorships of key heavy industrial enterprises were invariably listed among the positions coming under the jurisdictional control of the party Central Committee in Moscow. Thus despite the fact that the former economic ministries of the central government were abolished, the Central Committee in the capital could still supervise appointments and dismissals of top executives in the most important industrial plants in the Soviet Union.

Khrushchev supplemented this trend by putting his own supporters in crucial jobs outside the ranks of the party apparatus proper. The government changes of May 1960 mentioned earlier were a good example of this. Various other key positions were filled by Khrushchev's associates. General I. A. Serov, the head of the political police prior to 1960, had known Khrushchev in the Ukraine, as had R. A. Rudenko, who was the Soviet Procurator-General. Khrushchev's son-in-law, A. Adzhubei, was the editor of *Izvestiia*, the press organ of the government (*Pravda* represents the party).

It is true that Khrushchev, unlike Stalin, derived his power from the party, and did not stand above it as an independent dictator. His situation certainly acted as a curb on his acquiring the unbounded influence that had led to the worst excesses of the Stalinist era. However it should not be forgotten that the professional core of party secretaries and officials, numbering little more than 250,000, was not in any sense a democratic body by 1961. It was still autocratically controlled from the centre, and outside the inner circle of the central secretaries its representatives could still be appointed, promoted, and removed at a moment's notice. Unanimous approval of all central decisions was still the order of the day, though at the centre itself Khrushchev's lieutenants had a far greater share in the running of the state than had been the case under Stalin.

In the Soviet Union there are as yet no free institutions independent of the executive, so that democracy in the sense ascribed to it by John Stuart Mill does not exist. Nevertheless, the party has been taking increasing account of public opinion in recent years, and not only within its own ranks. This trend has been accompanied by some decentralization and a slight delegation of executive powers, although these can be recalled whenever necessary. At this point we may investigate some of the evidence for this tendency.

The Supreme Soviet, which is the legislative body for the USSR as a whole, is still tightly controlled by the party. For instance, the Soviet elected in March 1958 consisted of 738 deputies, of whom 563 were either members or candidate members of the party. In each local Soviet the regional party secretary was elected to attend the central meeting. However, three-fifths of the 1958 deputies were said to be workers or peasants, as compared to two-fifths in 1954: at least the social composition, if not the political make-up of the body was becoming more democratic. The power of decision still rested with the party alone, but an attempt was also made to associate the people with this process.

To this end more influence was given to the standing committees of the Supreme Soviet, especially in economic matters. In February

1957 a new committee was formed, the Economic Commission of the Soviet of Nationalities, to deal with the claims of the union republics on the central budget. Although rigged electoral practices did not change in Russia, deputies to the Supreme Soviet were at least respected citizens, carrying with them the prestige of the capital on their return to the localities and acting as vehicles for party policies.

In the provinces themselves it would seem that the firmer grip of the party over the grass roots led to some relaxation of control from above. At the more senior levels Khrushchev succeeded in building up his own cadres of secretaries, while at both higher and lower levels party influence was strengthened in agriculture and in industry as a result of the economic reorganization of 1957. Although the decisions of higher echelons are binding on lower ones, and meetings of the junior organizations are always prepared by senior bodies, members of primary party organizations have been known to reject candidates put forward by committees at the *raion* (district) level. Moreover the less-important meetings on the bottom rungs of the hierarchy are marked by more freedom of speech than is to be found at any other level except at the very top. Their decisions are of very minor significance in any case, so that the regime can easily afford the luxury of some semblance of liberal thinking.

Central control over the national minorities was also eased after 1956. The census of 1959 showed that less than 55 per cent of the Soviet people considered themselves to be Russian by nationality, and of these 85 per cent lived in the Russian Socialist Federated Soviet Republic. For the most part the minorities lived in well-defined groups along the border regions of the Soviet Union. There has been a tendency for Russians to move in ever-increasing numbers into these regions. In Kazakhstan, due to the opening of the virgin lands, the proportion of Russians to Kazakhs changed greatly between 1953 and 1960, so that by the latter year the Russians formed the largest single national group in the area.

In his secret speech to the Twentieth Congress, Khrushchev criticized Stalin's nationality policy, and in the course of the years after 1956 he took several steps to enlarge the rights of the minorities. The creation of the Economic Commission in the Soviet of Nationalities together with economic decentralization benefited the union republics as a whole and gave more responsibility to their national leaders. Although the Russian element still predominated in the large urban centres throughout the Soviet Union, Khrushchev gave the minorities a somewhat wider representation in the Presidium as it stood after the expulsion of the 'anti-party group', which incidentally was purported to have opposed the extension of further rights to the national republics. Thus in July 1957 the Presidium included:

A. Kirichenko, D. Korotchenko, A. Kirilenko	Ukraine
K. Mazurov	Belorussia
V. Mzhavanadze	Georgia
N. Mukhitdinov	Uzbekhistan
J. Kalnberzin	Latvia
O. Kuusinen	Finland
A. Mikoyan	Armenia

In addition to strengthening Khrushchev's popularity among the minorities, these moves also tended to reinforce his position as head of the party and the state, since many of his most faithful followers were to be found among the ranks of the non-Russian party officials, especially in the Ukraine, where he had spent so much of his career. Khrushchev's policies were not far-reaching in any respect: the Leninist right of self-determination still remained a fiction; national culture that bordered on revisionism was still branded as bourgeois nationalism, and the political whip still lay as firmly as ever in the hands of the Great Russians. But in all fields except politics national minorities appeared to have almost the same opportunities as Russians by 1961, and some regions in the Caucasus and Central Asia were decidedly privileged from the economic point of view. The situation had changed indeed since Stalin's liquidation of national minorities during the Second World War.

THE TWENTY-FIRST PARTY CONGRESS

According to the Constitution of the Soviet Communist party, party congresses are held every four years, yet only three years after the Twentieth Congress Khrushchev convened an extraordinary congress in January 1959. The official reason for this step was to give approval to the Seven-Year Plan, but the congress also served as a platform for the affirmation of Khrushchev's new authority and as an occasion for foreign Communist parties to engage in consultations of a kind that were becoming much more frequent than in the past. Seventy-two foreign party delegations came to Moscow in January 1959 compared with the fifty-six that had attended the previous congress.

In domestic affairs the Twentieth Congress had been mainly concerned with the practical influence Stalin had exercised. Questions of Marxist theory had been virtually confined to the sphere of foreign affairs. At the Twenty-first Congress the position was reversed. Khrushchev devoted some time to doctrine with regard to world affairs, but his chief interest now lay in the Soviet transition to Communism. Until 1959, according to Soviet theory the USSR was still a socialist as opposed to a Communist state: it relied on capitalist remnants like trade and money and included three types of property —state, co-operative, and private. The proletariat still received material goods according to its labour and not according to its needs, which is the Communist ideal. Also the state was clearly far from withering away in the Marxist sense.

At the congress Khrushchev diagnosed the Soviet system and asserted that the USSR had now entered the phase when Communism would finally be achieved. While insisting in orthodox style that 'the transition from the socialist phase to the highest phase takes place in accordance with the natural laws of the historical process, which may not be arbitrarily violated or circumvented',[1] Khrushchev listed specific tasks that would have to be carried out by the Soviet Union in order to build Communism.

Khrushchev outlined a vigorous programme. An abundance of goods would have to be created to ensure the flowering of the true Communist spirit. Class distinctions were to be eradicated. This would entail the fusion of the three existing kinds of property into property owned by the people as a whole, and the elimination of the distinctions between intellectual and physical labour and between peasants and industrial workers. The Soviet people would have to be conditioned by education to prepare itself for these changes. The time was not yet ripe for the withering away of the state, but a few minor functions of the central bodies could now be delegated to non-governmental organizations like the trade unions.

The reader may judge for himself from the relevant passages in this and other chapters to what extent Khrushchev's optimistic aims corresponded with the actual potentialities of Soviet institutions at the end of the 1950s. In the economic sphere his prophecies depended to some extent on the actual achievements of the Seven-Year Plan and on the feasibility of eliminating collective farms, private property, and the gulf between town and country. In the political field the goal of a stateless society could only be attained through the mediation of the Soviet Communist party, which firmly held all the government strings. The gap between intellectual and physical labour could be narrowed only if the whole of society were to be reorganized from the

---

[1] Stenographic record of the Twenty-first Congress.

occupational point of view and a revised educational system set up to ensure a future in which the rift would be closed.

Khrushchev's emergence as the chief spokesman on Communist ideology within the Soviet Union confirmed his position as Lenin's successor in doctrinal matters and filled the gap that had existed since the death of Stalin. Khrushchev's success in the struggle for political power was now crowned by the privilege to pose as the authoritative interpreter of Marxist ideology. His laurels were still green, however, and his supporters at the congress were anxious to consolidate his supremacy over his rivals in this new sphere. Kuusinen, a member of the Presidium, reminded the congress: 'I recall that... Molotov, who has never been capable of producing the smallest theoretical chick, reproached other Comrades for their "lack of attention to theory". Today... Comrade Khrushchev has enriched our theory with a number of clear ideas and new theses.'[1]

Incidentally the Twenty-first Congress was marked by a growing adulation of Khrushchev that was only different in degree from the personality cult of Stalin that had been condemned by Khrushchev at the previous congress. His chief flatterers were mainly recruited from the ranks of the party apparatus and had recently been introduced to high politics by Khrushchev himself. The same men also led the renewed campaign against the 'anti-party group' at the congress.

THE ECONOMIC THAW

What was the actual state of the Soviet economy by the time of the Twenty-first Congress? Just how sanguine were Khrushchev's hopes for material abundance and a speedy advance toward economic Communism? In order to answer these questions, we shall have to retrace our steps and survey both industrial and agricultural developments since 1956. Apart from some beneficial reforms in agriculture, reviewed in Chapter IV, no decisive steps to remedy blatant irrationalities and inefficiencies in the economic system had been taken during the period from Stalin's death to the meeting of the Twentieth Congress in 1956. Industrial growth was fast, but real progress was still held back by factors characteristic of the Stalinist economy—a haphazard price system, over-centralization, Utopian plans, and the pursuance of schemes for the sake of ideology rather than for economic profit. The squabbles within the collective leader-

---

[1] Stenographic record of the Twenty-first Congress.

ship group from 1953 to 1955 over economic questions prevented the emergence of a broad platform of new policies.

The first signs of post-Stalin relaxation in any sphere were apparent in the decline of the police following on Beria's fall, a decline that was relatively steep and irreversible. Next followed two half-hearted attempts to carry out other innovations: in the economy through Malenkov's abortive consumer goods policy, and in the literary field through the spontaneous efforts of Soviet writers. Neither essay was followed through—rather, each was drawn up sharply by the political leadership, some of whose members were at first apprehensive about the possible consequences of turning their backs too abruptly on past habits. By the time of the Twentieth Congress, however, when Khrushchev was virtually at the helm of the state, his secret speech on Stalin opened the floodgates for domestic policy change.

The Twentieth Congress witnessed the first glimmerings of an economic thaw that went beyond the makeshift steps taken between 1953 and 1956. A softening-up of rigid Stalinist economic theory in 1955 heralded the advent of the more practical measures taken in 1956. Late in 1955 a writer in *Voprosy Ekonomiki*, the leading Soviet economic journal, complained of the other-worldliness of debates on economic questions: 'Since the economic discussions of 1951, it has become customary in every work to refer to the objective character of economic laws of socialism, yet not a single work thoroughly examines in what the objective character of this or that law finds expression....'[1] At the Twentieth Congress itself a new pragmatic spirit was evident in delegates' reports on local economic conditions: the speakers were men of the calibre of Pervukhin or Saburov, experts between the ages of forty-five and fifty-five who had had the good luck to frequent technical academies and institutes that had not been available to older men like Kaganovich, and who were concerned less with theory and more with practical results.

At the congress attention was given to the directives of the sixth Five-Year Plan (1956–60) providing for the continued rapid growth of the economy. The coming five years were viewed as a transitional period. During this time Soviet workers would lay the foundations for a subsequent spurt of activity that would raise the USSR to the industrial level of the United States within ten to fifteen years after 1960. The economy would have to be readjusted technically in order to prepare for the future. Increasing emphasis was to be put on the industrial application of atomic energy, the replacement of coal by

[1] *Voprosy Ekonomiki* (No. 10, 1955), p. 8. Quoted in Alec Nove, *The Soviet Economy* (London: George Allen & Unwin, 1961).

oil and natural gas, and the speeding-up of the automation programme.

Administrative as well as technological changes were discussed at the congress. Both Khrushchev and Bulganin stressed that the decentralization programme embarked upon very hesitantly since 1953 would be continued on a greater scale. They referred to resistance to change in this matter, thus hinting at the reluctance of the state bureaucracy and economic circles to give up their Moscow empires. Already in his speech of resignation in January 1955 Malenkov the bureaucrat had admitted his 'insufficient experience in *local* work'.[1] Due to resistance from him and other political leaders, Khrushchev had only succeeded in setting up one or two local ministries in 1954 and 1955. Slightly more authority was delegated to republic governments in these years, enabling them to make detailed plans of their own and to fix production targets for given areas.

In connection with the drive for decentralization, Bulganin asserted that by 1960 Siberia and the Far East would produce more than a third of the country's power and cater to an extra three million workers. This projected industrial spread to the East was an acceleration of a trend that had gathered momentum during the Second World War and was no less urgent now—for strategic as well as for administrative reasons, in view of the possibility of another war.

Although the Twentieth Congress dealt a preliminary blow at traditional economic attitudes, the real breakthrough took place at the plenary session of the Central Committee held in December 1956, which we have already had cause to mention in connection with Khrushchev's rise to power. The economic situation at home and in the Soviet bloc at this juncture gave cause for concern. Industrial growth was beginning to slow down in the USSR, although this only became known to the general public in July 1957. Strains in the programme of economic integration for the bloc, which were already evident before the imposition of the over-ambitious sixth Five-Year Plan and the political troubles of 1956, got worse thereafter. If the Soviet Union was to maintain its political leadership in the bloc it would have to put its own economic house in order.

The title of the main resolution of the meeting reflected the new hardheaded factual approach: 'On Completion of Work on the Sixth Five-Year Plan and on Instructions for Making the Control Figures for 1956–60 and the National Economic Plan for 1957 more exact'. As a result the directives for the sixth Five-Year Plan and the

[1] *Pravda* (February 4, 1955).

plan itself were abandoned shortly afterwards. Work was begun on a new and more sober Seven-Year Plan covering the years from 1959 to 1965. A brake was put on the grandiose investment projects that had proliferated at an alarming rate in every sphere, and which had by and large remained uncompleted.

We saw earlier in this chapter that in one respect the December meeting looked to the past rather than to the future by reinforcing the powers of the central ministries. Lip service was paid to the theory of decentralization, but the action taken as a remedy appeared to have the opposite effect. Furthermore the chronic lack of co-ordination in central planning work was now accentuated by transferring more powers from the State Planning Commission (*Gosplan*), the organ responsible for long-term planning, to the State Economic Commission, which had been created as recently as May 1955, in order to deal with short-term economic schemes.

These retrograde trends were reversed in the spring of 1957 with the termination of highly-centralized economic administration. By May 10th the far-reaching 'Law on Further Improving the Organization of Management of Industry and Construction' was brought into force. The haste with which Khrushchev carried out his plans indicated how political impulse prevailed over economic discretion. In the course of the press discussion of the reorganization, an article in *Pravda* suggested that the scheme should be accomplished in two separate phases over a comparatively long period of time. In view of the very great implications of the changes, this would surely have been less disruptive from the economic point of view. But decentralization spelled a political victory for Khrushchev. By abandoning the sixth Five-Year Plan he took the problem of economic development out of the hands of Bulganin, who had been the plan's chief sponsor; and in putting through his own ideas on decentralization, he quickly withdrew much responsibility for the administration of the economy from his other rivals in the state bureaucracy and the economic interest groups.

Seen from the economic angle, decentralization was set in motion as a result of the flaws in the sixth Five-Year Plan, which cast more light than ever on inadequacies at the centre. The numerous specialized industrial ministries in Moscow were apt to cut themselves off from each other, a tendency to be found in any kind of bureaucracy and by no means confined to the Soviet version. However, the problem in the USSR was particularly acute. In the first place Soviet administration had failed to keep in step with the swift growth and diversification of the economy. Neither *Gosplan* nor the short-lived

State Economic Commission was strong enough to control and co-ordinate the expanding activities of the industrial ministries.

Secondly, since the early days of the Communist regime ministries had learnt from experience that supplies of vital materials were often inadequate or even entirely lacking. In the course of time each ministry had come to rely on its own sources as far as possible by building its own plants to provide scarce items. This system naturally led to the creation of isolated empires. Not only were the central ministries out of touch with one another; they were frequently slow in reacting to the needs of local enterprises under their control. These too had proliferated over the years and since the Second World War were scattered much more widely than before throughout the vast country—in the Urals, in Siberia, and in Soviet Asia.

The results of autarchy were harmful. The half-hearted attempt to give more authority to republican planning agencies between 1953 and 1956 had not succeeded in providing local administrations with enough responsibility to cut through the rigid ties binding the different areas to Moscow. That these ties caused inefficiency and waste was evident from the geographical dislocation of industry; each central ministry dispatched its own components hundreds of miles across the country from one factory under its control to another, components that could often have been put to good use in neighbouring factories under the control of another ministry. Valuable by-products were insufficiently exploited, since the ministries neglected to co-ordinate their plans.

The reform of May 1957, aimed at converting a structure based on the vertical principle, represented by the ministries, into one run on the horizontal principle. This was to be done by giving greater powers to each region. Republican governments were to nominate regional economic councils, known as *sovnarkhozy*, which were to be directly responsible for most industrial and construction enterprises in their areas. By the end of 1960 there were 103 *sovnarkhozy* in the Soviet Union. Their main task was to supervise the fulfilment of plans prescribed in Moscow. They were given some independent initiative with regard to the way in which they carried out the plan in their own areas, and they could consult other *sovnarkhozy* when necessary. Agriculture, transport and retail trade still fell outside their scope.

Regional links with the centre were maintained by the republicna governments. They controlled the *sovnarkhozy* within their domains and at the same time were responsible to the all-union government in Moscow. At the centre itself the number of ministries was reduced to fifteen. Six of them were all-union ministries, i.e. each of them managed a branch of the economy on its own account. The other nine were union-republican ministries operating through the corresponding ministries in the republics. The abolished ministries were in many instances replaced by state committees, which planned the work of all other administrative bodies in a particular sphere.

In 1957 *Gosplan* was reinstated as the chief co-ordinating organ for planning on a national scale. The State Economic Commission, a stronghold of the 'anti-party group', was discarded. *Gosplan* took over some of the functions of the old central ministries and in 1959 began to deal with agricultural planning as well. *Gosplan* supervised the draft output plans submitted to it by its equivalents at the republican level. Its powers were extensive, since it could either grant or refuse delivery authorizations for the whole country. In April 1960 *Gosplan*'s influence was diminished through the allotment of responsibility for long-term planning to the Economic-Science Council.

The rapid tempo at which partial decentralization was carried out also characterized subsequent efforts to bolster the economy. Although Khrushchev had been the severest critic of Malenkov's campaign for more consumer goods production from 1953 to 1955, he gave increasing attention to this sector after his victory over the 'anti-party group' in June 1957. Before that time, in May 1957, he had launched an optimistic scheme to catch up with the United States in the *per capita* production of milk, butter and meat by 1961–2 at the latest.

During the following twelve months programmes were announced for reducing the lack of balance between light and heavy industrial projects. At the end of July 1957, an imaginative if over-hopeful scheme to eliminate the housing shortage within ten to twelve years was set in motion. Early in 1958 a boost was given to the lamentable condition of the clothing industry with the establishment of an ambitious target for future raw cotton output. In May 1958, the Central Committee investigated the chemical industry and resolved to speed up the output of artificial fibres and plastics.

Although the economic targets for the future mentioned by Khrushchev in November 1957 set great store by an increase in consumer goods of all kinds, the control figures for the Seven-Year Plan published exactly one year later showed that at some point between these two dates the claims of heavy industry had been heeded rather more than expected. Priority still lay quite definitely with producers' goods. But at least the reforms had left an imprint on the plan, which included a wide variety of complex targets in all sectors of the economy. This was a far cry from the narrow-minded concentration on heavy industry in previous plans.

During the period after Khrushchev's victory extensive reforms were put through in some long-established heavy industries. The decision taken at the Twentieth Congress to shift the emphasis from coal to petroleum and gas production was acted upon; more significant still, in view of the sanctity that had been attached to hydroelectric schemes ever since Lenin's classic pronouncement that 'Communism is Soviet power plus electrification of the whole country', less prominence was given to electric power after a statement by Khrushchev in August 1958.

The reforms outlined above were intended to strengthen the Soviet economy, but they also had great political implications in the world arena. Being devoted historical materialists, the Soviet leaders view foreign policy through the prism of economic power. The United States is the main adversary of the USSR just because it is the greatest capitalist market. The USSR reasons that if its economy can overtake that of its American rival, the political influence of Russia will *ipso facto* outweigh that of the United States. Economic strength means three things for Soviet foreign policy: a good background for propaganda, a solid basis for trade and aid directed at the less-developed countries, and a precondition for military primacy.

Progress in rationalization and efficiency during the period from the Twentieth to the Twenty-first Congress set the Soviet Union firmly on the road to presenting a serious challenge to the United States, but by 1959 a variety of stumbling blocks still lay across its path. Some of them could be removed at will. Perhaps the greatest of these were the blinkers imposed by Communist ideology, which has a lot to say on the subject of economic theory, but is unfortunately conditioned more by the economic realities of Marx's nineteenth century than by later developments. The average Soviet citizen is apt to ignore subsequent mitigating influences on capitalism like the increase in social welfare and the rise of the trade unions.

Despite the economic thaw in Russia after Stalin's death, irrelevant theory still kept industry in shackles. The situation was far worse in agriculture, where the whole system of collectivization was constructed on the basis of a theory that resulted in the death of hundreds of thousands of peasants under Stalin and continued to cripple economic prospects in this sphere under the leaders who succeeded him.

Other stumbling blocks in the race with America were impossible to avoid. The enormous upsurge of Soviet industry in Stalin's time was partly due to the almost unlimited supply of manpower skimmed off the land into the young cities. By 1957 a shortage of labour was already apparent: the wartime decrease in the birth and survival rates continued to affect supply for some time afterwards.

The Soviet population did not cease to sacrifice its consumer needs to those of heavy industry after Stalin's death, but self-denial was less in some ways. Malenkov whetted the public's appetite through his New Course, and Khrushchev used the increase in consumer goods production in 1957-8 as a platform on which to build his popularity. After 1953 forced labour practically disappeared with the decline of the secret police and its private economic empire. The harsh labour laws regarding change of employment were modified, shorter hours were introduced, and the disorganized wage structure put into better order. All these sops to public opinion necessitated growing attention to aspects of the economy that did not contribute directly to industrial growth.

The years after the big leap forward in rationalization from 1956 to 1958 were spent in unspectacular consolidation of the ground gained. The economy still showed an upward trend, but there was no sign of achieving the 'abundance' of goods called for by Khrushchev at the Twenty-first Congress. Although he could affirm at the congress that by 1958 Soviet industrial production had overtaken that of Great Britain, France and West Germany combined, the control figures of the Seven-Year Plan published on February 8, 1959, showed that the accent still lay on heavy industry and military resources as against consumer goods production. The average growth rate for the former group was to be $9 \cdot 3$ per cent over the period covered by the plan, whereas consumer goods were to increase by $7 \cdot 3$ per cent.

There were three ways in which Soviet planners could develop consumer goods output more rapidly. The economic burden of the armaments programme could be cut back, foreign trade substantially increased, or foreign credit obtained for domestic expansion. The first and the last methods were unthinkable in the international political climate of the 1950s, and foreign trade was virtually restricted to the Communist bloc for the same reason. In 1957 the Soviet share of world trade was only $3 \cdot 5$ per cent, compared with $16 \cdot 9$ per cent for the United States.

The period from 1959 to 1961 was marked, in industry as in agriculture, by a curious combination of rational economic measures in accordance with the new spirit of post-Stalin planning and occasional moves that contained echoes of earlier times. On the retrogressive side were the over-optimistic figures given for capital investment in the Seven-Year Plan, a feature that had been all too prominent in previous Five-Year Plans. Then at the end of 1959 the term of the new plan that was intended to usher in economic Communism was extended from fifteen to twenty years; this period was far too long for accurate planning.

Progressive features included the introduction of more elastic planning by a decision of December 1960: as of 1962 the national plan was to be revised each year, although the pre-fixed annual targets were still to serve as a working basis. The economic thaw was continuing in the Soviet Union, but the habits of the past could not be shrugged off in a day.

AGRICULTURE

Soviet agriculture registered a 50 per cent rise in overall production between 1953 and 1958. This was due partly to economic incentives granted to the peasants, partly to the inauguration of the virgin lands scheme and the luck of the weather. By the time of the Twentieth Congress agriculture was still thriving, thanks to the vigour and speed with which Khrushchev had tackled the problems in this sphere from 1953 on. The impetus was kept going from 1956 to 1958 by further reforms, which are discussed below.

The improvement in Soviet agricultural production was spectacular, but it must be remembered that in 1953 the situation in the countryside was little short of desperate. Even as late as December 1958, Khrushchev admitted that 320 per cent more labour on state farms and 410 per cent more on collective farms was needed in Russia than in the United States to produce the same amount of potatoes. Furthermore, the improvement in collective farm production came mainly from the private sector, which Khrushchev was determined to suppress in the long run. In 1956, for example, free market sales of agricultural produce in Soviet cities amounted to over 38 billion roubles, of which under 10 per cent represented sales by the collective farms themselves, while the rest was made up for the most part of bargains in the produce from the peasants' private holdings.

At the Twentieth Congress Khrushchev stated. '... we must pay special attention to the development of state farms which represent the highest form of organized socialist agriculture'. Shortly afterwards a decision of the Central Committee and the Council of Ministers ordered the collective farms to cut down the subsidiary plots of land for the collective farmers' private use so that these small-holdings could produce no more than the family supply of vegetables and fruit. The possession of private livestock was also frowned upon.

The chief motive for this policy appeared to rest on ideological foundations, but there was also an economic reason that has often been overlooked. It has been estimated that between 1956 and 1959 approximately five and a half million persons left the countryside for the towns.[1] They provided a valuable source of labour for industry during a decline in the normal population supply. The effects of this continued large-scale rural exodus could be countered to some extent by converting collective farms into state farms, because the workers on collective farms only put in a minimum number of obligatory workdays in the year, whereas on state farms the peasants were full-time employees. Work productivity on the collective farms was about three to four times lower than that on the state farms.

Between 1953 and 1959 the number of collective farms was reduced by 23,500, of which 8,800 were transformed into state farms (others were amalgamated). In the years 1955–8 the increase in state farmland was in fact due more to transfers from the collective farms than to encroachment on the virgin lands in Soviet Asia. The virgin lands scheme should not be viewed in isolation, but as part of a wider plan to extend the state farm system, not only to Kazakhstan and Siberia, but also to European Russia where poor land previously in the hands of the collective farms had fallen into disuse.

Several agricultural reforms in the period under review helped to extend the more rational economic base that had been initiated not long after Stalin's death. Firstly, as from January 1, 1958, the compulsory delivery quotas on collective farmers' private plots, which had already been reduced in 1953, were abolished completely. Secondly, additional incentive was given to agriculture through higher government capital investment. In 1956 it amounted to 20·9 billion roubles, as compared with a total of 63 billion during the preceding five years.

The most important reform of this period came on January 22, 1958, when Khrushchev announced that the state-run Machine Tractor Stations were to sell most of their machinery to the collective farms (the state farms had always been provided with state machinery). By the end of the year over 80 per cent of the collective farms had acquired their own machinery from the MTS, either by cash purchase or on credit. The economic disadvantages of the MTS system, such as the lack of means of assessing machinery profitability

---

[1] For more details on these figures see B. Kerblay, 'La transformation des Kolhoz en Sovhoz et l'exode rural en URSS' an article in L'URSS: *Droit, Economie, Sociologie, Politique, Culture*, published by the Centre de Recherches sur L'URSS et les Pays de L'Est (Strasbourg, 1962).

and over-centralized control, had frequently been noted by Soviet economists; but they had been overridden in the past because Stalin considered that the transfer of state property to the collectives was a retrogressive step from the ideological point of view. Also the MTS had served as vital links for party supervision over agriculture; we have seen that in 1953 their powers were actually increased.

By 1958 there were good practical reasons for merging the MTS with the collective farms. In the first place, party influence in the countryside was much stronger by this time; it would not be jeopardized by the abolition of its main instrument of control from the past. Secondly, inefficient dual agricultural management was eliminated at the same time. Thirdly, the collective farms were now able to support the expense of operating the MTS machinery, thanks to the agricultural boom since 1953.

When the MTS were abolished, the state had to buy the produce of the collective farms that was previously handed over as payment in kind to the MTS. The necessity to review prices at this juncture presented an opportunity for further rationalization. In June 1958 the multiple-price system was abolished; under this system collective farms had to deliver a basic quota from their crop at low prices, receiving attractive prices only for output above planned requirements. The multiple prices were replaced by a single price for each item in each region. The law of supply and demand was allowed to make a welcome appearance with the institution of an annual review of prices according to the volume of production. The price system still contained a multitude of anomalies, but the 1958 reform, like the others mentioned above, represented a considerable advance over the short-sighted attitude toward agriculture that had been prevalent in Stalin's time.

By 1959, however, the agricultural sector of the economy was still causing the most concern among Soviet experts. During the first three years of the Seven-Year Plan (1959–61) agricultural production increased by only 1 per cent, compared with an 8 per cent rise in industry. After the upsurge from 1953 to 1958, stagnation had set in once more. But the new plan did not provide for agricultural price increases or for larger state investment, on the assumption that production would continue to grow after 1958 as it had done before. Only in 1960–1 was state investment augmented and the cost of some kinds of farm machinery reduced.

The slow-down in agriculture had a depressing effect on consumption, but the situation was different from that existing during the lean years from 1950 to 1953. By 1959 there were enough cereals and potatoes to eat, but animal products, vegetables and fruit remained in short supply. The actual amount of daily calories taken in *per capita* of the population was probably the same as in the United States, but the Soviet diet was far more monotonous and unbalanced than the American equivalent.

Khrushchev's categorical statements at the Twenty-first Congress on the need to convert the existing three kinds of property in the Soviet Union into state-owned plots had a braking effect on the incentive of the collective farmers. In 1953 Khrushchev had expanded, not contracted, the rights of the collective and private sectors, and the MTS reform of 1958 had further added to them. But in 1959 he put Communist dogma before economic viability.

There is no doubt that in the long run it is the intention of the Soviet leaders to turn all agricultural land into state property: Khrushchev's sudden application of pressure in 1959 was probably due to two factors—the need to demonstrate to the world that on the ideological plane the Soviet Union was not lagging behind the Chinese venture into the commune system, and the fear that the collective farmers might become too independent of party control after the abandonment of the MTS.

Khrushchev put forward concrete measures for gearing agriculture to the purpose he had in mind. Private plots were to be abolished; a higher proportion of collective farm revenue was to be reinvested instead of being distributed as extra income among the farmers; finally, the collective farms would be linked through joint power and irrigation schemes. This last step would compel the collective farmers to finance their own projects and would also lead to the creation of enlarged agro-towns—an old hobby horse of Khrushchev's, dating from 1951. Agro-towns, or urban-type farms on a massive scale, would serve a triple purpose: they would narrow the rift between town and country, an ideal championed by Marx; they would eliminate room for private plots; and they would increase the social gulf between the rank-and-file peasant and the farm managers, whose overall control would be strengthened in consequence.

The tragedy of the Soviet agricultural system lies in the problem of reconciling Marxist doctrine with economic profitability. So far in Soviet history the two aims have not been compatible. By the end of 1959 the economic effects of the campaign for ideological correctness were painfully clear. It was seen that 'the tendency toward accelerated transformation of the collective farms into state farms' was 'profoundly mistaken'.[1] Collective farmers' incomes had scarcely in-

[1] I. Vinnichenko in *Nash Sovremennik* (No. 4, 1959), p. 179.

creased. The curb on private plots cut back the most prolific source of goods in short supply, like meat and dairy products. Big farms were no more efficient than smaller ones—in fact they were often less so, as is the case in the United States. The peasants resented any sort of restriction on their profitable private allotments and looked upon the agro-town scheme with as much suspicion as they had done in the past.

The reckoning came at the plenary meeting of the Central Committee in December 1959. It was found that nearly 10,000,000 metric tons less grain had been delivered to the state in 1959 than in the previous year. The weather had been satisfactory, but the harvesting was badly organized. Other branches of agriculture fared little better.

Scapegoats had to be found. A. Kirichenko, a specialist in agriculture and one of Khrushchev's closest associates, was dismissed from the Presidium. N. Beliaev, the secretary of the Kazakhstan Central Committee, and those in charge of the party departments for agriculture in the union republics and the RSFSR also fell at the same time.

In June 1960, a large conference of agricultural experts met in Moscow to season Khrushchev's essays in theory with a little more economic good sense. They discussed practical methods of raising agricultural yields and of developing all collective and state farms up to the efficiency level of the leading farms. A plan to promote regional specialization in certain crops was established: the country was divided into thirty-nine agricultural zones and each farm was instructed to cultivate two to three crops only. For once a sound economic scheme also seemed as if it would reap political advantages as well, since concentration on one or two types of crop would make the peasants more dependent upon the state for their food supplies.

CHAPTER VI

THE KHRUSHCHEV ERA: FOREIGN POLICY

How did the brave new Khrushchev regime face up to the rest of the world beyond the Soviet borders?

By the time of the Twentieth Congress the Soviet leaders had departed more widely from Stalinist procedures in foreign policy than in domestic affairs. Persuasion rather than coercion was their unwritten slogan from the very start, with Molotov as the only significant dissenter. The new line, tentative and uncertain though it was between 1953 and 1956, and subject to violent fluctuations in Eastern Europe, nevertheless paid immediate and huge dividends in the less-developed countries. Only in Europe were Soviet aims not generally achieved. The German problem remained unresolved, while in Central Europe it seemed that Stalin's hold on his empire could not be gently loosened without opening wide the floodgates of separatism.

The Twentieth Congress was a watershed in foreign as well as in domestic affairs. Its function was to survey the previous three years' achievements in foreign policy, to draw conclusions from them, and to lay down steadier lines for the future. This had a stabilizing effect on Soviet foreign policy, but unfortunately this wholesome influence, at least in Eastern Europe, was negated by the repercussions following Khrushchev's secret speech on Stalin. Khrushchev intended his words for home consumption, but they were heard in anger by world Communism and acted upon violently. The subsequent upheaval in Eastern Europe took until the end of 1957 to subdue, leaving behind it a completely changed relationship between the Soviet Union and the European Communist camp. It took the Hungarian revolution of 1956 to shake off the weight of the Stalinist past.

Soviet relations with the Middle East and Asia continued to develop along much smoother lines, though the atmosphere of euphoria characterizing the years between 1953 and 1956 slowly dimmed. The Soviet Union came to realize that the new countries were not willing to go beyond a flirtation with Communism, while the recipients of Soviet favours learned that aid was not without its obligations.

Through the years from 1953 to the present time, two major problems clouded the international scene for the Soviet Union. In Europe the problem of a divided Germany remained unsolved and was a cause of mounting irritation between East and West, leading to the prolonged crisis over Berlin in 1958–60. In Asia, China gradually increased in strength and exerted increasing influence within the Communist camp as well as on her Asian neighbours, especially India. At a time when Russia was attempting to carry out a softer line in foreign policy and escape from the consequences of her Stalinist past, China stuck adamantly to Stalinist tenets and became even more rigid in her outlook after 1957. The growing rift between the two largest Communist states was to have repercussions both in Eastern Europe and in Asia.

The pattern of Soviet relations with other Communist states and with the rest of the world changed significantly between 1959 and the end of 1961, but in view of the proximity of events it is not easy to pick out any decisive trends. Within the Soviet bloc the catalyst of change was Communist China. In most of the less-developed areas of the world previously submitted to Soviet influence mutual relations grew even cooler than before, but this setback was more than compensated for by the opening up of new regions for Soviet diplomacy in Africa and Latin America, where in some instances the honeymoon atmosphere of earlier Indo-Soviet and Soviet-Egyptian contacts was once more evoked. The pattern of events at the summit of international politics took on a new sense of urgency in these years, threatening to bring the Soviet Union and the United States into head-on collision over the German question.

Since the Twentieth Soviet Party Congress in February 1956 dealt with peaceful coexistence and other ideological concepts closely related to the conduct of foreign policy, it serves as a convenient starting point for any treatment of Russia's position in world affairs during the Khrushchev era. The congress ushered in significant policy changes that were important to the future of foreign affairs.

THE TWENTIETH PARTY CONGRESS

At the congress the practical innovations in foreign policy that had occurred since Stalin's death, described in Chapter IV, were rationalized and distilled into theoretical generalities. Firstly, Russia had clearly enhanced her world position in the years from 1953 to 1956 by her increasing economic power and her acquisition of the hydrogen bomb, as well as by what appeared to be more satisfactory relations with Eastern Europe and the advance of the Communist cause in Asia and the Middle East. These factors convinced Khrushchev (though not Molotov) that the Communist bloc and its new friends outside the bloc were in a sufficiently strong position to avert war between the capitalist and Communist camps. In theoretical jargon this entailed rejection of the doctrine of the inevitability of wars between the two power blocs and adherence to the notion of peaceful coexistence.

Secondly, Russia's impulse to normalize contacts with Eastern Europe, leading to the reconciliation between Russia and heterodox Yugoslavia, was clarified in the ideological sense by Soviet admission of the possibility of different roads to socialism; it appeared that the Soviet model of development would never again be applied indiscriminately to other Communist states.

Thirdly, the evolution of Soviet policy in Asia and the Middle East from armed Communist aggression to the wooing of national bourgeois leaders found eloquent expression in Khrushchev's denial at the congress of the hitherto obligatory thesis that violent revolution was the only road to socialism.

Thus the Twentieth Congress presented an abstract résumé of the main lines of Soviet foreign policy since Stalin.[1] For the most part it did not launch a new series of changes, but rather altered the existing ideological line, which lagged behind the reality of political action. At the same time it provided a useful platform for explaining the deeper meaning of Soviet policy to the world: it attempted to impress the West (by the theory of peaceful coexistence), Eastern Europe (by the concept of different roads to socialism), and the uncommitted countries (by the theoretical rejection of violent revolution) that Stalinism had been abandoned.

As an essay in theory the changes made at the congress are of great interest, since they reveal the extent to which Stalinism was being rejected in another sense. We have seen how Stalin insisted on imposing ideological doctrines on his foreign policy despite their irrelevance to the actual situation as exposed by an economist like Varga. In Stalin's time ideology was often the primary factor in any estimate of the outside world. By 1956 reality was calling the tune to which time-honoured ideology had to adapt itself. The result was an increasing flexibility and subtlety in Soviet foreign policy. Like some mediaeval religious painter, Stalin paid scant attention to the contours of reality in describing his vision of the world. In comparison Khrushchev's sense of relative values amounted to a veritable renaissance in Soviet political action.

[1] It is interesting to note that in a recent Soviet textbook on foreign policy, the account of the Twentieth Congress is placed out of chronological order and is used as a preface to a chapter on foreign policy from 1955 to 1956. See *Mezhdunarodnye Otnosheniia i Vneshnaia Politika SSSR* (International Relations and the Foreign Policy of the Soviet Union; Moscow, 1960), pp. 4–14.

EASTERN EUROPE

At the congress Khrushchev's denunciation of Stalin had direct repercussions on the immediate future of Soviet foreign policy. His fulminating account of his late master's errors was almost entirely confined to the sphere of domestic policy, though brief mention was made of Stalin's 'shameful role' in the Yugoslav quarrel of 1948 and his neglect of India after her emancipation. But Khrushchev's speech contained no references to Stalin's method of dealing with the People's Democracies, and this implied that the Soviet leaders themselves would subsequently decide for Eastern Europe the extent to which the Stalinist heritage could be dismantled.

However, the matter was not settled so easily as that. By releasing violent criticism of Stalin at this particular juncture in East European affairs, Khrushchev committed what was perhaps the Soviet Union's biggest blunder in foreign policy since Stalin's lack of foresight in neglecting to prepare for the Nazi attack of 1941. He overlooked the fact that it was ludicrous to attempt to pin all the blame for the evils in the Soviet system on one man and that in denigrating Stalin he was also criticizing the whole regime. Exactly this point was made soon after the congress ended by no less a person than Togliatti, the head of the Italian Communist Party. He was backed up by Tito and Gomulka. Even worse, the uncovering of Stalin's mistakes sounded the death knell for his puppets, who in most cases were still in power in Eastern Europe. They had risen to the top on the crest of Stalin's infallibility; destruction of the myth involved their destruction also.

The undermining of the Soviet Union as the exemplary image of a socialist state, and the loss of prestige by Stalinist leaders in the People's Democracies, made revolution in Eastern Europe a practical possibility. A suitable climate for leanings toward independence had already been fostered by the economic and political détente of 1953-5 and the readmission of Yugoslavia to the Communist fold.

Soviet foreign policy pursued an unswerving course for a few months after the congress despite the shocked reaction of East European delegates to Khrushchev's speech. In April 1956 the Cominform, that erstwhile symbol of international Communist conformity, was finally dissolved, and in June the joint declaration of the CPSU and the League of Yugoslav Communists affirmed

> ... that the roads and conditions of socialist development are different in different countries, that the wealth of the forms of

socialist development contributes to their strengthening, and . . . that any tendency to impose one's own views in determining the roads and forms of socialist development is alien to both sides. . . .[1]

Six days after Tito left Moscow, riots broke out among factory workers in Poznan, Poland. As in Czechoslovakia and East Germany in 1953, economic grievances soon gave place to political outcries against Soviet domination. The Russians, still in a liberal mood, made concessions; many Stalinists were expelled from the Central Committee of the Polish United Workers' Party. Nevertheless, on October 15th, the Polish Politburo decided to elect Wladyslaw Gomulka as First Secretary; this was the man who had been imprisoned for some years for opposing Stalin.

In making a unilateral decision of this nature and refusing to go to Moscow for consultations, the Poles were openly defying the Soviet Union. The Soviet Presidium ordered Russian troops in Poland to move nearer to the towns and arranged for Konstantin Rokossovski, Russia's faithful supporter, to stage a coup if negotiations between Russia and Poland broke down. At this moment of crisis, the fragmented Soviet leadership rallied together temporarily. Khrushchev, Molotov, Kaganovich, and Mikoyan went to Warsaw to mediate with the Poles, who had their way by proceeding to elect Gomulka. Unlike the almost simultaneous uprising in Hungary, the bloodless October revolution in Poland triumphed. Gomulka's programme was more radical than Moscow would have liked, but at least it flowed naturally from earlier thaws in a domestic policy that left unscathed the two principles on which Soviet-Yugoslav relations had foundered in 1948—continued membership in the Soviet bloc and mutual agreement on the role of the Communist Party. Moreover, the Hungarian revolt in the same month had the effect of restraining the Soviet-Polish quarrel; the Poles curbed their demands for anti-Soviet measures in order to avert the fate of the Hungarians, while the Russians were too preoccupied with the rising in Budapest to assert their authority in Poland by force of arms.

In view of the see-saw reactions of Hungary to Soviet policy since 1953, described in the last chapter, it was not surprising that this unsettled country gave expression to the most pronounced rejection of the Stalinist past in all of Eastern Europe. The Stalinist Rákosi had to resign as First Secretary in June 1956, under the impact of Khrushchev's secret speech, but the policies of his successor, Ernö Gerö, were not sufficiently liberal for a people who had tasted more

---

[1] Text given in the *New York Times* (June 21, 1956), p. 10.

freedom under Nagy in the very recent past. On October 23rd, revolution broke out in Budapest.

Nagy was reinstated as Premier with the consent of Mikoyan, who was in Budapest with Suslov in order to control the revolution. For a period of six days the Hungarians enjoyed the luxury of a government that tried to be independent from Moscow. The reaction to Rákosi's 'hard' line was extreme. The Hungarians wished to end the political monopoly of the Communist Party and withdrew from the Warsaw Pact, thus putting themselves even further out of the Soviet grasp than the Yugoslavs had been from 1948 to 1955. This the Soviet Union would not allow. By crushing the November 4th revolt with tanks and troops against the will of a nation, Russia put a halt to the retreat from Stalinism—a halt as abrupt as its initiation had been at the Twentieth Congress and far more damaging to Soviet prestige. At the very moment when Russia was trying to eliminate some of the negative elements of her past, she had to reaffirm them in order to preserve the existence of the Communist bloc in any form. One is reminded yet again of the French Republicans: 'They believed themselves to be cosmopolitans; they were that only in their speeches ... the Revolution degenerated into an armed propaganda [*in the Russian case during the period from 1945 to 1953*], then into conquest ...' [*Hungary, 1956*].

The Soviet act in Hungary shed new light on the concept of different roads to socialism, which admittedly had not been outlined in any detail at the Twentieth Congress. By November 1956, it was at least clear that the Yugoslav agreement of June 1956 with the Soviet Union was not intended as a model for the rest of Eastern Europe, which would be obliged to contain its divergences from the Soviet prototype within certain limits. The definition of these limits formed the subject of the often painful dialogues that occupied Russia and her allies from the autumn of 1956 until the Moscow Declaration of the ruling Communist Parties in November 1957.

Before entering into the details of these discussions, we may stand back from our review of Soviet policy in Eastern Europe at this point and observe that the autumn of 1956 marked the turn of the tide in intra-bloc relations. Since that time the People's Democracies could no longer be considered as an unquestionable asset to the Soviet Union. Politically, some of them proved their unreliability in 1956, and the wounds that were then inflicted never completely healed. From the economic point of view the more generous trade and credit terms that Russia gave to her allies after the Hungarian and Polish revolts in order to pacify them represented a definite drain on her resources, a drain no longer compensated for by war reparations and Soviet-controlled joint stock companies—two among several forms of earlier Russian economic domination. In military terms, Soviet confidence in the reliability of East European troops waned after the events of 1956. For that matter the launching of an accurate intercontinental ballistic missile in the summer of 1957 heralded the close of an era when it was vital for Russia to retain Eastern Europe as a protective zone.

Nevertheless, the sudden release of the People's Democracies from the Soviet bloc would have struck a major blow at Soviet prestige and as an act of policy would have contradicted the ideological dream of world Communism and Russian national expansionist trends. In the autumn of 1956 the situation was very precarious. If the opposition to Russia in Poland, Hungary, and Yugoslavia had triumphed and joined hands across the national borders, Russia's geographical outlet to the more faithful Czechoslovakia and East Germany would have been restricted to the narrow eastern tip of Slovakia. With Western aid Germany could have attempted to reunite her two halves, and Austria might have retreated from neutrality in view of her new position in Europe vis-à-vis the two power blocs. Thanks to the lack of co-operation between the People's Democracies, the bloc remained under Soviet domination; this fragmentation of interests sprang from the national insularity that through the centuries had kept Eastern Europe weak against Russia, Austria and the Turks, and the Soviet Union had continued this policy of divide and rule.

Russia had to tread very warily after the Hungarian revolution. In the first months following the crisis it was a case of temporarily stemming the dike against revisionism until Communist inter-state relations could be re-established on some new and firmer basis. In an important speech of November 6, 1956, the Soviet ideologist Suslov made it clear that national roads to Communism were still permissible, but were subject to certain well-defined Marxist laws. These laws had been rigorously and successfully applied in the past to the Soviet Union; therefore some elements of the Russian experience had acquired universal meaning and were pertinent to the present situation in Eastern Europe.

This pronouncement was not specific in its references to individual countries. Articles that appeared on the same subject in the Stalinist East German and Czech press were, but even these did not accuse Gomulka personally when Poland refused to support the Russian position on the Hungarian question in the United Nations. Gomulka himself on October 20th supported the Yugoslav heresy at the Eighth Plenum of the United Polish Workers' Party, when he said: 'The model of socialism can also vary. It can be such as that created in the Soviet Union; it can be shaped in a manner as we see it in Yugoslavia; it can be different still.'[1]

The Soviet leadership was probably exercising pressure on the Czechs and East Germans in an effort to moderate their criticism. A middle way had to be found between the conflicting 'hard' and 'soft' lines of the various countries if the bloc was not to split up into two groups at loggerheads with each other, and with Russia as a hesitant bystander.

At this crucial moment in Soviet relations with the Communist bloc, China stepped into the arena. In an article of December 29, 1956, the newspaper *Jen Min Jih Pao* virtually reiterated Suslov's line of the previous month, making it doubly clear that while some local deviations from orthodox central policy might persist, they would not be allowed to override the general unity of the bloc under Soviet guidance. In one respect the article was more precise than Suslov had been. Yugoslavia was directly chided for attacking other Communist parties and causing a split in the socialist movement. From this moment it became increasingly obvious that Yugoslavia could scarcely be included in the revised Soviet system, even in the rather more liberal version that was about to evolve.

The Soviet Union now applied economic palliatives before concentrating on political problems. Soviet credits were handed out to critical sectors in Poland, Hungary, and East Germany. With an eye on the more distant future, Russia pumped new life into the Council for Mutual Economic Aid. In the summer of 1957 the Council drew up drafts of development plans for all of Eastern Europe for the next ten to fifteen years. Gradually the People's Democracies were allowed to play a greater role in the organization and even to dispute some of the Soviet proposals. Nevertheless, at the same time Russia began to make good use of the Council's multilateral conferences as a means of forcing majority decisions on recalcitrant members like Poland, who would not submit to pressure from a purely political body such as the revised version of the Cominform now suggested by the Soviet Union.

The idea of a new Communist International was naturally repugnant to the Poles and, above all, to the Yugoslavs, who had been the direct target of the Cominform. When the Soviet Union slowly sounded foreign Communist parties on this matter toward the

[1] *Nowe Drogi* (No. 10, 1956), p. 38.

end of 1956 and through 1957, it became apparent that the Chinese and the Italians were also reluctant to agree to the notion. Backing down somewhat, the Soviet Union proposed that a leading periodical for the Communist Parties should be established. (Apart from its distinctive anti-Yugoslav aim, the Cominform had consisted of little more than an editorial machine in Belgrade.) The Poles, the Italians, and especially the Yugoslavs still resisted but, in September 1958, the first issue of the *World Marxist Review* finally appeared—significantly, in faithful Prague and under a Soviet editor.

After the bitter experience of the recent past, the Soviet Union found it impossible to reintroduce a Communist political international organization with all that it implied of Soviet domination. The Italian idea of a continuous series of bilateral or multilateral meetings of Communist parties was finally adopted. Throughout the latter part of 1956 and most of 1957 Russia held bilateral meetings with the leaders of all the East European countries, at which she gradually formed her impressions of the way in which the wind would blow at a multilateral meeting.

Khrushchev's final victory over the 'anti-party group' inside Russia allowed him to take a more decisive line in Soviet foreign policy. The hesitations and blunders of the years since Stalin's death were due, as we have seen, as much to the rifts in the Soviet leadership as to growing recalcitrance on the part of the People's Democracies. After July 1957, Khrushchev was able to carry out his foreign policy compromise, which lay somewhere between Molotov's old-fashioned Stalinism and the unbridled revisionism that had affected some parts of Eastern Europe. Gone were the days when Molotov could try to thwart the executive through his control of the administration. In July 1957, Khrushchev said of his new Foreign Minister: 'Gromyko only says what we tell him to.... If he doesn't we'll fire him and get someone who does.'[1]

Softened by increasingly generous credits and noting that the Soviet Union now put revisionism in the same category as Nazi fascism—that *bête noire* of Eastern Europe which had been used so much by the Soviet Union as a rallying cry in the past—the individual countries, apart from Poland and Yugoslavia, were drawn once again to Russia's side.

The Polish and Yugoslav Communist Parties held a bilateral meeting of their own at Belgrade in September 1957, at which they expressed agreement with each other's views; but a wedge had already been driven between them as early as January 1957, when Gomulka

[1] In the words reported by Averell Harriman in *Life* (July 13, 1959), p. 33.

promised the Chinese Foreign Minister, Chou En-lai, mediating for Moscow in Warsaw, not to exacerbate Polish differences with the Russians. Tito, on the other hand, never flinched from holding up Yugoslav practical and ideological deviations from the Soviet line as examples for export to other East European countries, even if it meant the dissolution of the Communist camp. His purpose veered closer to the Hungarian heresy of October 1956 than to Gomulka's milder indiscretions.

By the autumn of 1957 Khrushchev could afford to gamble on the hope that at a multilateral meeting of the world Communist parties Yugoslavia could be safely isolated and Poland bludgeoned by a compelling majority to re-enter the Soviet fold. The launching of the first earth satellite on October 4, 1957, just before the convention in November of the leaders of sixty-four Communist Parties in Moscow to celebrate the fortieth anniversary of the Russian Revolution, gave a fillip to Russian prestige.

Yugoslavia remained stubborn. Tito sent Eduard Kardelj and Aleksandar Ranković to Moscow instead of coming in person, and the Yugoslav delegation refused to sign the important declaration of the twelve ruling Communist parties confirming Russian leadership. Poland found herself threatened by isolation, especially after Mao Tse-tung's open recognition of Soviet supremacy at the meeting. She bowed to the storm and signed the Moscow Declaration. However, the final document reflected some of her opinions in that the draft theses of the Soviet Communist Party were modified in the final version. The Soviet Union was more often referred to as merely the foremost state in the bloc and not as the leader; comments in the theses on the 'pernicious ideas' of 'national Communism' were replaced by less harsh reprovals of revisionism and dogmatism.

The 1957 November Declaration of the twelve ruling Communist parties on foreign policy and Khrushchev's victory over the 'anti-party group' in domestic affairs were parallel lessons in the dynamics of a totalitarian state and empire. After Stalin's death brief and dangerous ventures away from monolithic unity into collective leadership at home and political diversity abroad had proved disastrous; salutary bloodletting of the body politic soon led to wounds that might well have proved fatal had they not been closed up by a return to totalitarian 'normality'. However, it was not simply a case of *'plus ça change, plus c'est la même chose'*. The very steps taken to regain control of the situation were redolent of a changed spirit. In foreign affairs one has only to compare the restrained Moscow Declaration of 1957 with the Cominform's violent expulsion of the Yugoslavs in 1948. In domestic policy Khrushchev's appeal to a majority in the Central Committee and to Leninist principles in June 1957 contrasted strongly with Stalin's high-handed, secretive, and lethal methods of dealing with his opponents. After 1957 the return to stronger rule in Russia and abroad brought changes that bore the imprint of the disturbing years from 1953 to 1957.

With the Moscow Declaration of the Communist states behind her, Russia had little trouble in neutralizing the effect of the Yugoslav threat in 1958. When Tito expressed a negative approach to both the Warsaw Pact and Western capitalism in a new draft programme for Yugoslav Communism, and Ranković openly attacked the Soviet leaders at the Yugoslav Congress in April 1958, Khrushchev at last appeared to align himself clearly with the current Chinese attitude toward Tito by stating at Sofia on June 3rd that the Soviet Communist Party had never withdrawn its approval of the condemnation of Yugoslavia by the Cominform in 1948. On June 17th, after accusing Tito of having taken an active part in the Hungarian rebellion, the Soviet Union executed Nagy. In the same period Russia postponed two loans promised to Yugoslavia. Relations between the two countries sank to the low level that had characterized the interval between Stalin's death and the reconciliation of 1955.

By 1958 Poland had neither the strength nor the inclination to resist bloc pressure. She made a last stand at the Yugoslav Congress in April by refusing to walk out after Ranković's criticism of the USSR, but the execution of Nagy forced her into a choice between creating an open rift with Russia by continuing to support Nagy's image, or else acquiescing. Her historic urge to self-immolation was no longer powerful enough to make her cling to Tito's principles, which in any case differed in some ways from her own, and on June 28th, Gomulka criticized Tito and Nagy in a speech that reconciled Poland to the Soviet Union once again. The trend culminated in Gomulka's pro-Soviet speech at the Soviet Twenty-first Congress early in 1959. Poland hung on to the concessions granted her in 1957–8, but she was no longer an active source of friction in the bloc.

After six years of trial and error, the Soviet Union had partially succeeded in achieving its aims of consolidation and relaxation in Eastern Europe. The cost was high, and the final result not entirely satisfactory from the Russian point of view. Yugoslavia's continued neutralism was a reminder of the bitter disputes throughout East Europe that had taxed Soviet diplomacy to the utmost.

After the Twenty-first Congress it was no longer the revisionist countries in Eastern Europe that were embarrassing the Soviet Union, but rather those members of the bloc that were neo-Stalinist by inclination.

Why was this so? In the first place it should not be forgotten that Khrushchev's original aim in delivering the secret speech had been to steer Russia and the Communist bloc into a new political phase, leaving behind the legacy bequeathed by Stalin. Soviet suppression in Eastern Europe later in 1956, although reminiscent of Stalinist policy, was not deliberately prepared by Khrushchev, but was carried out in order to cut short a revolt that Russia had not foreseen. It represented an unpremeditated flashback to the past that merely held up the planned advance to a more liberal future. When calm was restored in 1959, it was seen that the neo-Stalinist countries were now the ones that were out of line with Soviet policy. On the neo-Stalinist wing, the similarity of views shared by East Germany, Czechoslovakia, and to some extent Bulgaria became more apparent. In June 1960, the Soviet leaders found it necessary to criticize 'dogmatism' through the press.[1] Scarcely veiled accusations were levelled at Ulbricht, the Secretary of the East German Communist Party.

Taken on their own, the dissenting views of these three countries were not sufficiently influential to cause the USSR much trouble; the real danger to Khrushchev lay in the fact that their opinions on ideology and foreign policy often appeared to veer closer to Chinese than to Soviet attitudes at a time when the Sino-Soviet conflict was blowing hotter. As we shall see when we come to consider relations between Russia and China in this period, the latter did not discard Stalinist tenets but rather flaunted them in Russia's face and rallied to the side of other Communist states that held similar political views. In the case of East Germany and Czechoslovakia, the ties were economic as well as political, since China relied to a great extent on supplies from them for crucial portions of her industrial programme.

The firm attitude of Czechoslovakia and East Germany had helped to re-anchor the bloc firmly to Russia after the uprisings of 1956, but their continued adherence to a 'hard' policy after 1957–8 was embarrassing to the USSR. The Soviet Union feared that these two countries might eventually imitate Stalinist Albania, who toward the end of this period allied herself directly with China against Russia.

Albania's position was in some ways similar to China's. She too suffered from economic and social backwardness in relation to the rest of the Communist world and to Russia in particular. Both

[1] *Pravda* (June 12 and 13, 1960).

Albania and China had taken on Communist governments without Soviet military aid, and neither of them could tolerate the existence of a neutral Yugoslavia—China mainly for ideological reasons, Albania chiefly on account of her traditional hatred of an overbearing neighbour. Together they struggled to win over other countries in the bloc to their point of view at inter-party meetings held in Bucharest in June 1960, and in Moscow in November of the same year.

The Stalinist countries in the Communist camp worried the Soviet Union in yet another way. Just when Khrushchev was making an all-out attempt to woo the less-developed countries into joining the new socialist commonwealth, which was painted in glowing terms for the outside world, China and her Communist sympathizers took pains to make it quite clear that their attitude toward new nationalist governments in the non-committed areas of the world did not differ very much from the line Stalin had taken between 1945 and 1953 with such disastrous effects. Once again the Soviet Union found it difficult to adopt a correct attitude between the extremes of left- and right-wing policies in the Communist camp.

By the time of the Soviet Twenty-second Congress in 1961, the East European Communist bloc, which had reached the height of its unity at Stalin's death, had now become a much more loosely-knit group of partly self-willed countries. The totalitarian empire was fast dissolving into a socialist commonwealth. We have noted the developments that led to this change; at the end of this section on Soviet relations with Eastern Europe it might be useful to give a brief sketch of the revised institutional framework still binding the camp to Russia.

By 1961 Soviet relations with the East European People's Democracies as a whole were marked by more reliance on formal institutions like the Warsaw Treaty Organization and the Council for Mutual Economic Aid, and less on the unofficial ties through party channels that had bound the bloc to the Soviet Union during Stalin's lifetime. New life was pumped into these two bodies, which in earlier years had been mere propaganda fronts, and ties with Moscow were put on a more normal inter-state basis; there was no place in the socialist commonwealth of the 1960s for Stalinist instruments of control like the Cominform.

Founded in May 1955, the Warsaw Treaty Organization included the eight European Communist states. It was intended as a bulwark against NATO and therefore rested on a military basis, providing for mutual assistance in the event of outside aggression. Before the Polish and Hungarian uprisings of 1956, Soviet troops were stationed in Eastern Europe regardless of the terms of the treaty, but after that time the situation was regularized in accordance with its provisions. The Political Consultative Committee established by the treaty met in 1956, 1958 and again in February 1960. It served as a focal point for the expression of opinions on foreign policy issues like West German militarism and disarmament, and it generally gave more weight to non-Soviet views as time went on.

The Council for Mutual Economic Aid became the primary agent for the economic integration of Eastern Europe after the death of Stalin. By 1961 it was the most active body for co-ordinating policies within the bloc, although, like the Warsaw Pact, it was confined to the eight European members. The original charter of the council contrasted greatly with that of its capitalist equivalent, the European Economic Community, in that its terms made no specific reference as to how decisions were to be reached. In the early years of its existence it remained a dead letter, except for a few measures imposed on it by the Soviet Union. But after 1956 its activities grew considerably, and open disputes between the member countries were allowed to develop over such controversial matters as price fixing and national specialization. Temporary national alliances within the bloc were formed to counter Soviet suggestions. A move of this kind would have been inconceivable in the Cominform. The Communist camp was still far from being a free commonwealth of sovereign nations in 1961, but it had travelled a long way since 1953.

THE GERMAN PROBLEM

The threat of a revived capitalist, and possibly militant, Germany, whether split in two or united, was instrumental in keeping Eastern Europe bound to the Soviet Union between 1956 and 1961. During these years divided Germany, the vital hinge between Communism and capitalism in Europe, created even greater problems than before. After abortive attempts during 1954–5 to solve the German question as a whole, and to its own advantage, the Soviet Union began to face up to the harsh realities of the situation: a regime under which the two Germanies became more entrenched and dependent on their respective protectors. Soviet long-term aims with regard to Germany did not change. The Soviet Union still appeared to envisage a German nation weaned from its capitalist traditions, but for the time being an effort was made to take advantage of the stalemate by pushing for short-term, piecemeal gains.

In the summer of 1957 Russia supported Polish plans for the neutralization of Central Europe. Rapacki, the Polish Foreign

Minister, proposed that Poland, Czechoslovakia, and East and West Germany should neither produce nor stockpile atomic weapons; outside powers would then promise not to use atomic arms against the area. At the same time Gomulka suggested that the Baltic should become a neutral sea. Rumania called on Bulgaria, Albania, Turkey, Greece, and Yugoslavia to join together in another neutral area.

The receptive Soviet attitude to a neutral bloc in Central Europe was probably motivated by Russia's acquisition in the summer of 1957 of an efficient long-range rocket, which led to a change in military strategy. Until 1957 the main Soviet deterrent consisted of the large armies placed on the western fringe of Eastern Europe and prepared at a moment's notice to overwhelm all of Europe and cut the continent off from American support.

The Communist plans were rejected by the West, which feared that Russia would try to lure the whole of the neutral area thus created into the Communist camp, using the somewhat aggressive manner she was now applying to the uncommitted nations in the Middle and Far East. A neutral Baltic, closed to all countries except Russia and Scandinavia, would also give the Soviet Union an enormous advantage in the region.

Reverting to less far-reaching schemes after the failure of the Rapacki plan, Khrushchev made a bid in November 1958 for the definitive recognition of East Germany and its frontiers by the West. The Soviet demands included the abrogation of all existing agreements on Berlin and the transference of Soviet rights as an occupying power to the East Germans. West Berlin was to become a 'free city' from which the Western powers would withdraw. Russia threatened to hand over her responsibility in Berlin to East Germany within six months. With characteristic realism, Khrushchev now saw that the earlier Russian plan for the 'democratic reunification' of Germany was plainly impossible to bring about in the immediate future. He even expressed the opinion in public that Communist government in West Germany was a necessary prelude to a united Germany.

This particular Soviet move was much more frank than Molotov's bid at Berlin in 1954 for the temporary establishment of two German states for a short period after the signing of a peace treaty. In 1958 Khrushchev based his argument on the need to acknowledge the *status quo* with regard to Germany, though the mere recognition of East Germany as a sovereign state would naturally involve a substantial change in the attitude of the West, which consequently rejected the suggestion.

In January 1959, the Soviet Union proposed a twenty-eight-nation peace conference to draw up a German peace treaty. The terms of this treaty were to be virtually the same as those put forward by Molotov in 1954 at the Berlin Conference. Russia's long-term aim of either neutralizing or communizing the whole of Germany and driving the Americans out of Europe had not changed one jot, although many devious short-term methods of arriving at this end had been employed since 1954. The gambit of January 1959 was made in the hope that the West would at least give diplomatic recognition to the East German Government.

Why was Khrushchev spurred on to renewed action in 1958–9? On the one hand it seemed likely that West Germany would receive atomic arms in the near future; on the other, China's 'harder' line in foreign policy was getting a more sympathetic hearing among the members of the Warsaw Treaty Organization. Moreover, the contrast between prosperous West Berlin and poverty-stricken East Berlin was increasing, while the exodus of refugees from East Germany through the city continued to grow.

The British Prime Minister, Harold Macmillan, attempted to pour oil on troubled waters by travelling to Moscow for consultations with Khrushchev on the Berlin and East German problem in February 1959. The two leaders tentatively agreed to look for some way of increasing security in Central Europe by limiting forces and weapons in the area, but they were mistrusted by the West Germans and the Americans. Khrushchev did his best to multiply signs of disagreement over the German problem in the West during his official visits to the United States and France in September 1959 and March 1960 respectively. In the United States he appeared to be leading up to a Soviet-American agreement that would ignore the interests of continental France and Germany; in France Khrushchev persistently reminded his audience that Germany had attacked France three times in the course of seventy years.

Khrushchev's efforts were not sufficient to split the West, which would no more cede to the Russian terms for a peace treaty in 1960 than in 1954. After the four wartime Allies and the leaders of the West and East German Governments failed to arrive at any solution of the German problem at the Geneva Conference of May–August 1959, a summit conference of the Soviet, American, French and British heads of government was convened in Paris in May 1960, at the suggestion of Khrushchev. Any hope of agreement was practically doomed before the event, and the pessimism of the West was soon confirmed. Khrushchev wrecked the meeting by using the incident of the American U-2 espionage plane shot down over Soviet territory shortly before the conference. Apparently pressure from the Chinese Communists and from certain members of the Soviet party hierarchy induced Khrushchev to act as he did.

After the failure of the summit meetings, the Soviet Union did not proceed to solve the German question unilaterally as it had threatened to do, but Soviet diplomatic notes and political speeches on the subject took on an increasingly hostile tone, including threats of military retaliation. The German problem remained totally unsolved by the time of the Soviet Twenty-second Congress in 1961.

THE MIDDLE AND FAR EAST

With the conclusion of the arms agreement with Egypt in 1955, the Middle East had been the scene of a major breakthrough for Soviet foreign policy, but the area proved to be less receptive to further advances in the period between 1956 and 1959 than the Soviet Union had expected. Until the period following Anglo-French intervention in the Suez Canal in October 1956, the future seemed bright. The arms deal opened the door for the Communists to several Arab countries. Large numbers of Soviet and Czech technicians followed the arms into Egypt and, in November 1955, Syria began to negotiate for a similar arrangement. Russia set up diplomatic missions in Libya, Ethiopia, and the Sudan.

The Suez crisis of 1956 was closely connected with Soviet aims in Egypt and the Middle East as a whole. The increasing warmth of Soviet relations with Egypt led to the withdrawal of the American offer to finance the Aswan Dam project in the summer of 1956. This blow embittered Nasser against the West and was undoubtedly a major factor in inducing his government to nationalize the Suez Canal one week later. By invading the Suez Canal area to assert their claims the British and the French were also aiming a direct blow against Russian policy, since they hoped to overthrow Nasser's ostensibly pro-Soviet government. The desperate nature of the action incidentally showed how far the French and the British were prepared to go in order to counter Soviet infiltration in their traditional sphere of influence. Like the Americans and the Russians themselves at this time, they tended to overrate the extent of the Arab countries' pro-Soviet leanings. The political results of this nervousness on the part of the West temporarily played into the hands of the Russians, although Soviet propaganda gains from the Suez fiasco were offset by worldwide criticism of Russian intervention in Hungary at the same time.

Flushed with her diplomatic success in the Suez crisis, Russia began to abandon her former carefully moderated tone. China's attitude toward wavering uncommitted countries, increasingly aggressive since the Bandung Conference of 1955, was not imitated by the Soviet Union, but it did begin to hint that it viewed neutralism as a merely temporary stage on the road to Communism. This attitude was reflected in December 1957, when the Soviet Union took part in the Asian-African People's Solidarity Conference held in Cairo. By October 1958, caution was thrown to the winds and a meeting for Asian and African writers was arranged on Soviet territory, at Tashkent.

Political crises in Syria and Iraq in 1957 and 1958, respectively, brought out the true nature of Soviet long-term aims in the Middle East. Both the Syrian Government and the nation as a whole turned of their own accord to a strongly pro-Soviet attitude in 1957, culminating in the take-over of military control in August by a group of left-wing officers. The trend was naturally welcomed in the Soviet Union; it was unusual for another country to move voluntarily toward the Communist camp. The phenomenon was all the more remarkable in a country that had made great economic progress since the Second World War, and where no civil strife or coercion from an outside Communist power was involved.

High Russian hopes were shattered when Nasser proclaimed the union of Syria and Egypt within the United Arab Republic on February 1, 1958 (Egyptian troops had already landed in Syria in October of the preceding year). Nasser's move was as unexpected as Syria's sudden enthusiasm for Russia. It represented the first major setback for the USSR in the Middle East since the inauguration of the policy of peaceful coexistence. Anti-Communist elements in Syria had worked for union with Egypt. The Soviet press, which had obviously expected the threat to the left-wing regime in Syria to come from a capitalist power like the United States or Britain, kept a surprised silence for some days after the merger before hailing the new United Arab Republic. Only two years later—when Russian disillusionment with regard to some of the uncommitted nations had reached a lower level and there was no longer as much need to conciliate Egypt in the hope of future gain—was Soviet judgment pronounced:

> With the purpose of maintaining their control, the ruling circles of the Egyptian bourgeoisie strengthen their ties with the more reactionary forces in the Syrian region, carry out repressive

measures against the Communists and other democratic elements, thus weakening the Arab struggle against imperialism.[1]

In July 1958 a revolution occurred in Iraq. The pro-Western government was overthrown and a new regime set up under Abdul Karim Kassim. The news was acclaimed in Moscow, since the Iraqi coup dealt a mortal blow to the Baghdad Pact. The previous government had been the central link in the pro-Western states near Russia's southern borders. More than that, Iraq's geographical position among the Arab countries was crucial from the Soviet point of view. Situated a mere 150 miles from the southern Russian frontier, she controlled important oil resources that could be denied to the West, though they were of little use to Russia, who was anxious to export her own oil surplus. The Soviet Union also possessed an unusual lever of influence in Iraq through the Kurds, a race that was striving for national identity though it was scattered over Turkey, Syria, Iraq, Iran, and the southern tip of the Soviet Union. The Soviet Union supported the Kurds' national aims and sent several thousand Russian Kurds to Iraq after the revolution, together with military equipment and advisers.

Egypt, Syria, and, after the coup of 1958, Iraq, were all neutralist areas, yet the Soviet Union was not treating them equally by the time of the Twenty-first Congress in 1959. Having extended an open hand to all neutralist countries of the world since 1954 on the alleged principle of disinterested aid to any nation that was not capitalist, Russia gradually began to separate the sheep from the goats. Iraq remained a friend of the first order, since she appeared to be moving politically closer to the Soviet Union; but the United Arab Republic 'deceived' Russian hopes because earlier *rapprochement* was not succeeded by a further swing to the Communist side.

With the passage of time it became more obvious that the Soviet Union never regarded neutrality (e.g. in Austria's case) or neutralism (as practised in the United Arab Republic or India) as permanent legal and political standpoints, but merely as useful steps away from the capitalist camp on the way to Communism. For the Soviet Union neutrality and neutralism were dynamic concepts, not static resting places. In the Communist system inter-state allegiances are primarily organic, not legal: the actual status of neutral and neutralist countries means little to the Soviet Union (it has frequently confused the two); more important are such factors as identity of views and informal political relations.

[1] *Mezhdunarodnye Otnosheniia i Vneshniaia Politika SSSR*, p. 231.

It is necessary to understand the Soviet position in order to understand the essence of peaceful coexistence, which aims at keeping the committed capitalist adversary at bay until the rest of the non-Communist world is finally brought into line with the socialist camp. There is no question of allowing the world balance of forces to remain as it is. Imre Horvath, the Hungarian Foreign Minister in 1957, stated the Communist point of view succinctly; with regard to Austria he said: 'We approve of the neutrality of certain capitalist countries since it signifies that they do not join the imperialist military blocs created with a view to starting a war.' But tilting at Yugoslavia, he continued: 'The neutrality of a socialist country must be assessed not only from the point of view of peace but also from that of the cause of socialism. While a true neutrality on the part of a capitalist country means standing apart from the conquerors and those ready to go to war, the neutrality of a socialist country represents an underhanded attack on the cause of peace and socialism and its betrayal.'[1] Thus the Communist interpretation of neutrality deprives it of all detachment. In the words of Khrushchev during his state visit to Austria in 1960: 'Neutrality is not a mountain range which can isolate one from the outside world.'[2] Between the time of the Twentieth Congress and the present day the neutralist countries in the Middle East and Asia have come to realize the implications of this interpretation.

Soviet foreign policy in Asia between the Twentieth and Twenty-first Congresses was not marked by the bright hopes and subsequent disillusionment that brought convulsive excitement to the scene in the Middle East. Rather there was a calm extension of Soviet influence through further consultation and economic assistance on the basis of the solid groundwork built up before 1956. The situation was not complicated by the local revolutions and acute Great Power jealousies that sparked the tinder in the Arab countries.

While improving its relations with India, Burma, and Afghanistan, the three countries that had attracted most attention in the earlier period, the Soviet Union also looked further afield for new spheres of influence. Indonesia was an obvious choice. With the third largest population in Asia after China and India, vast natural resources, and a strategic geographical position on the main Asian trade routes, Indonesia was a great prize in the race for Asia. In particular her protracted quarrel with the Dutch over the ownership of western Irian

---

[1] Budapest Radio, June 3, 1957.
[2] *New York Herald Tribune* (European edition), July 7, 1960.

gave the Soviet Union the opportunity to exploit its anti-colonial propaganda machinery to the full.

The Soviet Union recognized the Indonesian Government in 1950, but diplomatic relations were only established in 1954. The Communist Party of Indonesia won thirty-nine seats in the 1955 elections, thus taking its place as one of the four major parties in the country. After the shift in Soviet policy from a 'hard' to a 'soft' line in Asia, the Indonesian party was assigned a leading role in co-ordinating Asian Communist parties. In the autumn of 1956 President Sukarno made a state visit to Moscow, and Indonesia received a 100-million-dollar loan from the USSR. In 1958 when the Celebes rose up in revolt against economic hardships and corruption in the central administration, the Soviet Union sent jet planes and ships to Sukarno as a gesture of moral support. (The United States Secretary of State, John F. Dulles, had shown some measure of sympathy for the rebellion.) In February 1960, Khrushchev staged another carefully-timed blow against American prestige by visiting Indonesia two months after President Eisenhower had bypassed the country on his goodwill tour of Asia.

The reaction of Indonesian political leaders to increased Soviet influence followed the pattern already adopted by Nehru in India and U Nu in Burma, except that religious resistance to Communism seemed to be stronger in Moslem Indonesia. In an article of April 1958, Muhammad Hatta, the former Vice-President, wrote that his country was 'prepared to accept technical, material and moral help from any country whatsoever, provided only that the donor government does not interfere in our domestic affairs or weaken or threaten our independence and sovereignty'; but he added, 'Generally speaking, the Indonesian people place their faith in religion, and religion is basically a dike against the spread of Communism.'[1]

By 1958 India was becoming more openly critical of some aspects of Soviet behaviour. Russia's rough treatment of neutralist Yugoslavia caused Nehru to comment that dogmatism appeared to be gaining the upper hand in Soviet foreign relations. At the same time the Indian Communist Party began to take a firmer line with regard to the Congress Party. In April 1958, Ajoy Ghosh, the Communist Party Secretary, asserted that the Congress Party was no longer strong enough to hold India together and that 'the unity of India can today be maintained only by strengthening the Communist Party and democratic forces'.[2] By the end of 1958 the Soviet ambassador in

[1] 'Indonesia Between the Power Blocs', *Foreign Affairs* (April 1958), pp. 481–2.
[2] *New Age* (April 13, 1958), p. 13.

Peking was pointing to the need for radical reform from below in India if the government proved incapable of carrying out its programmes. The end of the honeymoon period in Indian relations with international Communism was soon to be marked by Chinese aggression against India's northern frontiers.

In the period after the Twenty-first Party Congress, Soviet relations with the countries of the Middle and Far East scarcely deviated from the direction they had taken after 1955, except that they appeared to lose still more of their earlier warmth. At the Twenty-first Congress Khrushchev came out into the open against Arab nationalism and criticized Nasser for accusing the Egyptian Communists of anti-Arab subversion. The hardening of the Soviet position reflected the general disillusionment with the less-developed countries.

In 1954–5 the so-called 'national bourgeoisies' in the Middle and Far East were in many cases still struggling for their existence against hostile sections of the populace at home, or against foreign pressures. By 1959 rulers like Nasser were firmly in the saddle, with the result that the *mariage de convenance* between the Communists and the 'bourgeois' threatened to break up.

It seemed probable that Nasser's power would be enhanced by the extension of Arab unity in the form of some sort of federation with Iraq. In May 1959, Khrushchev made it clear that the Soviet Union did not favour any more unions between Arab states until they adopted governments of a more socialist hue. Soviet-Egyptian relations broke down in the spring of 1959, but were patched up again in the autumn with the help of a cultural agreement and Nasser's personal expression of gratitude for Soviet aid on the Aswan Dam project.

On balance the Soviet Union was still gaining sufficient advantage from its ties with the countries of the Middle and Far East by 1961 to make it worth while to maintain friendly contacts. By virtue of the political impetus to the left that had brought them to power in the first place, the bourgeois governments were still as much committed to follow a progressive line in their domestic economic and social programmes as they had been in the early years of their rule.

Countries like Indonesia were still haunted by their colonial past in a very real sense. Since 1957 the Soviet Union has been more patient than China in facing the political situation in the developing countries. The serious border incursions into India in the autumn of 1959 were an open sign of China's growing irritation with the 'national bourgeois' governments. China was now applying force against the country that had agreed to the five principles of peaceful coexistence with her at Bandung in 1955. Khrushchev's Asian tour in the spring of 1960 was in part intended to offset the bad impression caused by a fellow Communist country. Khrushchev studiously avoided any mention of the Sino-Indian conflict. Referring to India, Indonesia, and even capitalist Japan as co-equals of Communist China in the Asian area, he intimated that Mao Tse-tung would do well to keep on good terms with his country's neighbours.

The impact of China's 'harder' policy had fewer repercussions in the Middle East, which lay outside her immediate sphere of influence, but it was sufficiently influential to embarrass the USSR. When the Iraqi Communist Party seemed as though it might acquire representation in the government of Iraq in May 1959, Khrushchev restrained its efforts; it might have induced the frightened Iraqi bourgeoisie to call on Egypt to intervene, as had happened in Syria in 1957. To the revolutionary Chinese, these tactics smacked of betrayal. During the celebrations in Peking on the occasion of the tenth anniversary of the Chinese Communist victory, Syrian Communists who were present were egged on to accuse their government of fascist tendencies.

At this point we may examine Sino-Soviet relations after the Soviet Twentieth Party Congress in 1956. China's increasing influence on Soviet attitudes during these years has already been observed with regard to Communist bloc politics and the German problem. What were the reasons for Russia's growing nervousness of her Asian neighbour?

CHINA

By the end of 1957 Communist China had embarked on a new stage in her relations with the Soviet Union. In terms of both ideological and power status, she effected a rapid climb during 1956–7 in relation to the most important country of the socialist camp.

Khrushchev's attack on Stalin at the Twentieth Congress crippled the reputation of the camp's erstwhile ideological leader, and it was not until the Twenty-first Congress in 1959 that an attempt was made to elevate Khrushchev to the status of a major theoretician. In the interval the only possible claimant, on the basis of long experience and originality of thought, was Mao Tse-tung. The Twentieth Congress enhanced Mao's standing by officially adopting his 'soft' line of that time toward the under-developed countries of Asia, although Lenin and not Mao was referred to as the authority for the change in policy.

In terms of sheer power, China was still a long way behind the

Soviet Union even in 1959, but gratifying progress in domestic programmes, which was not accompanied by as much violence and social upheaval as had been the case in Soviet history at a comparable stage, was now linked with growing diplomatic prestige abroad within the Communist orbit. China scored a success as the mediator in the Soviet discussions with Eastern Europe in 1956–7.

By weighting the scales more heavily against revisionism than against Stalinist dogmatism in the appraisal of international Communist relations as expressed in the Moscow Declaration of November 1957, Khrushchev prevented a possible cleavage in the bloc between Soviet and Chinese oriented satellites. Early in 1958 China adopted a much 'harder' political line. If, in November 1957, Khrushchev had championed the claims of revisionist Poland and Hungary, then Stalinist Czechoslovakia, Bulgaria, and Albania might conceivably have forsaken Soviet for Chinese leadership in the following year. In the event Russia maintained her leadership, although by 1960 Albania had indeed transferred her allegiance to China.

Like Russia, though much more wholeheartedly, China reverted to a 'harder' line after an experiment in relaxation. Mao's attempt to appease the Chinese intelligentsia by means of the 'Hundred Flowers' campaign, initiated in February 1957, unleashed criticism of the government that was soon hushed by a return to orthodoxy; but the new line was not a diluted version of the original, as was the case in Russia and most of Eastern Europe. The result was a growing discrepancy between Soviet and Chinese policies. With an eye on Formosa, still occupied by hostile Chinese Nationalist forces, China now insisted that local wars could not be avoided, whereas the Soviet Union believed they could. In the summer of 1958 it seemed as though the Chinese managed to persuade Khrushchev, on a visit to Peking, to give in slightly to their point of view. After Khrushchev's departure the Chinese campaign against Formosa was sharpened, with the full backing of the Soviet press. Russia also withdrew her request for a summit meeting between the major powers. But Sino-Soviet differences over Eastern Europe remained unsolved.

Strong bonds held the Soviet Union and Communist China together in a largely hostile world, but by 1961 the differences in their stages of economic and political development threatened to sever these ties; the differences had led to incompatible points of view. China's lower level of economic wealth, her fresher revolutionary zeal, and her particular hatred of white imperialism all served to estrange her from her Communist partner. The rift grew steadily from 1956, when China maintained a relatively 'soft' policy, and widened even more quickly after 1958 and her reversion to a 'hard' policy at home and abroad.

Indications of the Sino-Soviet quarrel appeared first on the ideological plane. Although the practical consequences of the split were potentially enormous, the divergence of views was confined for the most part to battles of words between the protagonists and was rarely converted into actual power politics before the Twenty-second Party Congress in Russia.

The idealogical battle was all the more fierce in that it was conducted on several fronts. From 1958 to 1960 the struggle centred on the question of the Chinese commune system and the related subject of Soviet and Chinese proximity to Communism. After 1960 interest switched once more to foreign policy and the appraisal of Communist world strategy. In August 1958, the Chinese resolution on the formation of communes announced triumphantly that 'the attainment of Communism in China is no longer a remote future event'.[1] After some initial prevarication, Khrushchev challenged the Chinese claim in July 1959, in the course of a speech made in Poland. He said that China had a poor understanding of how to build Communism, and he drew attention to the failure of the commune idea in the Soviet Union during the period of War Communism (1917–21).

Khrushchev had three motives in attacking China. In the first place, if Mao's commune idea was allowed to go uncriticized, it would seem as though Chinese Communist ideology was taking the initiative from the Soviet Union and that China was likely to achieve Communism before the USSR. Secondly, the commune system could be offered to the less-developed areas of the world as being more suited to peasant societies than the Soviet system. Thirdly, as a result of the first two possibilities, the Soviet Union might lose its position as the political and economic model for the Communist bloc.

Sino-Soviet differences on another important problem, that of Communist world strategy, came to a head in June 1960, at the Bucharest conference of the twelve Communist governments. They arose from China's reluctance to abandon the Leninist view that war between capitalism and Communism was inevitable. This notion had been discarded by the Soviet Union at the Twentieth Congress in 1956. China viewed peaceful coexistence as a mistaken policy. Mao could still see nothing but hatred for Communism in the West, whereas Khrushchev claimed that there were 'progressive' as well as 'reactionary' circles in capitalist countries. On the strength of his

[1] *Peking Review* (September 16, 1958), p. 23.

opinion, Mao stressed once again that at least local wars were inevitable and should be encouraged by the Communist bloc if it was a case of supporting new countries against neo-colonialists. Furthermore he mistrusted the 'national bourgeois' governments in developing areas. He maintained that Communist parties would have a better chance of coming to power through force than by acquiescing to such governments.

The Bucharest conference issued a very short communiqué that barely concealed the Sino-Soviet quarrel. At the Moscow meeting of eighty-one Communist parties in November 1960—the largest of its kind ever held—the Soviet Union managed to hold out against the Chinese, who apparently received full support only from Albania. The declaration issued at the end of the conference reaffirmed that Communism could still triumph without resorting to war; its cautious tone reflected the Soviet view that the time had not yet come for a decisive showdown with capitalism. Nevertheless, every effort was made to accommodate the Chinese, short of reverting to a policy of war.

Although a mounting battle of words divided China from the Soviet Union, its effect on the practical execution of policies was still small. However, relations between the two protagonists cooled to such an extent that the Soviet Union refused to deliver atomic bombs to China and to set up a joint Sino-Soviet naval command in the Pacific. Russia also withdrew many of her technical experts from China. Nevertheless, the full implications of the clash between the Soviet and Chinese lines in domestic and foreign policies had yet to be felt in the wider sphere of international relations.

AFRICA AND LATIN AMERICA

We saw how Soviet foreign policy embarked on a major departure from its previous course in 1955 by applying Communist expansionist tactics—hitherto concentrated on geographical neighbours in the Euro-Asian land mass—to more distant countries like Egypt, cut off from Russia geographically and politically by the countries in the Baghdad Pact. Between 1959 and 1961 this trend was intensified by increasing Soviet attention to African and Latin American countries.

Mikoyan's visit to Cuba in February 1960 ushered in a new age of Soviet foreign policy and reflected the changing balance of world power. Until that time the capitalist camp headed by the United States had kept its hands off the Soviet sphere of influence in Eastern Europe, and Russia had done likewise in the Americas. Now the

Communists established close relations with an island that lay geographically as close to the United States as Formosa to mainland China. The Soviet Union declared a propaganda war on the shades of the Monroe Doctrine.

The close ties that grew between Fidel Castro's revolutionary government and the Soviet Union were significant in other ways. Cuba could be the key to the extension of Soviet influence in Latin America, a sub-continent that had remained virtually untouched by serious Communist subversion (although the Guatemalan revolution of 1954 had leaned sharply toward Communism before the United States intervened). The peculiar rapidity with which Cuba passed from her semi-colonial status to a quasi-Communist dictatorship no doubt gave encouragement to the Soviet leaders, who were becoming impatient with the stubborn non-alignment of the uncommitted nations in the Middle and Far East. The Cuban experience also lent weight to their argument with China as to the feasibility of winning areas of the world over to Communism without resorting to war.

In Africa the immediate opportunities for Communist expansion were not so bright, but the scope was even greater than in South America. Between 1959 and 1961 newly-independent sovereign states emerged in ever increasing numbers. Very few Communist parties existed on the African continent, and they had closer contact with the Communist parties of the ex-colonial powers than with Moscow, but Russia had the chance, as in Asia and the Middle East in the years after 1953, of projecting a favourable image of herself on unstable and often rather naïve governments only just released from the colonial yoke. The heady spirit of Bandung was in the air again, but this time it could perhaps be manipulated with a subtlety culled from earlier experience.

Soviet methods of wooing the emerging states included action in the United Nations in support of their claims for independence, early diplomatic recognition, and official exchanges accompanied by offers of aid and trade. The troubles in the Congo after its attainment of independence in 1960 provided the Soviet Union with an opportunity to fish in troubled waters; its failure to secure a foothold in the area was offset by its remarkable success in Cuba.

POLITICS AT THE SUMMIT

Throughout the period covered by this book, resistance by the West, and the United States in particular, was the chief obstacle to the fulfilment of Soviet designs abroad. For many years after 1945 the United

States considered taking action against Soviet expansion in Eastern Europe. When this notion faded, her efforts were devoted to countering Soviet influence in Asia, the Middle East, and subsequently in Africa and Latin America. After the Second World War the Soviet Union soon realized that the United States would lead the capitalist camp against it. Through Marxist conditioning the Soviet Union is apt to view world forces preponderantly in terms of economic power; this led to its early recognition of the American role and also to its acute sensitivity about comparison between the economic strength of Russia and the United States.

Soviet clear-sightedness on this score led to an adjustment of policy after 1945. Before the Second World War Britain and France had been the butt of Communist propaganda. From 1945 onwards it was the United States. The Declaration of the eighty-one Communist parties of December 1960 described the United States as 'the world's biggest exploiter, the main bulwark of world reaction and present-day colonialism, the international gendarme and the enemy of all the peoples'. But hatred and fear of its only rival for world domination inculcated a certain respect in the Soviet Union. America came to be viewed as the only power within the capitalist camp worth negotiating with on a serious basis. That was why in the autumn of 1959 the world viewed the incongruous spectacle of Khrushchev's state visit to the United States.

Apart from Mikoyan and Molotov, none of the top Soviet leaders had ever visited the United States. American acceptance of Khrushchev in the United States as a top-level negotiator on equal terms with President Eisenhower greatly benefited the Soviet Union, which still suffered from an inferiority complex in international affairs. Khrushchev toured the country and held confidential talks with Eisenhower at Camp David. The two men managed to break the ice of Soviet-American relations. Khrushchev's first direct impressions of American economic strength probably deterred him from taking rash action against the United States.

The heads of the British, French, Soviet, and United States governments met at Paris in May 1960, in a similar attempt to lessen international tension, particularly over the Berlin problem. The slight progress achieved during Khrushchev's American visit was obliterated at Paris by the Soviet Union's exposure of American observation flights over Russian territory in U-2 planes. Khrushchev considered that he had been misled by American overtures of goodwill. He accused President Eisenhower of personal duplicity and broke up the conference.

With the failure of summit diplomacy after Khrushchev's meeting with the new American President, John F. Kennedy, at Vienna in June 1961, the Soviet Union renewed its threat to sign a separate peace treaty with East Germany before the end of 1961. In August the East Germans began to seal off their sector of Berlin by constructing a wall between the East and West sectors of the city. In this way they succeeded in preventing the flight of thousands of refugees each month. By the end of our period, Soviet pressure on the West with regard to the German problem had not diminished. The Soviet defence budget was increased in July 1961, and on August 30th Russia resumed the testing of nuclear weapons in the atmosphere, though this has since been stopped.

Global disarmament was frequently the subject of top-level negotiations between the USSR and the major NATO powers—Britain, France, and the United States—between 1953 and 1961.

Soviet disarmament proposals have always been part and parcel of Soviet politico-military strategy. Until 1949 the United States had a monopoly of the atomic bomb. The Russians consequently strove to abolish all nuclear weapons. After 1953, when Malenkov announced the explosion of a Soviet hydrogen bomb, Soviet negotiators changed their tune. Not having any of their own long-range rockets, they tried to get American rocket bases dismantled. Finally when the first efficient Soviet ICBM was launched in 1957, the Soviet Union proceeded to advocate total disarmament, which would remove United States conventional armed forces from Europe and the Pacific and make the Soviet land area less vulnerable. Disagreement between the West and the USSR next centred on the former's insistence on establishing some form of international inspection system for detecting nuclear explosions and guarding against surprise attack *before* nuclear weapons could be banned and American overseas military bases abandoned. Today the intricacies of the disarmament problem remain enormous, as proven by the hundreds of international meetings that have been held on the subject in spite of such few concrete results.

During his visit to the United Nations General Assembly at New York in the autumn of 1960, Khrushchev put forward a grandiose scheme for disarmament. The armed forces of all states would be demobilized within four years and replaced by national militias that would not be allowed out of their own countries; neither would any military ships or aircraft be permitted to pass their own borders. If this plan were to be carried out, United States forces protecting Western Europe, the Middle East, and Asia from possible Soviet aggression would be incapacitated, leaving the Russian land mass invulnerable. The West rejected the Soviet idea.

Khrushchev's decision to attend the United Nations General Assembly in 1960 was motivated by the need for a good platform for his disarmament scheme, rather than by any respect for the United Nations as such. After 1953 he paid little more attention to the organization as an outlet for multilateral diplomacy than Stalin had done. Since the early post-war years the Soviet Union had kept up a scarcely veiled hostile attitude to the United Nations, which was more often than not seen as the tool of the 'international gendarme', the United States. This remained the Soviet view even after the West no longer had what the Soviet Union referred to as a 'mathematical majority' in the General Assembly. The Soviet Union attacked Dag Hammarskjöld, the Secretary-General of the United Nations after 1953, for giving too much scope to the United Nations in the interests of the West. In 1960-1 he was accused of promoting United States interests in the Congo and of overstepping his powers by sending troops to the area. He was also criticized for appointing a commission to investigate the troubled situation in Laos.

On the death of the Secretary-General in September 1961, the Soviet Union brought up the notion of three Secretaries-General, an idea it had first proposed at the fifteenth session of the General Assembly in October 1960. The aim of the *troika*, as it came to be called, was to protect the interests of all hues of political opinion in the world by having capitalist, Communist, and neutralist representatives at the head of the United Nations. From past experience, however, it seemed likely that such an arrangement would paralyse the executive arm more than ever. The Soviet veto had been exercised over one hundred times in the Security Council since the war, and there was little likelihood that it would not be wielded for similar purposes by a Communist Secretary-General.

However, the Soviet proposal had propaganda value for the uncommitted nations, which were rapidly gaining more influence in United Nations affairs and were flattered at the thought of being represented at the top level. The Soviet Union continued to use the United Nations meetings as a platform for its powerful propaganda machine, although it nearly always bypassed the organization when implementing actual policies. Ever since its first contribution to the United Nations Expanded Programme of Technical Assistance in July 1953, the Soviet Union had employed the organization as one of its instruments for courting the less-developed countries of the world and drawing attention to the political errors of the capitalist powers.

How had the new tenets of Soviet foreign policy expounded at the Twentieth Congress in 1956 been adjusted to reality by the time of the Twenty-second Congress in 1961?

The doctrine of peaceful coexistence at first surprised non-Communist observers by its implication of sweeping changes in the Soviet outlook, but it soon became clear that the USSR still intended, as in the past, to persist in the struggle against capitalism with every means in its power; henceforth, however, armed warfare on a large scale would not be employed. The notion of peaceful coexistence was not a major ideological innovation; it did not follow from Marxist-Leninist ideology as was claimed, but was rather a tactical manoeuvre based on several shrewd political calculations. The urgent need for some measure of international relaxation while the succession crisis of 1953–7 was resolved helped to mould the new concept, as did Russia's stronger position in international affairs. We have seen that by 1961 an idea that was at first interpreted in a broadly literal sense by some countries in the socialist camp was partly retracted by the Soviet Union, redefined in the light of the bitter experiences of 1956–7, and handed gingerly again to a bloc that could no longer include revisionist Yugoslavia. The attempt to scotch the thesis that violent revolutions and upheavals were the only paths to socialism survived the years in better shape. Parliamentary channels were dutifully adopted by Communist parties struggling for power throughout the world. But toward the close of the period covered by this book increasing impatience was being shown in some quarters. China was strongly contesting the Soviet assertion.

CHAPTER VII

SOCIAL CONTROLS

By 1961 persuasion had largely replaced coercion as the main instrument of government in the Soviet Union. We have seen this trend at work in the decline of the secret police and in the increased participation of the population in some sectors of the political process. While Stalin remained alive, he alone was the ruling force in politics: the interest groups were his tools for use at will. Khrushchev rehabilitated the party and thus made his own fortune as well, but he remained too dependent on the party to be able to manipulate it as arbitrarily as Stalin had done in the period after 1945.

In this chapter we shall trace the swing from Stalin's use of coercion to Khrushchev's use of persuasion which led to changes in Soviet social life.

The political history of a non-Communist democracy may be written with little or no reference to its social aspects and yet remain complete in itself. If the same treatment were accorded to a totalitarian society, the result would be an unfinished painting. In the Soviet Union politics has a far more direct influence on all spheres of life than it does in the West. The legal system, education, even religion, are servants of the regime, to which they are bound in a functional whole. Soviet lawyers are employed by the state to work out a new concept of neutrality for application to the uncommitted countries of the world, the whole educational system is revised in accordance with the political aims of the Soviet ruling élite; religious sentiment is revived during a time of crisis like the Second World War to cement patriotic feeling.

Thus a review of Soviet social institutions is not only interesting in itself, but also mirrors various trends in political development. We have seen this to be the case for the period 1945–53. It was no less so in the years after Stalin's death.

INSTRUMENTS OF COERCION

Dictatorial control over the Soviet population was one of the first aims of the Communist party after it came to power, and in the final analysis it remains as important an aim to this day. This should not be forgotten in the course of the discussion that follows. Nevertheless it is true that control is now being exercised in a far more subtle and less brutal fashion, and that this process has been speeded up considerably in recent times.

The decline of the secret police, the most notorious instrument of coercion in Stalin's time, has been described earlier in this book in its chronological setting. Reforms in the legal system and the army and the changing official attitude toward religious belief are dealt with below.

The Legal System

Article 112 of the Soviet Constitution states that 'judges are independent and subject only to the law', but the true situation is otherwise, and even the theory is belied to some extent by Article 126 of the Constitution, which stresses the vanguard role of the party in the Soviet state. The position is given more correctly in a history of Soviet law that asserts that judges are dependent 'from the state or from the policy of the party and the government, since the court is an organ of power, and its activity is one of the aspects of state government'.[1] Important legislation requires the signature of a Central Committee secretary as well as that of the President of the Supreme Soviet: the economic decentralization of 1957 entailed significant legal changes, but they were arranged by the Central Committee before the Supreme Soviet met to endorse them. At the lower levels, so long as a one-party system persists in the USSR, defence attorneys in political cases are open to great personal risk if they attempt to produce an objective brief.

Although the party still maintains ultimate control over the law and could revert to more arbitrary action of the kind that characterized the Stalinist era, it is true that legal administration has been normalized to a certain degree since 1953. The curtailment of the supra-legal powers of the secret police led to the abolition of the latter's special courts in September 1953. In 1955 Soviet procurators were given greater powers of supervision over legal administration. Procurators occupy a position of special importance in the Soviet Union. As in the continental European legal system, their duty is to carry out impartial investigations of crime and make reports to the courts on their findings. Their opinions carry great weight, particularly in a political system that wields tremendous power through its state officials. In most legal cases, the procurators' advice to the judges

---

[1] M. V. Kozhevnikov, *Istoriia sovetskogo suda 1917–1956 gody*, 2nd ed. (Moscow, 1957), p. 277.

may aid the latter to arrive at an impartial decision, but whenever political offences are concerned (and the definition of a political offence is still wide in Russia), the procurators are apt to become mere instruments of state policy.

The slightly more liberal atmosphere in legal procedure was reinforced by a 1958 revision of the criminal law codes; this removed certain anomalies and some of the harsher elements of injustice. The measure that brought the most relief was the insistence that criminal proceedings be in complete compliance with the legal codes: previously, judges had been able to convict enemies of the regime on charges that had no basis in the law. Loopholes favouring arbitrary action still remained, however, as several of the provisions in the new codes were vaguely worded. Moreover, in 1961 sentences for economic crimes against the state were made more severe; for instance, currency speculation was now punishable by death.

Khrushchev's chief aim in promoting legal reform was the same as that of his general policy: to reject the darker aspects of the Stalinist past. By laying stress on 'socialist legality', Khrushchev implied that, unlike Stalin, he had come to power and was ruling by lawful methods. Throughout the years 1953–61 numerous bodies were appointed to investigate the cases of persons unjustly punished during Stalin's lifetime, and many of his victims were freed from prison or else posthumously rehabilitated.

In promoting legal reform, however, Khrushchev kept other motives in view. In accordance with the Engels theory of the withering away of the state, attention was paid to the order in which the various categories of law would dissolve with the approach of a true Communist society. At the Twenty-first Congress Khrushchev included legal institutions among the state organs that were to undergo this process. Pashukanis, a leading Soviet lawyer in the 1930s, had thought that civil law could be lopped off the state system, leaving economic legislation to regulate all relations. This notion was picked up once more in the late 1950s: lawyers debated whether people's personal affairs could slip from under the net of legal control so that, for instance, divorce could be dealt with outside the courts.

On a more practical level Khrushchev spurred on the process of dissolution by handing over various legal duties to non-professional bodies. Instead of the customary militia, people's 'vigilantes' now keep order in the streets of some provincial towns. In 1958 interest centred around the 'comrades' courts', disciplinary committees of laymen sitting in judgment on their fellows. These courts dealt mainly with minor infringements of labour discipline, acting as restraints on the workers in place of the much harsher labour laws that were partly abrogated after 1953. Until May 1961, the comrades' courts were supposed to be selected by the trade unions or local government organs, but the party no doubt had the last say in many cases. Again this was in line with Khrushchev's policy of strengthening party influence in all sectors of Soviet life. He withdrew some sectors of judicial procedure from the party's grasp and placed them ostensibly under the control of the general population; however, party members comprise the backbone of the masses and persuade or coerce them in the manner prescribed from above by the Central Committee. Thus in promoting the eventual withering away of the state, the party is at the same time maintaining its say as to how the law is to be administered.

The Army

The armed forces have played a less significant role in Soviet life than might be imagined, given the dictatorial nature of politics. They have rarely been used as an instrument of active coercion in the domestic arena, except in times of civil or international war. Troops were employed to safeguard the internal Soviet system during peacetime, but they were controlled by the security organs, not by the military. After the Second World War the Red Army's main task besides defence was to control the new Soviet satellites. Neither Stalin nor Khrushchev gave the Red Army a primary part in domestic affairs, and particularly after 1957 it appeared to play a passive role under the thumb of the party.

In the purely military field, its prestige was enormously enhanced by the Second World War, but this was not accompanied by a comparable rise in political influence. The reason for this was undoubtedly the close control that the party constantly exercised over the ranks of the military since the early days of the Soviet regime, and which it has never relaxed until the present day. Party supervision is exercised through special party representatives in the army: it was claimed in 1955 that 77 per cent of all servicemen were party or Komsomol members.[1] Top-ranking military personnel were permitted to occupy responsible posts in the highest party organs but were not encouraged to take a decisive part in political decisions. We have seen that at a moment of national crisis, during the 'anti-party group' struggle of 1957, the army was called in to play a secondary and fleeting political role, but that was all.

Just as the demise of the 'anti-party group' was accompanied by

[1] *Pravda* (February 9, 1955).

the encroachment of the party on the influence of the state bureaucracy and the economic hierarchy, so Zhukov's fall in the winter of 1957 was followed by an even further weakening of the military apparatus. Political controls in the army were immediately fortified. The reduction of the armed forces announced in January 1960, besides reflecting the shift of emphasis from conventional to atomic weapons, aimed a blow at the corporate influence of the military. As a result of the reform, nearly half the army officers were scheduled to be demobilized—a move that gave the party an opportunity to rid the forces of non-desirable political elements. In the spring and summer of 1960 many junior officers were promoted into the upper ranks, where there had been some muted opposition to party influence from other men besides Zhukov. At the present time it seems highly unlikely that the army will throw up a Soviet Bonaparte.

In an inconspicuous way, the armed forces serve as an instrument of persuasion in the interests of the Communist regime. Although the officer class is now largely recruited from the ranks of the intelligentsia, compulsory military service remains a useful tool of social and national integration in a multi-lingual state. During the Stalin era the army also supplemented the education of millions of peasant recruits, but this task has diminished with the raising of the school-leaving age and the accelerated urbanization of the masses.

Anti-Religious Measures

The two instruments of coercion so far considered serve the same purpose in any twentieth-century state system, although their relation to the government is very different in the Soviet Union. Turning now to the application of political coercion with regard to religious belief, we come upon a distinctive aspect of the Soviet totalitarian system, one in which men's minds as well as their bodies are subject to political control. The distinction only applies to this century, however; *cuius regio, eius religio* applied to all of Europe at one time.

Religion in the USSR is controlled by the state just as completely as are the law and the military. All forms are openly discouraged and discrimination is practised against their followers. Atheist propaganda is zealously disseminated by the party in order to propagate the Marxist-Leninist anti-religious creed. Official opposition to religious faith stems from Marxist tenets, but it receives further stimulation from the knowledge that it is grappling with a rival ideology no less all-embracing and demanding than Marxism itself. The Soviet Communist party still has reason to fear the influence of religion in

Russia. In 1958 a conservative estimate put the number of practising Orthodox Christians in the USSR between twenty and thirty million,[1] or more than the total membership of the Soviet Communist party. This figure does not take into account followers of the twelve other main religious faiths practised in the USSR.

The strength of Soviet believers does not of course reside in their material influence on the course of events, but in the fact that after more than forty years of effort the regime has not succeeded in winning over the minds of many of its subjects on a vital point of Communist ideology. The Soviet regime has had amazing success in transforming society, but in this and other ways human nature remains as impervious as it did in the wake of other great historical revolutions.

Communism aims at dispensing with fixed moral standards. In Marxist terms morality is a phenomenon which changes its values with the evolving economic basis of society. But in a state subjected to enormous upheavals in times of both war and peace since 1941, and indeed since the Bolshevik victory in 1917, large numbers of Russians have felt the psychological and spiritual need to cling to some faith with permanent moral values. Religious sentiment is strongest among the peasants, weaker in the lower social strata in the towns, and probably least active in the ranks of the intelligentsia. Women account for roughly 70 per cent of all believers and keep the flame of religion alive in their children and grandchildren.

The Russian Orthodox Church joined in the universal adulation of Stalin during his later years. As a useful state tool during the war it had been allowed to maintain a fraction of its former strength; for this small mercy it was grateful to the dictator who might have crushed it completely. After Stalin's death Russian Christians suffered somewhat less persecution for a time due to the weakening of the secret police, which had been the chief agent for intruding into people's private lives. The official body of the Church also gained a little more freedom in its relations with churches abroad after the initiation of peaceful coexistence as the mainspring of Soviet foreign policy, but it still had to remain a subservient handmaiden of state interests, just as it had been during the Second World War. Cordial exchanges between Russian and Yugoslav churchmen, for instance, were only encouraged during those periods when the Soviet party had an interest in refurbishing inter-party and state relations.

On the domestic scene the offensive against the Church suddenly became more intense in the summer of 1954. Anti-religious articles in the press took on a bitter tone. This new wave of persecution appeared

[1] *International Review of Missions* (October, 1958), pp. 442-3.

to be due in part to the return to neo-Leninism, with its accent on atheist militancy, and in part to policies associated with Khrushchev. So long as he had to face political opposition, especially from Bulganin and Zhukov, who did not approve of violent action against the Church, his hands were somewhat tied. But by the late 1950s he was in a position to implement his purpose. Atheist propaganda was stepped up once more. In 1960 G. Karpov, the chief Soviet supervisor of the Orthodox Church, was replaced by a younger and stricter man, while the official who occupied a corresponding position in the Church also gave up his job. The reasons for Khrushchev's particular antagonism to the Church were obscure, but perhaps they were connected with his general suspicion of all intellectual trends and his personal reliance on a pragmatic approach to life. Being in closer contact with the nation than Stalin ever was, especially with the rural regions through his frequent travels around the USSR, he no doubt realized the extent to which religious feeling still survived.

INSTRUMENTS OF PERSUASION

Coercive methods of rule were an absolute necessity in pre-war Russia if a universally feared and widely hated dictator was to maintain his grasp over the nation. Military victory in 1945, however, brought Stalin some measure of personal popularity; and it is interesting to note that in the early post-war years he could afford to rely on both repressive and persuasive methods in reconstructing the battered political system. His judicious mixture of violence and more gentle methods was described in Chapter II of this book.

After Stalin's death both Malenkov and Khrushchev tried to gain popularity for their individual causes. The secret police, the most hated instrument of coercion, was soon shorn of much of its influence. The legal system and the army were brought under closer party control, and the former purged of many of its Stalinist features. Khrushchev made good use of his popularity on his way to supreme power, and as the first man among the party leadership to denounce Stalin's arbitrary form of government, he became the champion of 'socialist legality'. Once Khrushchev had opened the doors to liberal trends, however, he discovered that both within the Soviet Union and in East Europe the subjugated populations were inclined to want reform at a faster pace than their masters did. Political counteraction in the shape of renewed coercion would have made Khrushchev look a traitor to his word. He was driven to it in Hungary in 1956, but in general he confined himself to less drastic measures.

Even in post-Stalinist Russia it remained a vital necessity to convince the people of the justice of one-party rule and Communist ideology in order to preserve the forms of totalitarian government; otherwise the floodgates of free thought would be opened, leading inevitably to the fragmentation of the monolithic political structure. Khrushchev paid particular attention to instruments of persuasion like state education and mass communication. An anti-intellectual himself, he showed considerable toughness in dealing with the supervision of men's minds, although he was the first to recommend paring the claws of state coercion in general terms. This feature of his character may explain his hard line on religious matters and his peculiar attitude to education, described below. At the same time he was also responsible for streamlining the organs of propaganda, especially the Soviet press.

The treatment of post-Stalin developments in what the author has called the instruments of persuasion includes a survey of the educational system and its most brilliant by-product, Soviet prowess in the sciences, followed by a discussion of the role of ideology among the people and its expression in mass communication and Soviet literature.

Education
Until 1958 secondary education in the Soviet Union for children between the ages of seven and seventeen was divided into ten grades. Education was compulsory until the age of fourteen, but many pupils finished the ten-grade course. Higher education was provided by over thirty-three state universities and eight hundred institutes, nearly all of them concentrated in the large urban centres. Extension study courses for persons already employed also played a considerable role.

The accent in university syllabi remains decidedly on lectures, the actual number of instruction hours per year being between 1,000 and 1,300, which is about twice as high as in the United States. The system leads to overstrain, and many students do not have time to read the excellent textbooks, which are plentiful in the Soviet Union and include the latest learning from abroad, sifted and translated by an organization like the Institute of Scientific Information. Most of a student's attention is devoted to his special subject, but between a fifth and a tenth of his time is given to political education, with a maximum of 3 per cent given over to sport. At the end of his course, which is usually a five-year one, a Soviet-trained university chemist, for example, is the academic equal of an American chemist with an MS degree.

In a country like the Soviet Union, state planning would be disrupted if graduates chose their own jobs and moved about the republics from one job to another at their own free will. In Stalin's time Soviet manpower was compelled to obey state needs under the pressure of harsh labour laws. In 1956 a law of 1940 preventing workers from changing their jobs without permission was repealed, but an enactment of 1955 still obliged specialists with higher education to stay for a short period in the posts to which they were assigned on finishing their university courses. This law was not as harsh as might appear, since most of those affected by it had received a virtually free state education, which (as is not always the case in the West) automatically ensured them higher salaries later on in life. Furthermore, after 1953 the carrots of financial advantage and prestige were used more often than naked compulsion in order to attract students into areas where they would be of most use to the state.

In 1955 the number of pupils graduating from the secondary schools was 750,000, compared with 232,000 in 1939, two figures that in themselves pointed to the enormous strides made in Soviet education since the Second World War. Over 60 per cent of Soviet university graduates were engineers or scientists, compared with 25 per cent in America. The proportion of science and engineering graduates in the USSR was approximately the same as or slightly higher than in the United States with regard to the relative industrial populations of the two countries, but this does not take into account post-graduate training and various other sources of technical manpower, which were more extensive in the Soviet Union.

Specialization, particularly on the scientific side, was one of the outstanding features of the Soviet educational system by the time of the Khrushchev era. The usual twenty to thirty branches of study taught in both Western and Soviet universities are subdivided in the USSR into microscopic areas, so that it is possible for an engineer to graduate as an expert in flat surface structures or a certain type of bridge construction only. A highly specialized labour force of this nature is easy to manipulate for the purposes of a planned economy, but it often leads to intellectual stagnation, as no less a figure than Ilia Ehrenburg pointed out at the time of the educational reform of 1958. The enormous concentration on scientific subjects in secondary schools tends to lead to mental constipation by the time students are preparing to enter the universities. The rather narrow utilitarian approach to education in the effort to oil the wheels of Russia's prolonged industrial revolution may also lead to the impoverishment of the Soviet citizen's humanistic background.

The goal of providing ten years of secondary education for every Soviet child was introduced at the Nineteenth Congress in 1952 and stressed once more at the Twentieth Congress. Complete courses were made more accessible for the children of workers and peasants by abolishing tuition fees and introducing a certain number of less purely academic subjects into the curriculum. During the same period, however, the number of places in higher institutions remained almost at the same level, and, more surprisingly, little attention was devoted to providing suitable jobs for the growing numbers of young people with full secondary education. The fact was that the great postwar expansion of Soviet education had in some ways outrun the nation's economic resources.

Attention was drawn to these difficulties in the press and through public discussion in the summer and autumn of 1958. Khrushchev published a memorandum on education on September 21st, which was followed on November 16th by the Theses of the Central Committee and the Council of Ministers. The definitive law of December 25th entitled 'On the Strengthening of the Links between School and Life and on the Further Development of the System of Public Education in the USSR' incorporated most of the ideas put forward in the two previous documents.

As a result of the educational reform the idea of universal ten-grade secondary education was to be abandoned over the following four or five years. The system was replaced by compulsory education for eight years only, in conjunction with reinforced polytechnical training schemes for those pupils who no longer took the ten-year course. At the university level, students were obliged to spend some of their time in practical work apart from their academic studies, but they could usually choose jobs that were connected in some way with their special interests.

The 1958 reform was partly intended to alleviate the excessive demand for university places and to cut down the number of young people educated to too high an academic standard to fit in with the requirements of the economy. The expanded polytechnical courses were worked out with an eye on the targets of the Seven-Year Plan, for which more skilled workers as opposed to experts with university training were urgently needed. Even in 1954, four years before the educational reform got under way, the ratio of experts to semi-professional persons was as high as 1 to 1·3. Too many Soviet students (and their parents) considered that 'they need not grow potatoes or milk cows';[1] they fully recognized the economic and prestige value of

[1] Khrushchev in *Pravda*, 1956.

higher training in a country with so much respect for education.

The 1958 reform also had political and ideological overtones: they could scarcely be absent in the Soviet Union with regard to an area of such vital importance for the future. The connection between ideology and politics was close. In the *Communist Manifesto* Marx had looked forward to the formation of an ideal society in which the division between intellectual and physical labour would be abolished. Khrushchev was adding his brick to the foundations of Soviet Communism by sending students to the factories and the farms. But he was also doing more than that. By hacking down the barriers between the systems for training workers of the mind and those for training the body, he was aiming a direct blow at the Soviet intelligentsia as a class. No better evidence of this aim could be given than the opposition to Khrushchev's memorandum from the doyen of the intellectual élite, A. N. Nesmeianov, the President of the Academy of Sciences. In the definitive law on the reform, some of Khrushchev's ruder blows against the student class were softened in deference to criticism of this kind, but the core of his proposals remained unaltered.

Khrushchev had his own reasons for weakening the corporate power of the Soviet intelligentsia. He was a self-made man with little formal education. His impatience with academic learning came to the surface in his rough treatment of Soviet writers, a treatment much less liberal than that proposed by Malenkov. Most of Khrushchev's opponents in the 'anti-party group' had closer affiliations with the intelligentsia than he had, both through their superior education and through their jobs in the government bureaucracy and their membership in the economic élite. At the time of the June crisis of 1957 it was clear that large numbers of students were sympathetic toward members of the 'group', especially Malenkov and Shepilov. Khrushchev, on the other hand, characterized its members as 'Marxist bookworms'.[1]

On more general political grounds, Khrushchev viewed the increasing influence of the Soviet intelligentsia in a better-educated and more technically complicated state structure as being nearly as serious a threat to the continued supremacy of the party apparatus as the encroachment of the government bureaucracy and the economic interest group. In many ways the danger came from the same source, since the latter two interest groups drew on the intelligentsia for their recruitment needs.

[1] *Le Monde* (July 14, 1957).

Science

It is often forgotten that the Soviet Union inherited a flourishing scientific tradition from the Tsarist past. Nearly all branches of science have included Russians of great merit, of whom the best-known in the West are probably the chemist D. I. Mendeleev (1834–1907) and the physiologist I. P. Pavlov (1849–1936). The upheaval caused by the Revolution disrupted intellectual work of any nature for a time, and the educational system suffered likewise, but by the Khrushchev era Soviet scientific education ranked second to none in the world.

Like everything else in the Soviet Union, science is closely controlled by the government. A committee on technology attached to the Council of Ministers advises the government on the allocation of men and funds for scientific projects throughout the country, while the famous Academy of Sciences directs basic research, both in the natural sciences and the humanities. The academy consists of the Soviet intellectual élite and wields great power through its close contact with the central authorities. It supervises the activity of well over 150 scientific research institutions and is allocated a large budget of unknown dimensions by the state.

The advantages of centrally directed scientific projects are obvious when one thinks of the waste and unnecessary rivalry in the United States. Given the enormous cost of present-day scientific research, even the two wealthy super-powers must tighten their purse strings in order to finance vital programmes. At the same time the Soviet system has its drawbacks. In the recent past there have been cases where significant Soviet breakthroughs in science have not been followed up immediately by further research, simply because the central administration can only keep in close touch with a limited number of bodies, most of them research institutes; and work which is not brought to their notice bears no fruit. For the same reason most of the best scientific studies in the Soviet Union have been carried out in these institutes and not in the universities, where the combination of teacher and student provides the ideal method of transferring knowledge to future generations. The Soviet Union has realized the disadvantages of over-centralization; in 1959 the Academy of Sciences approved a decentralized system of administering and planning scientific research.

Even Soviet science had to conform to ideological precepts in the rarefied atmosphere of Stalinist Russia. The Lysenko affair, described in Chapter II, was the most notorious example of this. Its harmful influence still permeates intellectual circles today: the President of the Academy of Sciences admitted not long ago that research in experimental biology remains in a stagnant state. Nevertheless intellectual honesty could occasionally prevail even before Stalin's death, as was shown in 1951 when a theory on the nature of cosmic rays was correctly refuted by Soviet scientists with the approval of the party, although the so-called discovery could have had propaganda value for Soviet science on a short-term basis. The period from 1945 to 1953 was in no sense a Dark Age for Soviet science as a whole. It was during these years that Russia began the intensive research on missiles that led to her later advantage over the United States. Scientists still disagree as to whether the Soviet Union or America was the first to explode a thermonuclear device in 1953, at a time when the post-Stalin thaw in the intellectual field had not yet taken place.

The details of the thaw in science after 1953 are not as well known as those relating to the literary world—partly because a trend of this nature is much easier to trace in writing and the arts, partly because despite incidents like the Lysenko affair, science is generally less subject to ideological pitfalls than literature. By 1957 it was clear that Soviet mathematicians and physicians, their prestige enhanced by mounting successes, were in a position to make a stand against what they considered to be excessive government control over the Academy of Sciences. They then pointed out that although a majority vote by academy members was supposed to direct research activities, in actual fact the latter were always decided on by the government beforehand. This resulted in wasted resources and inefficiency. Forthright criticism of this nature could only have come from men who were already sure of their worth to the state and were not afraid to take an independent line.

When the first earth satellite went into orbit on October 4, 1957, the non-Soviet world at last gave public recognition to the amazing development of postwar Soviet science. Behind the spectacular performance lay a wealth of solid achievement. In order to send the *sputnik* into space a very high level of expertise was required in mathematics, physics, chemistry, metallurgy and other fields, not to speak of skilful co-ordination among these various branches of science. The military as well as the scientific significance of this *sputnik* and its successors added to the psychological shock that reverberated in the West, and especially in the United States.

The effect of the venture was all the more shattering in that the full force of Soviet propaganda was employed to extol it. In 1955 the United States and Russia announced their plans for launching satellites. The American press thereafter was full of optimistic forecasts with regard to its national programme, but Soviet newspapers kept silent until the announcement of the *sputnik*, when the full blast of totalitarian propaganda was turned on for the benefit of the Soviet nation and the rest of the world.

The background to the launching of the *sputnik* is interesting. The United States employed German rocket scientists of the calibre of Wernher von Braun directly after the war, but only started on a large-scale missile project in 1953. The Soviet Union on the other hand continued to experiment after 1945 on the adaptation of their admirable wartime artillery and *katiushi* (short-range rockets launched from the back of military trucks) for use as missiles. The large size of Soviet rockets was due to a wrong technical judgment made at a time when it was considered impossible to construct small hydrogen bombs. In the long run the error proved to be an asset, since larger boosters could be fitted to the rockets, which were roomy enough to take bulky electronic equipment originally designed for military bombers. This mixture of skill and luck, combined with strong political and economic backing from a government that could prevent its resources from being used for raising the low standard of Soviet living, enabled Russia to outpace the United States in this field. The American government had to operate its space programme as part of a free enterprise economy. It was often hampered by competitive lobbying by industry and the lack of centralized control, at least in the early years.

The cost of the Soviet space programme is enormous. The American government has estimated that 40 billion dollars will be required to put a man on the moon. The Soviets may well use the same amount. Both countries now have the economic means to fulfil their programme. In 1957 the Soviet Union proved its scientific brilliance in one field only, but there is good reason to believe that the high level of scientific education, attracting the best brains in the USSR, will produce other major scientific achievements in the future.

Ideology
So far in this book we have noted the influence of ideology on the decision-making process only at the highest level in domestic and foreign policy. Its presence is also felt among the population as a whole. In the schools and universities, Soviet youth is submitted to special courses in Marxist-Leninist theory and examined on them. Communist theory permeates all textbooks: a subject like Soviet history may have to be learned anew in every generation, according

to the requirements of the party line; and the Lysenko case showed that the sciences were no more immune than the arts in this respect. Membership of the Young Communist League brings benefits like reduced prices, free holidays and better opportunities for future careers. At the same time it conditions the thought processes of those who join it.

Passing from the student to the adult world, the Russians are still fed on an abundance of ideological literature provided by state-controlled literature and the press. They remain virtually cut off from non-Communist opinion through the censorship of foreign writing and the slender chances of travel abroad. Accustomed by national tradition to submit to autocratic rule, they appear to offer little resistance to ideological indoctrination, although indifference is a rather more common trait. It is difficult for a non-Soviet citizen to judge the extent to which ideology plays a positive as opposed to a passive role in everyday life. Does the average Soviet citizen approach Communist ideology with the straightforward fervour of a Christian during the Middle Ages or with the Victorian's half-sincere, half-hypocritical conviction that churchgoing was good both for the soul and for trade?

There is little doubt that the generation of Communists that reached intellectual maturity before the Revolution—and part of the generation now between the ages of 45 and 60, which spent much of its adult life in the Stalin era—were raised on an ideal that gave them a purpose in life and a belief. The younger generation, or rather that part of it which has come to the attention of the non-Soviet world, is more difficult to understand. It has been nurtured entirely under Soviet conditions and has received a solid grounding in Marxist theory, but it has felt more than a breath of the post-Stalin pragmatism that has influenced high politics, the economic outlook, and the literary scene. At the same time the Twentieth Congress gave fresh impetus to theoretical study through the introduction of neo-Leninist principles, and the Twenty-first and Twenty-second Congresses gave evidence of renewed interest in the birth of actual Communism in the USSR.

A case might be made out for maintaining that if Soviet influence and Marxist ways of thought were withdrawn from Eastern Europe after only twenty years' impact, Communist ideology imposed from abroad would leave no greater residue than had Prussian methods on the Polish mind or Turkish civilization on the Serbs. But half a century of experience based to a large extent on the application of a theory, which, although German in origin, has grown deep into the national heart, has left indelible traces on the mind of the Soviet people. The semi-religious ardour of the earlier years of the Soviet regime may have cooled somewhat, so that ideology must wrestle harder than before with the pressing facts of life in an atmosphere of increasing worldliness, but Communist ways of thinking remain 'secreted in the interstices'[1] of the system, just as Western ideas of democracy do in the United States and Western Europe.

Mass Communications

As Hitler knew so well, the press and the radio have proved to be the greatest boons of the twentieth century to leaders of totalitarian societies. Mass communications have been the main conditioning force of opinion in the USSR. Khrushchev has called the national press the 'furthest-reaching weapon' for influencing the people. The Soviet government pays more attention than any other nation in the world to methods of disseminating information and commenting on it. Lenin referred to himself as a journalist in his passport, and Stalin and Molotov carried on the tradition by becoming editors of *Pravda*. The importance of the press has increased with the years. In 1917 roughly three-quarters of the population could neither read nor write; by 1961 the illiteracy rate was one of the lowest in the world. Furthermore, the partial replacement of coercion by persuasion after the death of Stalin induced the Soviet leaders to take a livelier interest in the propaganda machinery, which remained wholly within their grasp.

Mass communications in the Soviet Union are controlled by the agitation and propaganda section of the Central Committee Secretariat. In addition to supervising the kind of media to be found in the West, this body sees to the distribution of wall-sheets in factories, farms and public places, and organizes the activities of 'oral agitators', who spread the party line by word of mouth among their fellow-men. All press, radio and television editors are ultimately responsible to *Agitprop* for what they publish. The news material they handle is arranged in accordance with general party directives, the requirements of the censor, and specific instructions on matters of topical interest. Unlike their Western counterparts, they are free from economic competition and financial troubles, and so do not have to give the public what it will pay for; but they must take care to comply with political direction from above. Their influence is very great. The number of all newspapers in the USSR rose from 8,000 in 1952 to

[1] An expression used by A. Ulam in an article entitled 'Soviet Ideology and Foreign Policy', published in *World Politics* (Center of International Studies; Princeton University, January 1959).

9,936 in 1958, and their circulation from forty to fifty-eight million over the same period. The daily circulation of *Pravda* alone was five and a half million in 1956.

Significant changes have taken place in the Soviet press since Stalin's death. The external form of newspapers has been made more attractive. Photographs and witty captions now supplement long, unbroken columns of stultifying and repetitive propaganda. *Komsomolskaia Pravda* and especially *Izvestiia* under the editorship of A. Adzhubei, Khrushchev's son-in-law, both benefited from the new look. In some ways the actual content of the press has altered too. More space has been given to foreign news and to non-political items. The increasing sensitivity of the regime to public opinion can also be traced in Soviet newspapers. In Stalin's time the newspapers acted almost entirely as retailers of political orders from above, printing government and party decrees, legal documents and diplomatic reports. Recently more space has been given to public discussion of innovations like the reform of education and the abolition of the Machine Tractor Stations. Letters of complaint appear with increasing frequency and range over many subjects, many of them taboo before 1953. For example, the cry for consumer goods is often voiced: 'Rockets, rockets, rockets!—who needs them now! For the time being to hell with the moon; let me put something better on my dinner table instead.'[1] The assistant editor of *Izvestiia* went so far in January 1960 as to suggest that Soviet editors should themselves take the initiative in choosing topics for discussion in the press without waiting for ideas from the government. This idea does not appear to have been acted upon, but it is obvious that Khrushchev discovered in the press a useful method for sending up trial balloons in order to gauge public opinion and take political action accordingly.

Literature

Whereas the press, safely under centralized government control, has remained a faithful ally of the regime in its propaganda campaigns, the literary world has turned out to be an unruly child. As an instrument of persuasion in the hands of Zhdanov before 1953 it played a moderately successful role in the eyes of the political leaders, but after that time took so much of the leaders' time in being persuaded to conform that it was of limited value as a medium for influencing the general reading public along orthodox party lines.

Stalin's death was followed by signs of ferment among Soviet

[1] From a letter sent to *Komsomolskaia Pravda*, June 11, 1960. The writer was severely rebuked for his attitude in the same edition of the newspaper.

intellectuals and writers, although cultural problems did not figure as largely on the stage of high politics as they had done under Zhdanov in 1946-8. The end of the Stalin regime was followed by two consecutive waves of what appeared to be a spontaneous revolt against the bonds imposed by Zhdanov: the first broke in the autumn of 1953, the second in 1956. They were separated by an attempt on the part of Khrushchev and the party apparatus to crush or at least subdue the first wave. In 1953 Soviet artists tried to infuse their work with human values that had been neglected or frowned upon in Stalin's time. By 1956 they were bold enough to embark upon a programme of social and even political criticism of a very limited nature.

In October 1953, speeches containing definite liberal tendencies were made at a meeting of the Board of Soviet Writers. These were followed by a spate of literary works in which the cardboard virtues of the Soviet hero were replaced by sincere attempts to portray human nature. Plays and poems predominated, since they could be written more quickly than novels. It was the first part of Ilia Ehrenburg's novel *The Thaw*, however, that gave a name to the new phenomenon and set the critical tone of the period:

> An author is not a piece of machinery registering events. An author writes a book, not because he is a member of the Union of Soviet Writers and may be asked why he has published nothing for so long. An author does not write a book because he has to earn a living. An author writes a book because he finds it necessary to tell people something of himself, because he is pregnant with his book, because he has seen people, things, and emotions that he cannot help describing. . . .

The counter-attack was not long in coming. In January 1954, *Literaturnaia Gazeta* reiterated the old Stalinist attitude and in May the central press organs and other literary journals entered the lists. In October 1954, the Writers' Congress reaffirmed the orthodox party line, which was adhered to more or less until Khrushchev's secret speech to the Twentieth Congress in 1956 touched off the second wave of revolt. But the clock could not be put back, and cautious experimentation went on in the years from 1954 to 1956.

The intellectual thaw was a spontaneous reaction to long years of repression and had no direct connection with government policy in 1953. However, it became apparent in the later and more crucial stages of Khrushchev's struggle against Malenkov that the latter was more sympathetic toward the intellectuals than was Khrushchev.

Even in this early period there were signs of some divergence of views. At the meeting of the Board of the Union of Soviet Writers in October 1953, many speakers referred to Malenkov's statement at the Nineteenth Party Congress calling for more criticism of Soviet life. When Malenkov lost his post as chairman of the Council of Ministers in February 1955, his protégé Alexandrov, the Minister of Culture, fell at the same time. It was the two organs of the party, *Pravda* and *Party Life*, that led the attack on the first thaw.

The extent of the literary thaws of 1953 and 1956 was sufficient guarantee that the days of the *Zhdanovshchina* would not return during the Khrushchev era, but the thaws did not usher in a really liberal atmosphere. Party brakes were applied with particular vigour late in 1956 when the harmful effect of Khrushchev's secret speech at the Twentieth Congress became apparent. By the spring of 1956 the second part of Ehrenburg's *Thaw* already gave evidence of a retreat from the defiant attitude adopted in the first part. The literary journals began to criticize writers who demanded greater freedom after the Twentieth Congress, and outright attacks were made on individual authors after the revolts in East Europe. It was pointed out to those who interpreted Khrushchev's condemnation of Stalin in too liberal a sense that even before 1953 many Soviet writers had succeeded in producing great work.

This sentiment was echoed by middle-aged writers who had a stake in the Stalinist era and who were therefore inclined to side with the party pundits against younger men in protecting at least some of the cultural standards they had helped to establish. The more conservative authors continued to adhere strictly to party directives and served as vehicles for promoting official policy. A typical product of this school of thought was the novel *The Brothers Ershov*, which came out in the summer of 1958. It was written by V. Kochetov, a young man, but one who had already ingratiated himself with the regime. The novel was aimed against those intellectuals who were agitating for reform, and it contained scarcely veiled derogatory allusions to non-orthodox characters in Ehrenburg's *Thaw* and Dudintsev's controversial novel *Not by Bread Alone*. After a second edition of a half-million copies of this latter book was published, an announcement was made that *The Brothers Ershov* would be presented in a stage version at the time of the Twenty-first Congress. The scheme naturally had the full approval of the Ministry of Culture, but was openly criticized by writers of the hue that came under fire in Kochetov's book.

Whereas writers favoured by the regime acted as its polemicists, the more independent elements among the *literati* gave expression, within the limits imposed by the censor, to sentiments prevalent outside the charmed circle of high politics. They contrived to mix critical and conformist trends in their work, thus escaping the wrath of the party leaders or at least being able to retrieve their positions after being sent into the wilderness for a period. Evgeni Evtushenko and Vladimir Dudintsev fell into this category. Other less cautious authors like Boris Pasternak went beyond the bounds of what the regime would tolerate and suffered in consequence.

When Dudintsev's novel *Not by Bread Alone* was first published in 1956, its controversial subject matter was apparently acceptable to the censor, but in the following summer Khrushchev declared that the novel gave too much emphasis to the darker side of Soviet life and Dudintsev fell from grace. The honest hero of Dudintsev's book falls a prey to Soviet industrial bureaucracy and political careerism of a kind that cut too near the bone for comfort. In the slightly more relaxed conditions existing by 1959, however, Khrushchev admitted at the third Writers' Congress that Dudintsev had been right in many ways although he had made some errors.

A young poet like Evtushenko, appearing rather later on the literary scene than Dudintsev, could take advantage of the progressively more liberal attitude of the party, so long as he played his cards carefully. Although he stood up against the harsher aspects of government control of literature on several occasions, he succeeded for a considerable period in remaining in favour both with the regime and with the student class that reads his poems. As a symbol of the new Soviet generation, he has been sent on official visits to Cuba, Ghana, and Finland. Inside Russia editions of his work have been eagerly bought up by young intellectuals avid for poetry. Despite a rebuke from the Soviet literary establishment, Evtushenko continues to produce attacks on bureaucrats.

The now famous case of Boris Pasternak was in effect merely one incident in the course of an extended tussle between the party and recalcitrant Soviet writers. The name of Pasternak only became well known to the general public in the West in the autumn of 1958, when his novel *Dr Zhivago* was awarded the Nobel Prize, although it had not been published in Russia. Pasternak at first accepted the prize, but was immediately subjected to a barrage of severe criticism in the Soviet press. Party orthodoxy was offended by the negative attitude to the 1917 October Revolution expressed in the book. Pasternak appeared to hold the view that the Russian intelligentsia had been dealt a death blow in 1917 from which it had never been allowed to recover. To the party, his revolt against politics was bad enough in itself, but salt was rubbed into the wound when the novel was acclaimed in the capitalist world.

In October 1958 the executive committee of the Writers' Union expelled Pasternak, who wrote personally to Khrushchev three days later with the news that he had renounced the Nobel Prize. His submission was of no avail and after this time he was repeatedly accused of treason. He died in 1960, to all appearances a broken man. With the Pasternak case the Soviet authorities set a clear limit to the degree of literary freedom they would tolerate.

A year before this episode, in August 1957, another party lesson was handed out in the form of a summary of Khrushchev's speeches to unruly authors in the spring after the second thaw. Under the title 'For a Closer Link between Art, Literature and Life', these speeches eventually took on almost as much significance as Zhdanov's directives of 1946, although, judging by the Pasternak affair and other instances, they were not as feared. Indeed the 'conspiracy of silence' entered into by various eminent writers who objected to the curtailment of the second thaw was still in existence in 1958. They must have known that Khrushchev, unlike Zhdanov, was not for the most part prepared to back up his policy of firm persuasion with coercive measures.

Khrushchev timed the publication of his article for just after the fall of the 'anti-party group', which, as we have seen, was as a whole more sympathetic to the writers' struggle for freedom of expression than was Khrushchev. Once the 'group' was safely disposed of as a political force, Khrushchev attempted to assert the hegemony of the party apparatus over the intellectuals. The gist of the article was that both dogmatic adherents of the old school and rebellious innovators would receive short shrift from the authorities: writers had to align themselves according to the golden mean of cautious development in the arts, dictated by the party. Such an attitude must have seemed very tame to adventurous intellectuals spurred into activity by Khrushchev's secret speech at the Twentieth Congress.

At the third Writers' Congress in May 1959, Khrushchev showed that in some minor respects he was willing to soften his position and thus subscribe in reality to the notion of cautious development in the arts. Dudintsev was rehabilitated, and one or two of Khrushchev's remarks even hinted at conciliation with Pasternak, though his name was not mentioned. The party's literary darling, Kochetov, was relieved of his post as the editor of *Literaturnaia Gazeta* and A. A. Surkov, the conservative chairman of the Writers' Union, replaced by the more liberal Konstantin Fedin. More surprising still,

Khrushchev admitted that literature was not his *forte*, a fact only too well known to his audience, which had often laughed behind his back at his philistinism.

The uneasy relationship between the political leadership and the writers did not come to an end in 1959. The party had the feeling, undoubtedly justified, that in making attacks on the Stalinist era some authors also included by implication criticism of the political system as it appeared in the early 1960s. The writers were still at the mercy of the party, but they had come a long way since 1953. Beginning with a desire to infuse more human values into their work in 1953, they embarked on social criticism in 1956, dissecting the troubles of the ordinary citizen faced with the harsh realities of Soviet life. By the end of the 1950s a bold vanguard started to investigate the higher strata of society represented by the bosses in the Soviet system. Of all the liberalizing elements in the USSR that have come to light since the death of Stalin, the influence of the writers races on ahead of the rest, offering hope to the masses whose lives they portray and posing a problem for the future of the political system under which they work.

How did the social controls reviewed in this chapter affect Soviet citizens in their daily lives? In a totalitarian state the interests of the individual are placed far below that of the regime; this extreme relationship has changed in the Soviet Union since Stalin's death, and the means of enforcing it are now rather different. The regime still aims at preventing the formation of any grouping of private interests and is apparently successful in its purpose; but the arbitrary methods of the secret police, and the existence of special courts and fierce labour laws, have been set aside—apart from exceptional cases. In their stead the party octopus, supplied with more tentacles than ever before, reaches down among the masses and exhorts rather than coerces them into acting in the interest of the state. No doubt there are still many people who succeed in evading pressure from the political centre—the peasant who falsifies his returns in order to qualify for a bonus, the young writer who escapes the rigours of the censor, the economic manager who spends state money on his wife—but the high tension between private citizens and the agents of social control that existed under Stalin has been relaxed to a great degree.

The rift between the state and the individual has been narrowed by encouraging the people to take part in administration at the lower levels. Soviet citizens are now slightly better informed with regard to political affairs, both on the domestic and the international levels.

Other placatory gestures since Stalin's death include the growing concern over the quality and quantity of consumer goods. Not only is the regime taking action to remedy the pitiful state of affairs in this sphere, but it is actually permitting the general public to express its dissatisfaction in print. Indeed on this and several other matters devoid of vital political importance the censor has shown leniency; in other areas, however, only assent, not dissent, may be voiced.

Of the three broad social classes in the Soviet Union the intelligentsia is the darling of the regime, receiving the greatest financial reward and prestige; at the same time it pays the highest price by having to forfeit its most precious possession, spiritual independence. Soviet workers, who in 1954 formed approximately 36 per cent of the population, were originally the favoured ones of the Communist dictatorship, but a gradual and unconscious shift back to bourgeois values has deprived them of much of their previous standing. Yet they fare infinitely better than the peasants, traditionally the depressed class. Even by 1961 the peasants were still underpaid, neglected, cut off from urban civilization. Simultaneously persecuted both for their stubborn adherence to religion and for their private holdings, they continue to lag far behind the ideals set by the Communist state in the middle of the twentieth century.

CHAPTER VIII

THE TWENTY-SECOND PARTY CONGRESS AND CONCLUSION

The Twenty-second Party Congress, which opened at Moscow in October 1961, was intended to concentrate most of its efforts on a discussion of two instruments for moulding the Soviet future—the draft of the new party programme and the revised Party Rules. In the event, ghosts from the Soviet past intruded and claimed much of the delegates' time. This congress is a suitable point at which to conclude this study of postwar Russia, since it dealt in turn with the long perspective of Russia's political past and future.

DOMESTIC POLICY

The Political Past
At the congress the muddy waters of Soviet history were stirred once again by new revelations concerning the Great Purge of the 1930s. Khrushchev and other spokesmen added embellishments to the condemnation of Stalin made at the Twentieth Congress. It was now made known that Stalin had been directly responsible for the death of S. M. Kirov, and that Marshal Mikhail Tukhachevsky had been tried and executed on the evidence of false documents planted by the Nazis. On the strength of these and many other new disclosures the congress voted that Stalin's body should be removed from the Lenin Mausoleum on the Red Square. The myth that had toppled at the Twentieth Congress was shattered beyond repair at the Twenty-second. Khrushchev also dispensed with Stalin's 1937 thesis that the sharpening of the class struggle was a concomitant of the progress of socialist construction, the principle that had served as an excuse for the terrorism of the 1930s.

Another ghost from the more recent past was the 'anti-party group', which came in for yet another attack at the congress. In addition to further disclosures concerning its opposition in 1957 and afterwards, mentioned in Chapter v of this book, its members were also heavily involved in the responsibility for the purges. Malenkov's close ties with Ezhov, Stalin's head of the security service, were laid bare; Molotov, Voroshilov, and Kaganovich were all blamed for their parts in the crimes of the Stalin era.

The Political Future

The discussion of the new Party Rules at the congress looked to a brighter future. It was decided that at all regular elections at least one quarter of the members of the Presidium and the Central Committee would henceforth be replaced; the lower ranks of the party hierarchy were to be renewed at an even faster rate. This reform had a threefold aim—to prevent the recurrence of a personality cult, to promote young men to positions of seniority, and to root out party leaders who attempted to organize 'family circles'.

On a superficial view it seemed as though some element of genuine democracy was creeping into the government. But although the new measures undoubtedly ruled out the possibility of a return to the atrophied character of the political machine in the last years of Stalin's dictatorship, they still left many loopholes through which the head of both the party and the state could maintain his grip over the rank and file. Khrushchev presumably could use the new rules to carry out regular, undramatic purges. An escape clause in the new rules permitted men of outstanding ability to keep their posts for longer than the ascribed period; presumably Khrushchev included himself in this category.

The question of promotion brings us to a related problem; who would succeed Khrushchev and how would the succession take place? By the time of the Twenty-second Congress the Soviet leader was 68 years old, but the strength of the opposition until 1957 had given him little time to plan for the future.

In 1961 Frol Kozlov seemed to be Khrushchev's heir-apparent. It was he who gave the speech on the new Party Rules at the Twenty-second Congress, and his name began to be listed directly after Khrushchev's in party announcements. Kozlov occupied a key position in the party Secretariat that had lifted Stalin and Khrushchev to power in their time. He had an advantage over the other two men in that the party now reigned supreme over all other interest groups, which was not the case in 1924 and 1953. If the succession could be carried out quickly and smoothly, it appeared likely that the strong hegemony of the party would be perpetuated.

With the fall of the 'anti-party group', the state bureaucracy and the economic élite had been shorn of their leaders, although Malenkov was young enough to stage a return to power if conditions permitted it. The places of the old guard in the non-party interest groups were taken over by men transferred from the party apparatus. Leonid Brezhnev was President of the Soviet Union, Alexei Kosygin head of *Gosplan*. As it turned out, these two men were destined to take over the reins of power from Khrushchev in the autumn of 1964, when Brezhnev became First Secretary of the party and Kosygin was appointed Chairman of the Council of Ministers.

Another question concerned the form of post-Khrushchev government: would there be a return to one-man rule in the Soviet Union after an interregnum presided over by an oligarchy, as had been the case after Lenin's and Stalin's deaths, or would an oligarchy survive to conduct affairs of state? In 1961, no conjecture could be made in this respect. The whole question of Khrushchev's fall from power is beyond the scope of this book.

The Third Party Programme

While the new Party Rules looked to the immediate future, the party programme approved by the Twenty-second Congress outlined the general course of Soviet domestic affairs for the following twenty years. A draft of the programme appeared in July 1961, and was widely discussed in the press before its adoption at the congress. It was the successor to the first party programme of 1903 and the second of 1919. Obeying the dictates of his native caution, Stalin never committed himself to a new programme that might restrict his scope for future action, although the Eighteenth and Nineteenth Party Congresses resolved to work one out. Khrushchev was acting in character when he embarked on this venture in the very year that saw the failure of his boast of 1957 that Russia would overtake the United States in the production of meat, butter, and milk *per capita* of the population within four years.

The dangers of prophesying the future could clearly be seen from the fact that many of the unfulfilled aims of the 1919 programme were reintroduced in the third party programme. The main features of the new programme had already been spelled out by Khrushchev at the Twenty-first Congress (see Chapter v), but now a definite period was set for their realization. More specific details were given with regard to the changes that were expected to take place in the structure of the state and in the psychology of the Soviet people under Communism.

After some initial prevarication on the subject at the Twenty-first Congress, Khrushchev finally asserted in the autumn of 1961 that the Soviet state structure would in fact soon begin to wither away. It would be replaced by communal autonomy. No coercive state organs would remain, although economic activity would still be directed from the centre: 'The view that the system of self-administration in a Communist society is a decentralized system is a revisionistic anarcho-syndicalist distortion of Marxist-Leninist teachings on the socialist state and structure of society in the highest phase of Communist society.'[1]

Not only would the economy stay centralized, but it would be run by the party even under Communism, as would the many 'public organizations' that were expected to take over the administrative functions of the state. Party supervision of legal activities taken out of the hands of the lawyers and pressed upon laymen was one of the first examples of this trend. In making this claim for the party, Khrushchev effected a major innovation in Communist ideology, since Marx, Lenin, and Stalin had affirmed that the party as well as the state would wither away under Communism. Khrushchev argued thus: 'The party has a foundation more powerful than the state organs. It arose and exists not as a result of any obligations of a legal nature. Its development is based on circumstances arising from the political views of peoples, that is, from the demands of the moral factor, and mankind will always need moral factors.'[2]

Like Stalin before him, Khrushchev heaped privileges on the party apparatus through which both men rose to power, but Khrushchev went much further in his exaltation of the party. Having risen through it he did not proceed to abase it as Stalin had done; and in 1961 he promised the party a brilliant future under Communism in his first original contribution to ideology.

The advent of Communism was to usher in a change for the better in human nature as well as in political relations. If the idea of a state without coercion seems Utopian, the hope that the old Adam in man can be rooted out within a certain period through education and ideological indoctrination is yet more vain. Nevertheless the Soviet leaders believe that under Communist conditions people's characters will change radically. Instead of thinking of themselves, Soviet citizens will begin to put the common interest of society first; losing interest in personal possessions, they will live in communal houses, only use public cars, and forsake their country *dachas* for holiday homes set up by the withering state.

Selfishness, egoism, and vanity will dissolve with the trappings of the old socialist state. Not since the eighteenth century has such optimism in human nature been expressed. One is reminded of Condorcet: 'The perfectibility of man is in fact unlimited and can

---

[1] *Radianska Pravo* (No. 4, 1959), p. 18.
[2] Khrushchev in an interview with the editor of *The Times* (Radio Moscow, February 15, 1958).

never be reversed.'[1] Like the French revolutionaries before them, the Soviet leaders are so intoxicated by the great political and economic changes they have made that they feel as though human nature must alter too. But it is clear from literary and religious developments in post-war Russia that the new social order has left virtually untouched vast areas of the human intellect, not to speak of the deeper recesses of the spirit.

The Economic Outlook
There was perhaps less that smacked of Utopianism in Soviet prognostications for the industrial future of Russia over the following twenty years. Looking back at the recent past, the speakers at the Twenty-second Congress were able to congratulate themselves on having achieved a 10 per cent growth in overall industrial production in the first two years of the Seven-Year Plan, or 1·7 per cent more than planned. Looking to the future, they confidently divided the twenty-year period into two broad stages—the first ten years would see the establishment of the material and technical base of Communism, while by 1980 the Soviet people would be provided with an abundance of material and cultural goods. Heavy industrial output was planned to rise 540 per cent by 1980. This was no idle boast. If previous rates of growth for steel, electricity, and various other basic products were projected into the future, this target was within the realm of the possible.

Consumer goods output was to increase by 400 per cent over the same period, thus allowing for a 'considerable convergence' between heavy and light industrial production. In view of the sad history of light industry in the Soviet Union, this estimate appeared to be too optimistic; and even if it were to be achieved, it would not lead to an abundance of goods on the American or the West European scale. Much hangs on the meaning of abundance, however. For the Soviet peasant who has known of little besides privation and war during his ifetime, the earthly paradise is relatively modest in its proportions.

Over the twenty years real income *per capita* of the population was scheduled to rise more than three-and-a-half times—a large increase, but one which would only bring Soviet cash incomes in 1970 up to between 40 and 47 per cent of the 1961 average United States income; however, it has to be taken into account that under the terms of the Soviet programme public services in 1980 will provide about half the total volume of personal income. Besides welfare services now

[1] M. de Condorcet, *Esquisse d'un tableau des progrès de l'esprit humain* (Paris, 1883), Vol. I, p. 19.

obtainable in a country like Sweden, the Soviet people of 1980 may hope to receive free gas, heating, and local transport, in addition to rent-free apartments.

In the light of past experience the agricultural estimates for the twenty-year programme were not as sober as those for industry. It was expected that agricultural output would rise two and a half times in the course of the first ten years, and that productivity would increase even faster than in industry. The desperate need for more and better animal feeding stuffs was mentioned by Khrushchev at the congress, but no allusion was made to his idle boast of 1957 with regard to meat production. As at the Twenty-first Congress, the need to close the gap between town and country was emphasized, but no specific reference was made to the future of the collective farms. The first agricultural figures to come in after the meeting of the congress indicated that in this sphere at least the Soviet Union would have difficulty in fulfilling the twenty-year programme. In the first half of 1962 meat production only rose 12 per cent over the figure for the first half of 1961, although Khrushchev had called for an increase of one-third over the same period. Tractor production also fell below the required amount.

Whereas the political aspect of the Soviet future was still heavily overladen with theoretical considerations, the economic outlook was surprisingly free of ideological involvement in comparison with previous blueprints for the attainment of Communism. In view of the manner in which theory had often acted as a brake on economic development in the past, this was a hopeful sign. The post-1955 efforts to rationalize the economy were beginning to take solid roots.

Let us try to extricate ourselves from the Soviet Union's own view of its economic future and review the positive and negative factors that will determine whether the goals of the new programme are achieved or not.

The mere fact that the Soviet Union lags behind the United States in the economic sense gives the Russians an advantage, as Soviet resources in manpower and raw materials have not yet been efficiently tapped in many ways. Overproduction is not nearly so common a phenomenon in the USSR as it is in the United States. Other advantages stem from the Soviet economic and political system. A high and steady rate of investment can be maintained more easily in the USSR than in the West, which often falls a prey to recessions and the whims of the consumer; in Russia, as is well known, the preferences of the public have been disregarded to a notorious degree. This incidentally helps the Soviet planners in another way: as they have no qualms about the uncertain influence of economic demand, they can apply automation to an exceptionally wide range of standardized products over long periods of time.

The Soviet economic system is especially well suited to the production of basic materials, and it is in this sphere that Russia is first likely to overtake the United States. For political and military reasons great stress has been placed on this sector since the birth of the Soviet regime; it has never ceased to be in the vanguard of each successive plan. The great feats of Soviet education have lent extra impetus to developments in heavy industry. With the increasing application of scientific research to production, judicious Soviet investment in technical training is bound to pay ever-increasing dividends.

The chief handicap to fast economic progress in the Soviet Union stems from the very nature of the system, just as do most of the advantages mentioned above. In the rapidly maturing Soviet economy, centrally-planned administration tends to become overwhelmed by the magnitude and intricacy of the tasks it has to face. Yet despite some attempts at decentralization, the absence of real market relations in Russia inevitably forces locally appointed authorities to refer back to the centre on most vital questions. It would appear that the vicious circle can only be broken by resorting to market relations, thus running counter to Marxist economic doctrine. Ideology here creates a dilemma that may in time become as problematical as the tussle between collectivized agriculture and the drive for economic efficiency. So long as the party has a vested interest in prolonging the present economic structure and the ideology on which it is based, it is hard to see just how these problems can be resolved.

As the Soviet economy pushes ahead, the need to diversify production will create further headaches for the central administrators, and at some stage the suppressed demands of the consumer will inevitably have to be taken into consideration to a greater extent, thus complicating the direction of the economy. The further industrialization reaches out into the vast hinterland of the Soviet Union, the more new towns and communications networks develop, the more the outlay in human investment will become increasingly burdensome.

At the Twenty-second Congress the Soviet Union forecast that productivity in Russia would rise to the American level by 1970. As early as 1960 it was estimated that Soviet industrial production equalled 60 per cent of the American total. This figure was disputed in the West, but the argument did not affect the fact that at some unspecified time in the future it seemed not inconceivable that the USSR would become the greatest industrial power in the world.

FOREIGN POLICY

There was a ghost at the feast of the Twenty-second Congress. The Albanian Communist Party was not invited to send a delegation and came in for prolonged and bitter criticism during the debates. Supported by most other Communist parties, the Soviet Union assailed the Albanians for not adhering to the policy of peaceful coexistence and thus attempting to subvert the principles laid down at the Twentieth Congress of 1956. Gone were the days when Stalin could say of the Albanians 'They can be as faithful as a dog; that is one of the traits of the primitive.'[1]

The Soviet Union magnified Albanian recalcitrance because it had much in common with the Chinese point of view. In attacking defenceless Albania, the Soviet Union was pointing an accusing finger at Mao Tse-tung as well. Also, since Molotov's notions of foreign policy coincided with Chinese opinion, he too was the subject of much criticism at the congress. Although the Soviet attack on China was indirect, it was pointed enough to induce Chou En-lai, the head of the Chinese delegation, to leave the congress before the proceedings ended.

The Albanian episode, which led to the disruption of Soviet-Albanian diplomatic relations after the congress, was a vivid reminder of the schisms that endangered the unity of the Communist bloc. When Palmiro Togliatti, the head of the Italian Communist Party, spoke of polycentrism in the bloc in 1956, his judgment seemed premature, but by 1961 his vision had become a reality. In the latter year political consciousness of this fact appeared to be lagging somewhat behind the actual state of affairs.

Not only was there the threat of a political rift between those parties that agreed with the Chinese 'hard' line and those that still remained faithful to Russia, but a geographical barrier of sorts was also growing between European and Asian Communists. Omens of the future were obvious at the congress when the Vietnamese and North Korean Communist delegations supported China in her quarrel with the Soviet Union, while the European parties backed Russia. Albania did not fit into the geographical pattern, but the political motive was stronger than other factors in her case. Vietnam

[1] V. Dedijer, *Tito Speaks* (London: George Weidenfeld & Nicolson, 1953), p. 312.

and North Korea were bound to China by the mutual pull of culture, geography, and politics.

The emergence of Communist China as a great power acknowledged by the Soviet Union had led to the creation of a genuine forum in the Communist bloc for the discussion of ideological issues. The change was reminiscent of the Protestant challenge to the Papacy at the time of the Reformation. Like the earlier movement, the Sino-Soviet quarrel was concerned with power politics and the impact of nationalism as well as with theoretical matters.

The extent of the Sino-Soviet conflict should not be minimized, especially with regard to the treatment of the emergent nations: the soft handling of bourgeois nationalist governments reminded the Chinese Communists unpleasantly of Stalin's support of Chiang Kai-shek against themselves for many hard years before the Chinese revolution. But in 1961 Russia and China were still drawn together by some common ties. They faced a common enemy and depended on each other for military strength and Communist prestige. China's economic future could be affected considerably by the amount of Soviet help she received. Their geographical spheres of influence in foreign policy were different for the most part, and even where they threatened to clash, as in Africa and the Middle East, Chinese interest was still in an embryonic stage.

Soviet policy toward the less-developed countries received scant attention at the Twenty-second Congress, and the question of economic aid and trade was neglected. Sino-Soviet differences on the subject probably had something to do with this reticence, but the Soviet Union's own dissatisfaction with various aspects of political developments in the uncommitted countries was also growing. Soviet leaders still had not learned to differentiate among these countries, nor had they appreciated the fact that neutralism was not necessarily a step on the road to Communism. Ever since Bandung the Soviet Union had pursued the mirage of uncommitted nations slowly moving into the Communist camp. In reality the less-developed areas were greatly fragmented even within the same continent, as was proven by the dissension between the Monrovian and Casablanca blocs in Africa.

Yet two-thirds of the world was bound together by poverty, a tie that was more solid than any political unity, and one which set up an enormous gulf between it and the prosperous third of the globe. It may well be that in the distant future the dominating rivalry between capitalism and Communism described in this book will fade into the background under the impact of a more basic, physical difference of this nature, which divides men more than political theories ever can. Nehru drew attention to this:

> Capitalism today is very different from what it was even fifty years ago, much more than it was a hundred years ago. It has changed very much. So, in fact, have the Communist countries, at any rate the older ones. I don't say they are giving up their basic economic policies, but they are changing, they are really approaching each other. The real difference today in the world is between the well-to-do countries and under-developed countries. The other difference is a temporary one.[1]

The twenty-year programme announced with such confidence by the Soviet leaders contained a very important escape clause in case of its non-fulfilment. It was stated that if 'international complications' disturbed the peace of the world, it would be difficult to carry out the programme. In this way the policies of the capitalist states could be used as scapegoats for failures encountered on the road to Communism.

By 1961 perhaps the most striking fact with regard to the struggle between the two super-powers was that neither of them had succeeded in dominating large areas of the world, either intentionally or accidentally. Each had their well-defined spheres of influence free from interference by the other, though the Cuban affair boded ill for the future. If the under-developed areas of the globe, with or without China, succeeded in maintaining their new-found independence from both the Soviet Union and the United States and broke down internal barriers within themselves, George Orwell's prophecy of a world divided into three major power blocs might yet come true.

In 1961 it did not seem as if Soviet foreign policy aims would change radically in the near future. Eastern Europe would remain under Russian control; Germany remained the biggest problem inherited from the Second World War, and looked as though it would continue to be so even if the Berlin question could be solved. Total disarmament remained a dream only: and the Soviet Union's great opponent remained the United States, despite the economic rehabilitation of Western Europe and the prospect of future economic and political union through the medium of the Common Market. Inside Russia there seemed little chance of any brusque changes in the Soviet attitude to the outside world. Increasing industrial wealth had done little to modify the political structure, which was still firmly under the thumb of the party. Soviet public opinion was altering with regard to

[1] J. Nehru in *The Listener* (January 21, 1962).

domestic affairs to some degree, but hardly at all vis-à-vis foreign policy—a phenomenon not confined to the USSR; national attitudes everywhere are apt to be more conservative on foreign than on home policy.

It has been estimated that the territorial expansion of the Russian state has gone on at the rate of an average of 50 square miles a day for the last 400 years. In the years from 1945 to 1960 alone, 830,000,000 people joined the Communist camp of nations. Small wonder, therefore, that Khrushchev considered that the balance of world power had shifted decisively to the Communist side. His policy could be summed up in the optimistic words of Lunacharsky, written as long ago as 1932:

> When we built the biggest blast furnace in Europe, when we completed the largest dam in the world, when we set up the biggest ball-bearing factory in Europe, each occasion was a great struggle won, a bloodless struggle. We are giving concrete proof that a planned socialist economy, even in a technically backward country with a low level of culture that has been enslaved for centuries to one of the most barbarian governments the world has known, can produce brilliant results in a short time. We are able to set up a heavy industrial base, and once this task has been accomplished, we shall develop our light industry, we shall promote our agriculture and the living standards of our people on a socialist foundation.
>
> For us war is an encumbrance. We have no need of it. We need tranquillity. We need to concentrate our powers on our main business. By achieving this aim, we shall win over tens and hundreds of millions of workers, who, convinced of the justness of our course, will establish in all the earth the order of things we consider to be sensible.[1]

Russia now intends to conquer men's hearts by persuasion, and not, as previously, to control their bodies by force. The world will be a happier and safer place to live in if she continues to renounce the use of violence.

---

[1] A. Lunacharsky, *Stat'i i Rechi po Voprosam Mezhdunarodnoi Politiki* (Moscow, 1959), p. 360.

A SELECTIVE BIBLIOGRAPHY

The Anti-Stalin Campaign and *International Communism*. Russian Institute (eds.), New York, Columbia University Press, 1956.

BAUER, R., and INKELES, A., *The Soviet Citizen*: Daily Life in a Totalitarian Society. Cambridge, Harvard University Press; London, Oxford University Press, 1959.

BAUER, R., INKELES, A., and KLUCKHOHN, C., *How the Soviet System Works*. Cambridge, Harvard University Press, 1956.

BEREDAY, G. Z. F., and PENNAR, J. (eds.), *The Politics of Soviet Education*. New York, Praeger; London, Stevens, 1960.

BERGSON, A.. and KUZNETS, S., *Economic Trends in the Soviet Union*. Cambridge, Harvard University Press; London, Oxford University Press, 1963.

BERMAN, H. J., *Justice in Russia*. Cambridge, Harvard University Press, 1950.

BOFFA, G., *Inside the Khrushchev Era*. London, Allen & Unwin, 1960.

BRUMBERG, A. (ed.), *Russia Under Khrushchev*. New York, Praeger; London, Methuen, 1962.

BRZEZINSKI, Z. K. (ed.), *Political Controls in the Soviet Army*. Research Programme on the USSR, New York, 1954.

The Soviet Bloc. Cambridge, Harvard University Press; London, Oxford University Press, 1960.

CAREW HUNT, R.N., *The Theory and Practice of Communism*. London, Bles, 1956; New York, Macmillan, 1958.

A Guide to Communist Jargon. London, Bles, 1957.

CONQUEST, R., *Power and Policy in the U.S.S.R*. London, Macmillan; New York, St. Martin's Press, 1961.

COUNTS, G., *The Challenge of Soviet Education*. New York and London, McGraw-Hill, 1957.

COUNTS, G., and LODGE, N., *The Country of the Blind*. Boston, Houghton Mifflin, 1949.

DALLIN, A., *German Rule in Russia 1941–5*. London, Macmillan, 1957.

The Soviet Union at the United Nations. New York, Praeger; London, Methuen, 1962.

Soviet Conduct in World Affairs. New York, Columbia University Press, 1960.

DEUTSCHER, I., *Stalin*. London, Oxford University Press, 1949.

DeWITT, N., *Education and Professional Employment in the USSR*. National Science Foundation, Washington, 1961.

DINERSTEIN, H. S., *War and the Soviet Union*. London, Stevens, 1959.

DJILAS, M., *The New Class*. New York, Praeger; London, Thames & Hudson, 1957.

ERICKSON, J., *The Soviet High Command*. New York, St Martin's Press, 1952.

FAINSOD, M., *How Russia is Ruled.* London, Oxford University Press, 1963.
'The Party in the Post-Stalin Era.' *Problems of Communism*, January-February, 1958.
'What happened to Collective Leadership?' *Problems of Communism*, July-August, 1959.
FISCHER-GALATI, S. (ed.), *Eastern Europe in the Sixties*, New York, Praeger; London, Pall Mall, 1964.
FLORINSKY, M. T., *Towards an Understanding of the USSR*, New York, Macmillan, 1951.
FRIEDRICH, C. J., and BRZEZINSKI, Z., *Totalitarian Dictatorship and Autocracy.* Cambridge, Harvard University Press; London, Oxford University Press, 1956.
GARTHOFF, R. L., *How Russia Makes War.* London, Allen & Unwin, 1954.
Soviet Strategy in the Nuclear Age. New York, Praeger; London, Stevens, 1958.
GOODMAN, E. R., *The Soviet Design for a World State.* New York, Columbia University Press; London, Oxford University Press, 1960.
GRANICK, D., *The Red Executive.* London, Macmillan, 1960.
Management of the Industrial Firm in the USSR. New York, Columbia University Press, 1954.
HAMM, H., *Albania—China's Beachhead in Europe.* London, Weidenfeld & Nicolson, 1963.
HARPER, S. N., and THOMPSON, R., *The Government of the Soviet Union.* New York, Van Nostrand, 1949.
HAZARD, J. N., *Law and Social Change in the USSR* London, Stevens, 1953.
The Soviet System of Government. Chicago University Press, 1960.
INKELES, A., *Public Opinion in Soviet Russia*—a Study in Mass Persuasion. Harvard University Press; London, Oxford University Press, 1950.
JASNY, N., *Soviet Industrialization, 1928–1952.* Chicago University Press, 1961.
The Socialized Agriculture of the USSR. Stanford, Stanford University Press; London, Oxford University Press, 1949.
KARDELJ, E., *Socialism and War.* London, Methuen, 1961.
KAUTSKY, J. H., *Moscow and the Communist Party of India*: a Study in the Post-war Evolution of International Communist Strategy. New York and London, Wiley, 1956.
KAZNACHEEV, A., *Inside a Soviet Embassy.* New York, Lippincott, 1962.
KELLEN, K., *Khrushchev—A Political Portrait.* New York, Praeger, 1961.
KHRUSHCHEV, N. S., *On Peaceful Co-existence.* Moscow, 1961.
KOLARZ, W., *Religion in the Soviet Union.* London, Macmillan; New York, St. Martin's Press, 1961.
KRUGLAK, T. E., *The Two Faces of Tass.* Minneapolis, University of Minnesota Press, 1962.
LABEDZ, L., and HAYWARD, M. (eds.), *Literature and Revolution in Soviet Russia 1917–62.* Oxford University Press, 1963.

LAPENNA, I., *State and Law*: Soviet and Yugoslav Theory. London, Athlone Press, 1964.
LAQUEUR, W., and LABEDZ, L. (eds.), *The Future of Communist Society*. New York, Praeger, 1962.
LAQUEUR, W. Z., and LICHTHEIM, G. (eds.), *The Soviet Cultural Scene, 1956–57*. New York, Atlantic Books; London, Stevens, 1958.
LEONHARD, W., *The Kremlin Since Stalin*. London, Oxford University Press; New York, Praeger, 1962.
LEVIN, D., *Soviet Education Today*. London, Staples Press, 1959.
LIDDELL HART, B. H., *The Red Army*. New York, Harcourt Brace, 1956 (published in Great Britain under the title *The Soviet Army*, London, Weidenfeld & Nicolson, 1956).
LOWENTHAL, R., *Khrushchev in Command. Commentary*, June, 1958.
Party versus State—The Permanent Revolution is on Again, *Problems of Communism*, September-October, 1957.
MACKINTOSH, J. M., *Strategy and Tactics of Soviet Foreign Policy*. New York, St. Martin's Press; London, Oxford University Press, 1962.
MEHNERT, K., *Soviet Man and His World*. London, Weidenfeld & Nicolson, 1961.
MEISSNER, B., *Russland unter Chruschtschow*. Munich, Oldenburg, 1960.
MOORE, B., *Soviet Politics*, the Dilemma of Power. Cambridge, Harvard University Press; London, Oxford University Press, 1951.
MORGAN, G. G., *Soviet Administrative Legality*. Stanford University Press, 1962.
Imre Nagy on Communism: In Defence of the New Course. New York, Praeger; London, Thames & Hudson, 1957.
NEMZER, L., The Kremlin's Professional Staff: the Apparatus of the Central Committee, *American Political Science Review*, March, 1950.
NOVE, A., *The Soviet Economy*: An Introduction. London, Allen & Unwin; New York, Praeger, 1961.
PALOCZI-HORVATH, G., *Khrushchev: The Road to Power*. London, Secker & Warburg, 1960.
PETHYBRIDGE, R. W., *A Key to Soviet Politics*—The Crisis of the Anti-Party Group. London, Allen & Unwin, 1962.
PISTRAK, L., *The Grand Tactician*: Khrushchev's Rise to Power. New York, Praeger; London, Thames & Hudson, 1961.
RAUCH, G. von, *A History of Soviet Russia*. New York, Praeger; London, Stevens, 1960.
RIGBY, T., 'Khrushchev and the Resuscitation of the Central Committee', *Australian Outlook*, September 1959.
ROBERTS, H. L., *Russia and America*: Dangers and Prospects. New York, Harper; London, Muller, 1956.
RUSH, M., *The Rise of Khrushchev*. Washington, Public Affairs Press, 1958.
SALISBURY, H. E., *Moscow Journal*: The End of Stalin. Chicago University Press, 1961.

SCHAPIRO, L., *The Communist Party of the Soviet Union*. London, Eyre & Spottiswoode, 1960.
SCHAPIRO, L., *The Government and Politics of the Soviet Union*. London, Hutchinson, 1965.
SCHLESINGER, R. (ed.), *The Nationalities Problem and Soviet Administration*. London, Routledge & Kegan Paul, 1956.
SCHWARZ, S. M., *The Jews in the Soviet Union*. Syracuse University Press, 1951.
Labor in the Soviet Union. New York, Praeger, 1952.
SCOTT, D. J. R., *Russian Political Institutions*. London, Allen & Unwin, 1958.
SHULMAN, M., *Soviet Foreign Policy Reappraised*. Cambridge, Harvard University Press; London, Oxford University Press, 1963.
SLONIM, M. L., *Modern Russian Literature*. London, Oxford University Press, 1953.
SOUVARINE, B., *Stalin*. New York, Alliance Book Corporation, 1939.
SPULBER, N., *The Soviet Economy*. New York, W. W. Norton, 1962.
TOWSTER, J., *Political Power in the U.S.S.R.* New York, Oxford University Press, 1948.
TREADGOLD, D. W., *Twentieth Century Russia*. Chicago, Rand McNally, 1959.
ULAM, A., *The New Face of Soviet Totalitarianism*. Cambridge, Harvard University Press, 1963.
ULAM, A. B., *The Unfinished Revolution*. New York, Random House, 1960.
UTECHIN, S. V., *Everyman's Concise Encyclopaedia of Russia*. London, J. M. Dent, 1961.
VARGA, E., *Twentieth Century Capitalism*. London, Lawrence & Wishart, 1963.
WOLFE, B., *Khrushchev and Stalin's Ghost*. London, Constable; New York, Praeger, 1957.
ZAGORIA, D. S., *The Sino-Soviet Conflict 1956–61*. Princeton University Press, 1962.

PERIODICALS

Current Digest of the Soviet Press (weekly). New York.
Problems of Communism (bi-monthly). Washington.
The Russian Review (quarterly). Hanover, New Hampshire.
Soviet Studies (quarterly). Glasgow.
Survey—Journal of Soviet and East European Studies (bi-monthly). London.

INDEX

Abakumov, V. S., 69, 135
Adzhubei, A. (editor *of Izvestiia*), 171, 235
Afghanistan, 47, 150, 207
Africa, 151, 214
agriculture
  effects of Second World War on, 21–3; collective farms controversy, 55; in post-Stalin period, 129–35; in Eastern Europe, 139; in Khrushchev era, 183–7: *see also*: 'agro-towns'; collectivization; Machine Tractor Stations; peasants; Virgin Lands
'agro-towns', Khrushchev's proposal for, 55, 186
Akhmatova, Anna, attacks on writings of, 72
Albania, 103, 141, 165, 200, 249
Andreev, Andrei, 51, 52, 55
Andrianov, V. M., 53
'anti-party group' (opposition to Khrushchev), 57, 135, 242, 243; Khrushchev's struggle with, 161–9
anti-Semitism, 80
Arab-Israeli conflicts, Stalin and, 115–16
Aristov, A. V., 127
armed forces
  Stalin's policy for, 25; soldiers surrender during German advances, 27; psychological effects of service abroad, 28–9; expansion of, 31; and the CPSU, 66; in Khrushchev era, 222–3
Asia
  Russian aims in, 43–6; Stalin's ambitions in, 106–15; in post-Stalin period, 147–52; in Khrushchev era, 188–90: *see also* entries for individual countries; Middle East
atomic weapons, Eastern Europe's attitude to, 202
Austria, 91, 206, 207

Babaevsky, Semion, official approval of writings of, 72

Baghdad Pact, 150, 213
Balkan countries
  Anglo-Soviet agreement on spheres of influence in, 36, 40; in post-Stalin period, 141: *see also* entries for individual countries
ballistic missiles, 216
Baltic States
  German armies welcomed in, 27; as Soviet republics, 36; underground movement and deportations in, 67; opposition to collectivization in, 67; advantage to Russia of neutrality in, 202
Bandung Conference (1955), 149–50
Beliaev, N., 127, 187
Belorussia
  welcomes German armies, 27; and UNO, 43; postwar situation in, 67
Beneš, Eduard (Czech statesman), 100–1
Beria, Lavrenty
  and the Politburo, 51; and the collective farms, 55; and the secret police and the purges, 69, 80, 81; and the Doctors' Plot, 125; and the Council of Ministers, 124; arrest and execution, 125–6
Berlin blockade, 101
Brezhnev, Leonid, 243–4
Bulganin, Nikolai
  and the Politburo, 51; as Marshal of Soviet Union, 66; in post-Stalin period, 124, 129, 141, 144, 150; in Khrushchev era, 162, 163, 166, 225
Bulgaria
  Russia's reparation demands, 37; Stalin's pressure on, 93, 94; collective farms in, 104; in post-Stalin period, 138, 144; in Khrushchev era, 165, 170, 199
Burma, 111, 149, 150, 207

casualties (Russian) in Second World War, 18
Caucasian nationalities, deportations of, 26–7
Ceylon, 149

Chiang Kai-shek, 107–8
China
  Soviet attitude to, 45; independent Communist revolution in, 47; Stalin and, 107–9, 112–13; at Bandung Conference, 149–50; in post-Stalin period, 152–3; in Khrushchev era, 195–200 *passim*; disagreements and rivalry with USSR, 210–13: *see also* Chou En-lai; Mao Tse-tung
Chou En-lai, 149, 197
Churchill, Winston
  Soviet's insulting attitude to, 31; at meetings at Potsdam, Teheran and Yalta, 33–5; and postwar Poland, 39; and establishment of UNO, 42; on Russia's expansionist aims, 47; his 'Iron Curtain' speech to USA, 94, 95
Clay, General Lucius, and zoning of Germany, 41
'Cold War', the, 30, 85, 92, 93–6, 152
collaboration with occupying forces by Soviet population, 26, 27
collectivization system
  peasants' hatred of, 24, 25, 130; renewed propaganda on, 30; opposition to, in Soviet-controlled areas, 67; in Eastern Europe, 104; in post-Stalin period, 131; partial relaxation of, 139; in Khrushchev era, 183–6
Cominform, the, 97, 198
Comintern, Stalin abolishes the, 24
Committee for the Liberation of the Peoples of Russia (Nazi body), 27
Communist ideology, 232–4; Soviet campaigns in, 69–78
Communist Party of the Soviet Union
  wartime increase in, and policy of, 25–6, 57; Stalin and the old line, 29–30; declines in importance beside the government machine, 57; wartime changes in, and postwar administration, 57–60; and the State bureaucracy, 60; and the economic reconstruction, 60–6; and the army, 66; and occupied areas, 67–8; the 19th Congress, 78–9

concentration camps, Stalin sets up in Eastern Europe, 103
consumer goods production
  effects of Second World War on, 21–3; programme for increasing, 130, 135, 139; opposition to Khrushchev's plans for, 162; developments during Khrushchev era, 180, 182
Council of Ministers, 124–5
Council for Mutual Economic Aid, 74, 200, 201
CPSU: *see* Communist Party of the Soviet Union
Cuba, USSR and, 213–14
Czechoslovakia
  Stalin's ban on Marshall aid for, 21, 96, 100; Stalin's take-over of, 100–1; nationalized labour force in, 104; in post-Stalin period, 138; in Khrushchev era, 165, 194, 195, 199

deportations of nationalities of uncertain loyalty to USSR, 26
disarmament proposals, 216–17
'*divide et impera*', Stalin's policy of, 50
Djilas, M. (Yugoslav Communist), 98–9, 107
'Doctors' Plot', the (1952), 57, 60, 80, 104, 124, 125
domestic policy
  Stalin's, 49–82, 242; in post-Stalin period, 123–35; in Khrushchev era, 157–87
Dumbarton Oaks Conference, 43

East Germany
  Soviet defectors in, 66; Stalin's policy in, 91; formation of Democratic Republic in, 102; strikes and disorders in, 138; in Khrushchev era, 165, 194, 199, 202
Eastern Europe
  Stalin's policy in, 35–9, 74, 84–90, 96–106; strained relations between countries of, 96; Soviet purges and terror campaign in, 102–4; strikes and disorders in, 125, 138; in post-Stalin period, 137–43; in Khrushchev era, 165, 191–201:

see also entries for individual countries
Economic Problems of Socialism in the USSR (Stalin), 74–5, 78, 122
economic reconstruction, 60–6; the 'economic thaw', 175–83; the outlook, 246–9
Economy of the USSR during World War II (Voznesensky), 19
Eden, Anthony
 at Moscow Conference (1943), 40–1; at Geneva, 144, 145
education, 25, 69–70, 226–9
Egypt, Soviet aims in, 204–6
Ehrenburg, Ilia, 23
Eisenhower, President Dwight, 144; Khrushchev and, 215
electrical power production, effects of Second World War on, 19
European Advisory Commission on zones of occupation, 41

Fadeev, A. (Soviet writer), 71, 72
Finland, USSR and, 36, 47, 147
'Five Principles', the (Sino-Indian agreement), 149
Five-Year Plans, 19, 23, 79, 130, 132, 161; for East European countries, 104, 139
forced labour imposed by Stalin in Eastern Europe, 103
foreign policy
 under Stalin, 83–119; in post-Stalin period, 135–43; in Khrushchev era, 188–218; summary of, 249–51
France
 Communism in, 92–3; and Indochina, 111–12

Germany
 destruction of Soviet towns and factories by, 20; exploitation of USSR by, 20; Russians' pro-German feelings at beginning of Second World War, 27; occupation of USSR by, 26–7; USSR's victorious offensive against, 31–3; Stalin's fear of, 36, 40, 41–2, 101; Russia's reparation demands, 42, 93; problem of postwar zoning of, 40–2; Russia and question of reunification of, 91, 102, 144; Stalin and the Berlin blockade, 101; as main postwar problem, 145 ff, 189–90, 201–4; *see also* East Germany; West Germany
Gomulka, Wladyslaw, 138, 191, 194–5, 196–7, 198
Gosplan (State Planning Commission), 131; Khrushchev and, 143, 170, 180, 243
Gottwald, Klemens (Czech politician), 101
'Great Russians' sent to Baltic States, 67
Greece, postwar situation of, 40
Greek Orthodox Church, Stalin's rehabilitation of the, 25

Hitler, Adolf
 policy towards occupation of USSR, 27; reaction to evidence of Russian military strength, 33
Ho-Chi-Minh (Indochinese Communist leader), 111–12, 113
housing, effects of Second World War on, 21, 22
Hungary
 Russia's reparations demands, 37; and her acquisitions in, 47; the 1956 uprising, 137; reaction in post-Stalin period, 140–1; in Khrushchev era, 165, 192–3, 195
hydrogen bomb, the, 216

Ignatiev, S. D., 69, 125
India, 109; Stalin's view of, 110; independence granted to, 111, 112; at Colombo meeting, 149; Soviet leaders' visit to, 150; Soviet improves relations with India, 207; Nehru on Soviet foreign relations policy, 208; China's attitude to, 209
Indochina, Communism in, 111–12, 113, 149
Indonesia, 149, 207–8, 209
industry
 transplantation of plants in Second World War, 20–1; in post-Stalin period, 128–9; in Khrushchev era, 175–83 *passim*

intellectuals, the
  Stalin and, 72–8; in Poland, 104–5; Khrushchev's attitude to, 229: *see also* literature; science
Iran
  Russian occupation and release of part of, 47; Stalin and, 116–17
Iraq, 205, 206
'Iron Curtain', the (Churchill's phrase), 30–1, 94, 95
iron and steel industry, effects of Second World War on, 19, 21, 23
Italy, Communism in, 92–3, 196
Izvestiia, 171, 235

Japan
  Britain and USA bear whole burden of war against, 43; Soviet attitude to, 44–5
Jasny, Dr Naum (Soviet agricultural expert), 22

Kaganovich, Lazar
  and the Politburo, 51; replaces Khrushchev in Ukraine, 55, 57; in 'anti-party group', 57; in post-Stalin period, 124, 129, 135; in Khrushchev era, 159, 160, 163, 164, 165, 168, 192
Kalinin, Mikhail
  and the Politburo, 51; and postwar indoctrination of Soviet citizens, 70
Katyn massacre (of Polish officers by Russians), 38
Khrushchev, Nikita
  'secret speech' denouncing Stalin, 24, 159–60, 191; criticizes the 'personality cult', 50; and the Politburo, 51; rivalry with Malenkov, 52, 54–6; and the 'Leningrad Affair', 53, 54; in the Ukraine, 54–5; agricultural policy, 55, 131–5; early career of, 56; and Varga's economic theories, 75; Stalin and, 78; rise to power after Stalin's death, 124–35 *passim*; and Asia and the Middle East, 148–55 *passim*; domestic policy and final struggle for power, 157–87; and the 'economic thaw', 175–83; foreign policy, 188–218; and USA, 215–16; and UNO, 216–17; anti-religious policy, 223–5; and the Third Party Programme, 244–5; fall from power, 169
Kirichenko, A., 163, 169, 173, 187
Korean War
  Stalin and, 114–15; China and, 152
Kosygin, Alexei, 243–4
Kozlov, Frol, 243

Latin America, 213–14
legal system, 220–2
'Leningrad Affair', the (purge), 53–4, 60, 81, 104, 134, 135, 165
literature, Soviet control of, 71–2, 235–41
Lysenko, Trofim, controversy on theories of, 73, 230

MacArthur, General Douglas, 45, 94, 114
McCarthyism (USA), 93
Machine Tractor Stations (agriculture), 131, 184–6, 235
Macmillan, Harold, and the German problem, 203
Malayan Communist Party, 111
Malenkov, Georgi
  and the Politburo, 51; career of, and as Stalin's aide, 52; rivalry with Khrushchev and Zhdanov, 52–6 *passim*; his part in the purges, 53, 81; in the Secretariat, 52, 56; as member of the 'anti-party group', 56–7; Stalin and, 78–9; in post-Stalin struggle with Khrushchev for power, 124–35 *passim*, 139, 144, 148; declining power of, 158–65 *passim*, 168
Manchuria, Soviet aims in, 106, 107–8
Mao Tse-tung
  Russian attitude to, 45, 210; and Marxism-Leninism, 113: *see also* China
Marr, N. (Soviet philologist), Stalin's attack on theories of, 73–4
Marshall aid, Stalin bans Eastern Europe's acceptance of, 21, 96, 100

INDEX

Marxism and Marxism-Leninism
  Stalin's philosophy, 30, 69–78; Mao Tse-tung and, 113; Khrushchev and, 174–5, 194; and agriculture, 186; and anti-religious measures, 223–4
Masaryk, Jan (Czech statesman), 101
Middle East, Soviet policy in the, 82, 115–16, 151, 153–6; in the Khrushchev era, 204–10 *passim*: *see also* entries for individual countries
Mikolajczyk, Stanislaw (Polish Premier), 37
Mikoyan, Anastas
  and the Politburo, 51; in the post-Stalin period, 129, 135, 141; in the Khrushchev era, 161, 163, 173, 192, 193, 213
Molotov, Vyacheslav, 18; and the German problem, 40–1; and the Politburo, 51; as member of the 'anti-party group, 56–7, 135; declining power of, 57; in post-Stalin period, 124, 129, 135, 141; on foreign policy, 142–3; waning influence of, 146, 158–65 *passim*, 168, 192
Moscow Declaration, the, 197
MTS: *see* Machine Tractor Stations

Nasser, President, and the USSR, 204–5
national minorities, Khrushchev and, 172–3
nationalism, Stalin fosters spirit of, 24, 45, 66–7, 70
NATO: *see* North Atlantic Treaty Organization
Near East, Soviet aims in, 46–7, 106: *see also* entries for individual countries
neutrality, Communist views on, 207
North Atlantic Treaty Organization, 102, 143, 147

oil industry, effects of Second World War on, 19
'Old Bolsheviks', 51, 58
Orgburo, disbanding of the, 78

Pakistan, 111, 149, 150
Party Rules, the New, 79–80, 243, 244

Pasternik, Boris (Soviet writer), 238–9
'peaceful coexistence', Soviet policy of, 75, 79, 83, 115, 144, 150, 157, 218
peasants
  hatred of collectivization system, 24; and in Eastern Europe, 91; Stalin's wartime policy, 25: *see also* agriculture
'personality cult', the, 50
Pervukhin, Mikhail, 51, 161, 162, 163, 168
Poland, the USSR and, 36, 37, 38–40; Stalin bans Marshall aid for, 96; Communist purge in, 103; Stalin and intellectuals in, 104–5; the 1956 uprising, 137, 192; in the Khrushchev era, 165, 194–8 *passim*
Politburo, the
  composition of, 50–1; replaced by the Presidium, 78–9
population, high natural increase of, in USSR, 18
Potsdam, Allied leaders' meeting at, 31, 35, 41, 42, 145
Pravda, 171
Presidium, as successor to the Politburo, 78–9
press, the, 234–5
propaganda
  in schools, 25; postwar re-indoctrination campaign, 70–1; Communist drive in Eastern Europe, 104–5; and the press, radio and television, 234–5
purges
  the Great Purge (1930s), 18; conduct of the, 52–4, 80; effects on the party, 60; of the intellectuals, 73; by Stalin in Eastern Europe, 102–4: *see also* 'Doctors' Plot'; Leningrad Affair; *Zhdanovschina*

radio and television as propaganda media, 234
railway system, effects of Second World War on, 19–20
rationing of foodstuffs, 22
religion, political control of, 223–5: *see also* Greek Orthodox Church; Roman Catholic Church

INDEX

reparations demands and plans by Allies, 37, 42, 93

Roman Catholic Church, Stalin's attacks on, 104

Roosevelt, F. D.
postwar optimism of, 31; Russia's insulting attitude to, 31; meetings with Churchill and Stalin, 33–5; and Poland, 39; and establishment of UNO, 42; and Russian claims against Japan, 43, 44; death of, 49

Rudenko, R. A., 127, 171

Rumania
Soviet claims to, and reparations demands, 36, 37, 47; Communist-inspired government established, 40; Stalin's pressure on, 93, 94; collective farms in, 104; Khrushchev and, 165

Saburov, Maxim, 51, 54, 161–4 *passim*, 168

science, 230–2

'scorched earth' (Stalin's wartime decree), 20

SEATO: *see* South-East Asia Treaty Organization

'Second Baku', the (oil-producing area), 19

'Second Front', USSR's pressure on allies for the, 44

secret police
in USSR, 68–9; in Eastern Europe, 103, 140; in post-Stalin period, 125

Secretariat, the
rivalries in, 52, 56; Zhdanov and, 71; Khrushchev and, 124–5

Semonov, Konstantin, official approval of writings of, 72

Serov, I. A. (police chief), 127

Seven-Year Plan, 180, 182, 185

Shepilov, D. T. 127, 129, 168

Sino-Soviet treaties (1945 and 1950), 45, 113

Slansky, Rudolf (Czech party secretary), 104

Socialized agriculture of the USSR (Jasny), 22

South-East Asia, 109–11

South-East Asia Treaty Organization, 148, 149

Soviet-German Non-Aggression Pact (1939), 33, 36

Soviet-occupied areas, postwar situation in, 67–8

Stalin, Joseph
'scorched earth' decree during war, 20; his disregard for human lives, 18, 23; postwar changes in policy, 24–6; and the Communist Party line, 29–30; meetings with Churchill and Roosevelt, 31, 33–5; his fear of Germany, 36, 40, 41–2; and World Government, 42–3; domestic policy, 49–82; the 'personality cult', 50; policy of *divide et impera*, 50; postwar policy for the army, 66; his nationalist feelings, 71; and the intellectuals, 72–8; and the purges, 18, 53, 80–1; and Marxism, 69–78; foreign policy, 83–119; and Eastern Europe, 84–90; attitude to Marshall aid, 96; rift with Tito, 97–100, 136, 142; and Asia, 106–15; and China, 106–9, 112–13; brutal take-over in Czechoslovakia, 100–1; attitude to UNO, 42–3, 116–18; and the Middle East, 115–16; his last years, 81–2; significance of death of, 121–3

Stalingrad, battle of, 31; Virta's book on, 72

Suez crisis, 204

'summit' meetings and diplomacy, 143–6, 214–18

Syria, 205

Teheran, Allied leaders' meeting at, 42, 44, 47

territorial expansion of Russia, 252

Thaw, The (Ehrenburg), 23

Third Party Programme, 244–6

Tito, Marshal: *see* Yugoslavia

Togliatti, Palmiro (Italian Communist leader), 92, 191, 249

transport industry, effects of Second World War on the, 19–20

INDEX

Trotskyism
  Stalin's attitude to, 26, 37; and German Communism, 47; Zhdanov and campaign against, 51; muzzling of, 76
Truman, Harry S., 35
Truman Doctrine, 92, 95–6
Tukhachevsky, Mikhail, 26, 242

Ukraine, the
  welcomes German armies, 27; and UNO, 43; Khrushchev and, 54–5; Kaganovich and, 55, 57; underground movements in, 67
underground groups in Soviet-occupied areas, 67
Union of Soviet Writers, 71, 72
United Nations Organization
  Stalin's attitude to, 42–3, 116–18; and the Korean War, 114–15; Khrushchev and, 216–17
United States of America
  Stalin 'welcomes' American troops on Russian front, 24; USSR views as symbol of imperialism, 30; and war against Japan, 43; monopoly of the atom-bomb, 93; McCarthyism in, 93; military aid for the Balkans, 95; Churchill's appeal for co-operation against Soviet menace, 94–5; military and economic aid for Europe, 95–6; as chief obstacle to Soviet aims, 214–15: *see also* Eisenhower; Roosevelt; Truman

Varga, E. (Hungarian economist), 75, 110
Virgin Lands scheme (agriculture), 21, 132, 133
Virta, Nicholas, official approval of writings of, 72
Voroshilov, Kliment, 51, 135, 149, 163, 167
Vosnesensky, N. A., 19, 126; and the Politburo, 51; decline and death, and the Leningrad Affair, 53–4

Warsaw Pact and Treaty Organization, 147, 193, 198, 200, 203
West Germany
  formation of Federal Republic, 102; joins NATO, 147
Western Europe, Stalin's policy in, 92
Western influences
  Soviet re-indoctrination campaign against, 70; effects of, in Eastern Europe, 140
World Federation of Trade Unions, 111
World Government, Allied leaders plans for, 42–3

Yalta
  Allied leaders' meetings at, 31, 34–5, 38, 41, 44, 45; Declaration on Liberated Europe, 39; and Stalin's Asian acquisitions, 106; agreement on China, 110
Yugoslavia, 37
  independent Communist revolution in, 47; rift with USSR, 97–100, 136, 142; collectivization in, 98; and UNO, 117; in post-Stalin period, 141–2; in Khrushchev era 165, 169, 191–2, 195–200 *passim*

Zhdanov, Andrei
  struggle with Malenkov, 52–3; and campaign for control of literature, 71, 72, 235; and the intellectuals, 72–3; and anti-Semitism, 80; and the Cominform, 97; death, 53: see also *Zhdanovschina*
Zhdanovschina (purges), 73, 93, 104, 105
Zhukov, Grigori, 33, 66, 162, 164, 166, 225
Zorin, Valerian, 101
Zoshchenko, Michael, attacks on writings of, 72